PROCESS THIS!

Also by Jean Anderson

The Doubleday Cookbook* (with Elaine Hanna)

The Family Circle Cookbook (with the food editors of *Family Circle*)

The Grass Roots Cookbook

Jean Anderson's Processor Cooking

Half a Can of Tomato Paste and Other Culinary Dilemmas†
  (with Ruth Buchan)

The New Doubleday Cookbook (with Elaine Hanna)

The Food of Portugal‡

Micro Ways (with Elaine Hanna)

The New German Cookbook (with Hedy Würz)

The Nutrition Bible (with Barbara Deskins, Ph.D., R.D.)

The American Century Cookbook §

The Good Morning America Cut the Calories Cookbook (co-edited with Sara Moulton)

Dinners in a Dish or a Dash

*Winner, R.T. French Tastemaker Award, Best Basic Cookbook of the Year (1975)
  and Best Cookbook of the Year Overall (1975)

†Winner, Seagram/International Association of Culinary Professionals Award,
  Best Specialty Cookbook of the Year (1980)

‡Winner, Seagram/International Association of Culinary Professionals Award,
  Best Foreign Cookbook of the Year (1986)

§Finalist, James Beard Cookbook Awards and Julia Child Cookbook Awards (1998)

PROCESS THIS!

New Recipes for the
New Generation of Food Processors
+ Dozens of Time-Saving Tips

Jean Anderson

WILLIAM MORROW
An Imprint of HarperCollinsPublishers

HarperCollins books may be purchased for educational, business, or sales promotional use. For information please write: Special Markets Department, HarperCollins Publishers Inc., 10 East 53rd Street, New York, NY 10022.

FIRST EDITION

Designed by Mary Austin Speaker

Printed on acid-free paper

Library of Congress Cataloging-in-Publication Data

Anderson, Jean
    Process this! : new recipes for the new generation of food processors : + dozens of time-saving tips / Jean Anderson.—1st ed.
      p.   cm.
    Includes index.
    ISBN 0-06-018565-1
    1. Food processor cookery.   I. Title.

TX840.F6 A54   2002
641.5'89—dc21

                                              2001057925

02   03   04   05   06   QW   10 9 8 7 6 5 4 3 2 1

Contents

Acknowledgments

I should like to thank, first of all, the following individuals and companies without whose valuable cooperation this book could not have been written: Paul Ackels and Mary Rodgers at Cuisinart, Stamford, Connecticut; Brian Maynard and Justin Newby at KitchenAid, St. Joseph, Michigan; and Rachel Litner of Rachel Litner Associates, Livingston, New Jersey.

In addition, I'd like to thank Tex Harrison, proprietor, Complements to the Chef, in Asheville, North Carolina, who provided professional discounts on much of the equipment used in testing recipes for this book; also Connecticut chef, artisanal baker, and award-winning cook book author Charles van Over, who so graciously shared his contacts and clout. I'd also like to thank Joanne Lamb Hayes, trusted friend and colleague, who was a valuable source of information throughout this project; Sara Moulton, best friend, confidante, and sounding board for nearly twenty-five years; Jeanne Voltz, distinguished cookbook author and taste-tester extraordinaire; my niece Kim Anderson for retesting and double-checking some of the recipes; also friends and family, willing guinea pigs all whenever there were recipes to taste and appraise.

Finally, I'd like to thank Patricia Adrian, editorial director of *The Good Cook*, who thought that the new generation of food processors deserved an all-new food processor cookbook; Barney Karpfinger, for many years my agent and anchor, who supported this project from the start; and my editor, Harriet Bell of William Morrow for her editorial wisdom, guidance, and boundless enthusiasm. Every author should be so lucky.

In closing, a tip of the toque to the late Carl G. Sontheimer, who introduced a new kitchen appliance at the 1973 Chicago housewares show that would revolutionize the way we cook. He called it "the food processor."

PROCESS THIS!

Introduction

COMPARED TO TODAY'S racy new food processors, those early machines hailed as miracle workers back in the 1970s look positively Smithsonian.

Instead of on-off switches, there were stop-start mechanisms in the lid locks. And "stovepipe" feed tubes that required meticulous trimming of any food put into them. Motors sometimes stalled because they weren't powerful enough to deal with the load. Blades dulled faster than they ought, and most work bowls didn't hold very much.

Still, we loved our food processors because they shortcut many long-winded recipes. Coleslaw, so tedious to prepare by hand, was suddenly a snap. Ditto scalloped potatoes and all manner of dips and spreads to say nothing of the whole repertoire of pâtés, purées, cream soups, and sauces. We were on a roll.

All because Carl Sontheimer, an American traveling in France, happened one day upon something called Le Magimix, a scaled-down version of Le Robot-Coupe. This was an industrial strength machine that chopped, shredded, sliced, and puréed, streamlining the labor-intensive classics of *haute cuisine*. French chefs loved it. American chefs called it "the buffalo chopper."

Sontheimer, a retired engineer who knew his way around the kitchen, immediately saw what a reconfigured Magimix could do for the American cook. He shipped some home to Connecticut, began tinkering, and came up with a food processor that would serve restaurant chefs and home cooks alike.

The grand unveiling took place in 1973 at the National Housewares Exposition in Chicago, but strangely, Sontheimer's new Cuisinart food processor generated no buzz. Indeed, it was only after Julia Child, James Beard, and other culinary supernovas began using the food processor that it would become the hot new kitchen "toy." And spawn slews of imitations.

By the time Carl Sontheimer died in 1998 at the age of eighty-four, he'd seen his food processor become a kitchen staple, he'd seen clones come and go, and he'd seen many refinements and improvements.

One of the earliest (after the addition of an on-off switch) was a pulse button coupled with faster braking action, which made it easier to control the coarseness or fineness of a chop. Next came the mini food processor, a pint-size powerhouse ideal for chopping a handful of fresh herbs, mincing a clove or two of garlic, or buzzing up a cup of mayonnaise.

Work bowls for full-size processors grew bigger and bigger and feed tubes ballooned until they could swallow an apple whole. This presented problems for long skinny foods, but there was a solution: a small inner feed tube down which carrots, bananas, and the like could be fed one by one, producing camera-ready slices almost every time.

As the twenty-first century approached, there was a strong new contender for market share. KitchenAid, long known for the supremacy of its electric mixers, launched a line of food processors. In no time several competitors, and Cuisinart in particular, began reinventing their machines. With nearly thirty years of hindsight, they knew what had worked on the early models and what hadn't. They knew, too, the kinds of innovations it would take to make their new machines shine. These are on the market now and they are something (see About the New Generation of Food Processors, page 000).

Consumers, alas, have failed to keep pace. Some are still using antiquated food processors. Some have banished their machines to the top pantry shelf because they never learned to use them properly. And others have never used a food processor at all.

I for one couldn't cook without one. I've been working with food processors since the early 1970s and I've tried almost every brand, the wimps as well as the workhorses. Today I keep three at-the-ready for the recipes I must test for cookbooks and magazine articles: a big, heavy-duty professional model for yeast breads and quantity recipes, a medium-size machine for every-day dishes, and a mini for small jobs. (I call them "Bridie," "Gracie," and "Mary" after those tireless assistants in the New York recipe test kitchens of *The Ladies' Home Journal* where I began my career—pre-processor. Bridie, Gracie, and Mary were our "food processors," chopping, slicing, and shredding whatever we needed.)

In the two years I spent developing recipes for this book, I learned much about the new generation of food processors and how to adapt recipes to suit them. In baking, for example, I discovered that if I turned certain cake and cookie recipes upside down and completely changed the method of mixing, I could prepare them almost entirely by food processor. I learned, too, that I could turn my food processor into a bread machine.

In the pages and recipes that follow, I pass along the techniques and tips I've learned. I am also absolutely up-front: If I don't think a food processor is the tool to use for a particular food or a particular job, I say so.

My aim, quite simply, is to teach you to use the new generation of food processors to best advantage and to the hilt.

How To Use This Book

■ Before beginning any recipe in this book, read the recipe through carefully, and make sure that you understand exactly what you are to do.

■ To save time, have all ingredients measured and partially prepped (i.e., peeled and chunked) before you begin cooking. Whenever I'm baking, I assemble all the dry ingredients (flour, sugar, leavening, seasonings) in a large spouted measure and all the "wets" (milk, eggs, vegetable oil, etc.) in another so that they can be added to the work bowl with little risk of spilling. Small amounts of "dries" can be placed on a double thickness of wax paper, then lifted and tipped into the work bowl. Saves on dishwashing.

■ Do not substitute one ingredient for another unless a recipe suggests it.

■ Do not substitute one pan or casserole for another unless a recipe suggests alternatives. I am quite specific about pan shapes and sizes because they are essential to a recipe's success.

■ When a recipe directs you to "cool" something, bring it to room temperature.

■ When a recipe says to "chill" something, refrigerate it, or set it in an ice bath, until uniformly cold.

■ Allow 20 minutes for an oven to preheat.

■ Allow 15 minutes for a broiler to preheat.

Unless specified to the contrary:

■ Eggs are large.

■ Butter is unsalted.

■ Flour is all-purpose, sifted before it is measured even if the label says "pre-sifted." Flour compacts in shipping and storage, and if you don't sift it before you measure it, your quick breads, pastries, cakes, and cookies won't be as tender as they should be.

■ Cornmeal is the granular yellow type most supermarkets carry.

■ Brown sugar is measured by tightly packing it in a dry measuring cup and leveling off the surface with the edge of a knife or metal spatula.

■ Lemon, lime, orange, and grapefruit juices are freshly squeezed.

■ Vanilla is always pure vanilla extract, never imitation.

■ Black pepper is freshly ground.

■ Freshly grated Parmesan cheese is Parmigiano-Reggiano.

Getting Down To Basics

INCLUDED HERE ARE pointers to guide you in buying one of the new-generation food processors as well as tips on using it safely. I also offer handy reference charts that list the foods best suited to these new machines, then tell the best ways to prep, slice, chop, grind, and purée them. As an additional help, I've added a chart of equivalents so you'll know exactly how many slices of bread it takes to produce one cup of crumbs, how many apples for one cup of slices, and so forth.

On the preceding pages, I also list the things you should know in order to use this book wisely. Read it, please, before trying any of the recipes.

ABOUT THE NEW GENERATION OF FOOD PROCESSORS

These new machines combine the best features of their predecessors with cutting-edge innovations that make them more versatile, more powerful, and more reliable. In addition, they're quick to clean, thanks to their streamlined designs. Here's a quick rundown of the most capable and readily available models.

KitchenAid has introduced mini bowl and blade inserts for its 9- and 11-cup food processors, even for its compact 5- and 7-cuppers—inspired space-savers that make one machine do the work of two. In addition, there's a timesaving chef's bowl insert for its top-of-the-line professional model. Work bowl dirty? Just slip in the chef's bowl and continue processing. For serious cooks, amateurs as well as pros, there's KitchenAid's "Chef's Chopper," a powerful 3-cup mini with reverse spiral action and scalpel-sharp blade to ensure uniform chopping with little or no bowl scraping. Just the thing for a single onion, a few carrots, or a handful of parsley.

KitchenAid has also created a reversible thin slicing/shredding disk that's standard equipment for all of its machines, with separate medium slicing and shredding disks for the 11-cup models. Its new slip-on citrus juicer attachment (with a small reamer for lemons and limes and large reamer for oranges and grapefruits) really works. Finally, its see-through plastic accessories box means no more disks and blades jumbled up in a drawer.

LeChef, Ronic's food processor with eleven functions, has some welcome innovations, too. Its work bowl's sloping sides eliminate that right angle where foods being processed in straight-sided bowls so often collect. Moreover, its S-shaped metal chopping blade is serrated and one end of it turns up like the wingtip of many airliners. This combination helps keep food in the middle of the bowl and in the path of the blade, so you don't have to stop the machine as often to scrape the work bowl—a time and nuisance saver. On the downside, this French food processor's work bowl is fairly small. It holds up to five cups of semi-liquid ingredients, and twice that of sliced or shredded foods.

After twenty-seven years, Cuisinart has completely overhauled its workhorse with an Italian design that's as racy as a new Ferrari. Gone are the old dirt-catching pulse and on/off levers at the base of the machine, and in their place, a smooth easy-to-clean keypad at the front. Cuisinart's biggest breakthroughs, however, are a slower "dough mode" for kneading yeast doughs and a reconfigured dough blade made of metal instead of plastic. The expanded feed tubes with small inner feed tubes remain (just the thing for slicing and shredding long skinny foods) as do the big work bowls. There are two models in the new line: the Prep 11 Plus with an 11-cup work bowl and the pricier PowerPrep Plus 14 with a mighty 14-cup work bowl. And here's truly good news, the blades and disks of earlier Cuisinarts are not obsolete; they fit the new machines.

Cuisinart's mini food processor (a true mini holding just a shade over 2½ cups) is both chopper and grinder, thanks to its reverse-action motor and two-sided blade: dull for grinding coffee beans and whole spices, sharp for mincing garlic, fresh herbs, and so forth. But there are a couple of drawbacks: the work bowl quickly scuffs in the grind mode and genuinely hard spices—cinnamon sticks, for example—do not grind to powder, only to coarse crumbs.

Cuisinart, KitchenAid, and LeChef food processors all offer a load of attachments, some optional, some included—everything from egg whips to vegetable juice extractors to julienners and french-fry cutters. In addition, there's a wide range of shredding and slicing disks from coarse to fine and from thick to thin. Recipe booklets come with each machine; KitchenAid and Cuisinart also include how-to video tapes with their full-size processors.

All of the new food processors come in "basic white," but for certain models KitchenAid offers as many as nine decorator colors (from Onyx Black to Majestic Yellow and Empire Red to Almond Cream). Cuisinart's color choices, limited to its mini and 11-cup machine, are white, black, blue, and brushed chrome. All 14-cup machines are white—so far, at least (except for the shiny cast zinc number commissioned and sold by Williams-Sonoma).

Which processor should you choose? I can't recommend a particular brand, but I will say this: If you are a dedicated cook and are serious about adding a new-generation food processor to your kitchen, or if you're hoping to replace an old one, talk to friends and neighbors who may already have plunged. Then ask if you can test-drive their new food processor. If that fails, request a personal demonstration—either by a friend or at a local kitchen shop.

Consider, too, the type of cooking you do, then let your particular needs guide you in your choice. If you bake yeast bread or frequently cook for a crowd, you should spring for the machine with the most powerful motor, the most heavily weighted base, and the biggest work bowl. Otherwise a less Herculean 7- to 11-cup model will serve you well.

Top-quality food processors are expensive, it's true. But if you think of them as a lifetime investment, learn to use them correctly, and treat them kindly, you won't be disappointed.

HOW TO USE YOUR FOOD PROCESSOR SAFELY

Before you use your food processor, read and reread the user's manual, then keep it handy for future reference. It spells out everything you must do to use your food processor safely. Instead of repeating those safeguards here, I'll offer the additional safety tips I've learned over the years.

■ Beware the metal chopping blade! It is lethal. Most cuts occur when people grow cavalier about the chopping blade and handle it carelessly outside the bowl as well as in.

■ When scraping the work bowl or stirring anything in it, use a stiff long-handled plastic spatula, skirting the blade at all times.

■ When loading the chopping blade into the dishwasher, lay it flat and in full view on the top rack where you won't accidentally bump into it.

■ When switching from the chopping blade to the slicing or shredding disk, set the blade well out of reach, or better yet, slip it inside a heavy-duty plastic zipper bag.

■ Unless your processor has a storage box, store disks and blades in separate heavy-duty plastic zipper bags, and label each so you know at a glance exactly what's inside. As a further safeguard, I cover the cutting edge of each slicing disk with a piece of pressure-sensitive paper, which can be used over and over again.

■ Always leave the metal chopping blade in place when lifting the work bowl from the power base (this is to prevent leakage around the central spindle).

■ When pouring or tipping anything from the work bowl, anchor the blade with your second or third finger. Just insert it in the central tube on the bottom of the work bowl, then farther up into the blade's hollow spindle.

■ After processing something with the metal chopping blade and emptying the work bowl, remove the blade and set it out of harm's way before you scrape the bowl with a rubber spatula.

■ Never force your processor beyond its capability, for example by exerting too much pressure on the pusher when slicing or shredding something hard.

■ Set the food processor at the back of the counter where it's less likely to "walk" and drop off the edge while processing heavy loads.

■ Keep your eye on the processor at all times, especially when kneading yeast doughs. Under heavy loads, nonstop churning can stall the motor. It can also overheat and kill the yeast. For that reason, I often knead in 20-second increments, letting the machine and the dough rest in between.

■ Never uncover a work bowl until after the blades or disks have come to a complete stop. People have been cut by opening the work bowl too soon. The newest processors do brake more quickly; still, it's best to err on the side of caution.

■ Never force a stuck work bowl lid—those plastic latches are sharp enough to cut. Instead, spritz the locking mechanism with nonstick cooking spray. As a preventive, I routinely spray the work bowl rim and locking mechanism before every use. Try it, it works.

■ Never leave the food processor lid in the "locked" position or any of the buttons depressed. Doing so can damage their delicate spring-lock mechanisms.

A DICTIONARY OF FOODS AND HOW TO PROCESS THEM

When food processors first entered our lives in the early seventies, we were so smitten with these new miracle workers that we tried to make them do everything. Miraculous they were—and the latest models are even more so. Still, there are certain jobs they do not do well—and I'm not talking just mashed potatoes here. In the pages that follow, I focus on those foods and functions that let the new generation of food processors strut their stuff.

Processors vary from brand to brand, even from model to model. Some have powerful motors and quick braking action. Others don't. Some have pulse buttons so sensitive you can use staccato bursts of speed. Others don't. Moreover foods, even the same foods, vary in degrees of hardness and dryness, both of which affect processor times as do the quantities and combinations of food put into the work bowl. In addition, no two cooks will have the same mastery of the processor keypad.

Thus, the processor times and techniques given here should not be taken as gospel but used as a guide. As you familiarize yourself with your machine and your aptitudes, you will learn just what it takes to chop onions or parsley, grate Parmesan, or reduce bread to crumbs.

ALMONDS, WHOLE Prep: To blanch almonds, submerge in boiling water 30 seconds, drain, and slip off skins. Spread the almonds on paper toweling and dry 1 to 2 hours, replenishing the toweling as needed.

Tool to use for chopping/grinding: Metal chopping blade.

Technique: Churn the nuts, no more than 2 cups at a time, allowing 8 to 10 seconds for a coarse chop, 12 to 15 for moderate, and 20 to 25 for finely ground.

ALMONDS, SLICED OR SLIVERED Prep: None needed.

Tool to use for chopping/grinding: Metal chopping blade.

Technique: Pulse the nuts, no more than 2 cups at a time, 5 to 10 times for coarsely chopped nuts, 10 to 15 for fairly finely chopped. For ground nuts, use two 10-second churnings.

Tip: If a recipe contains sugar, pulse ¼ to ½ cup of the sugar with the almonds; it helps keep them from churning to paste. Fine dry bread crumbs can perform the same function as can a bit of flour.

APPLES Prep: Peel the apples, halve, and core. If they are to be chopped, cut into slim wedges or 1- to 1½-inch chunks. If they are to be sliced, leave as halves or halve each half lengthwise.

Tool to use for chopping: Metal chopping blade.

Technique: Pulse up to 2 cups of apple chunks 2 to 3 times for a coarse chop; 5 to 6 for a finer one.

Tool to use for slicing: Thin, medium, or thick slicing disk, whichever the recipe specifies. The medium slicing disk, standard equipment on most processors, is the workhorse and the one you'll use the most.

Technique: With concave sides all facing the same way, stand as many apple halves or quarters in the feed tube as will fit snugly. Exerting gentle pressure on the pusher, pulse the apples through the slicing disk. Repeat until all of the apples are sliced.

Tip: To keep chopped or sliced apples from discoloring, sprinkle immediately with 1 to 2 tablespoons fresh lemon juice and toss lightly.

APRICOTS See Peaches.

AVOCADOS Choose firm-ripe avocados if they are to be chopped or sliced; soft ones if they will be puréed. The small, dark-skinned, nut-flavored Hass is always my first choice.

Prep: For chopping and puréeing, halve the avocados and pit. For slicing, peel the halved avocados, then halve each half lengthwise. If the avocados are large, cut each half into thirds.

Tool to use for chopping/puréeing: Metal chopping blade.

Technique: Using a tablespoon, scoop the flesh of up to 4 small avocados into the work bowl, and sprinkle with 1 tablespoon fresh lemon or lime juice (to prevent browning). Pulse briskly 2 to 3 times, then using a plastic spatula and avoiding the blade, scrape the work bowl and stir. Pulse 2 to 3 times more until lumpy.

Note: Avocados don't chop cleanly. What you'll get is something on the order of guacamole. To purée, churn the avocados until smooth—10 to 15 seconds should do it.

Tool to use for slicing: Medium or thick slicing disk.

Technique: For short slices, stand the avocado quarters in the feed tube, fitting in enough of them so that they don't wobble. For long slices, lay the quarters on their sides, arranging and piggybacking so they don't slip. Exerting extra-gentle pressure on the pusher, pulse the avocados through the slicing disk. Repeat until all are sliced.

Note: If the slices must be clean-cut for a recipe where visuals count, hand-slice the avocados.

Tip: To keep sliced avocados from darkening, sprinkle with 1 to 2 tablespoons fresh lemon or lime juice, and toss gently.

BANANAS If bananas are to be sliced, choose firm-ripe specimens; if mashed or puréed, select soft ones.

Prep: Peel the bananas. If they are to be sliced, halve crosswise. For mashed or puréed bananas, cut the peeled halves into 1-inch chunks.

Note: I don't recommend chopping bananas. Even the firmest of them will mash.

Tool to use for slicing: Medium or thick slicing disk.

Technique: If your food processor has a small inner feed tube, pulse the bananas down it one at a time, exerting light pressure on the pusher. To keep the slices from darkening, toss gently with 1 to 2 tablespoons fresh lemon or orange juice.

Note: Unless I have a bunch of bananas to slice, I find it easier to slice them by hand.

Tool to use for mashing/puréeing: Metal chopping blade.

Technique: Add up to 2 cups banana chunks to the work bowl, sprinkle with 1 tablespoon fresh lemon juice, and churn 5 to 10 seconds to mash—the bananas should be lumpy. To purée, churn until smooth, about 15 seconds in all.

BEANS, GREEN OR WAX Prep: Wash and tip the beans, then cut into uniform lengths the width of the feed tube—3 to 4 inches depending on the brand and model.

Tool to use for frenching: Medium slicing disk.

Technique: Lay the beans on their sides in the feed tube, arranging them as neatly as possible and filling to within a half inch of the top. Insert the pusher, and exerting steady pressure, pulse the beans through the slicing disk. Repeat until all beans are frenched.

Note: Cooked beans, like most other cooked vegetables, can be puréed. For directions, see Purées in this section.

BEETS Beets are messy and there's no getting around it. But I have learned a few tricks to minimize the scarlet spatter. For starters, select either beets that are small enough to fit into the broad feed tube or babies that can be dropped whole into the small inner feed tube.

Prep: Parboil the beets in their skins with the root ends and 1 inch of the tops intact until firm-tender, about 20 minutes. Or roast them (see page 107). Peel and trim the beets, slice or shred, and finish as recipes direct.

Tool to use for slicing: Medium slicing disk.

Technique: Place whole peeled beets in the outer or inner feed tube, filling to within an inch of the top and arranging as snugly as possible. Exerting firm pressure on the pusher, pulse the beets through the slicing disk. Repeat until all the beets are sliced.

Tool to use for shredding: Medium shredding disk.

Technique: The same as for slicing.

Note: To purée cooked beets, see Purées in this section.

BREAD CRUMBS See Crumbs.

CABBAGE Prep: Trim the cabbage of its coarse outer leaves, quarter, and cut off the core at the point of each quarter. If the cabbage is to be sliced, cut in columns that can be laid cut-side down in the feed tube. If it is to be chopped or shredded, cut into 1- to 1½-inch chunks.

Tool to use for slicing: Thin or medium slicing disk.

Technique: This is a bit tricky, a test in spatial arrangement. To get crisp slices of more or less the same size, you must lay the column of cabbage in the feed tube so that the disk will slice across the layers of leaves. Arrange as much cabbage in the feed tube as you can for a snug fit, then using firm pressure on the pusher, pulse through the slicing disk. Repeat until all the cabbage is sliced, emptying the work bowl as it fills.

Tool to use for chopping/shredding: Metal chopping blade.

Technique: Place chunks of cabbage in the work bowl (no more than 2 cups, 4 if your work bowl is large), and pulse 5 to 6 times for a coarse chop, 8 to 10 times for a fine one. Empty the work bowl as each batch is chopped.

CARROTS Prep: Trim and peel the carrots. If they are to be chopped, cut into 1-inch chunks. If they are to be sliced into rounds, cut in lengths to fit the smaller inner feed tube; if sliced into strips, cut in lengths that can be laid flat in the large feed tube.

Tool to use for chopping/grinding: Metal chopping blade.

Technique: Place up to 2 cups chunked carrots in the work bowl and pulse 2 to 3 times for a coarse chop; 4 to 5 for a moderate one; and 6 to 10 for fine or very fine. To grind carrots, let the machine run 15 to 20 seconds nonstop.

Tool to use for slicing: Thin, medium, or thick slicing disk.

Technique: For precisely cut slices of uniform thickness, pulse the carrots down the small inner feed tube one by one, exerting steady pressure on the pusher. For soup and stew carrots, stand as many as will fit in the wide feed tube, reversing the directions so that some carrots are large end up and others large end down. This makes for a tighter fit. Pulse through the slicing disk exerting firm pressure on the pusher.

For strips, simply lay the carrots on their sides and fill the feed tube to within about 1 inch of the top. Pulse through the slicing disk, exerting firm, steady pressure on the pusher.

Tool for shredding carrots: Medium shredding disk.

Technique: The same as for slicing.

Note: To purée cooked carrots, see Purées in this section.

CELERY Prep: Trim off the tops and ½ inch or so of the bottoms. If the celery is to be chopped, cut into 1-inch chunks; if sliced, cut in lengths to fit the feed tube (the small inner feed tube if appearance is an issue).

Tool to use for chopping: Metal chopping blade.

Technique: Drop up to 2 cups celery chunks in the work bowl. For a rough chop, use 2 to 3 pulses; for a moderate chop, 4 to 6 pulses; and for a fine one, 8 to 10.

Tool to use for slicing: Thin, medium, or thick slicing disk.

Technique: Stand as many pieces of celery in the large or small feed tube as you can, with concave sides facing the same way. Exerting steady pressure on the pusher, pulse through the slicing disk. Repeat until all celery is sliced, emptying the work bowl as it fills.

CELERY ROOT (CELERIAC) Choose small, firm specimens.

Prep: To remove the tough, fibrous skin, slice off each end of the celery root, then stand on a cutting board. With a sharp knife, peel by cutting from top to bottom, following always the shape of the root. If the celery root is to be shredded, halve the celery root lengthwise, place cut-side-down on a chopping board, and cut into blocks the height and width of the feed tube. If the celery root is to be sliced, divide into columns that will fit in the small inner feed tube.

Note: I've never come across a recipe that calls for chopped or minced celery root, but the technique would be the same as for carrots (see page 11).

Tool to use for shredding: Coarse or medium shredding disk.

Technique: Stand enough chunks of celery root in the feed tube as needed for a snug fit, then pulse through the shredding disk, exerting firm pressure on the pusher. Repeat until all of the celery root has been shredded, emptying the work bowl as it fills.

Tool to use for slicing: Medium slicing disk.

Technique: Pulse the columns of celery root one by one down the small inner feed tube, exerting firm, steady pressure on the pusher. Because celery root is so hard, I find this method less apt to dull or deform the blade, less likely, too, to stall the machine.

Note: To purée cooked celery root, see Purées, in this section. Also see Potato and Celery Root Purée (page 179).

CHEESES Prep: Cut Parmesan, Romano, and other hard cheeses into 1-inch cubes. Cut medium-hard cheeses (Cheddar, Gruyère, Jack, etc.) into blocks the size of the feed tube and chill well or partially freeze. Soft cheeses are better sliced and shredded by hand.

Tool to use for grating hard cheeses: Metal chopping blade.

Technique: Some owner's manuals call for dropping the cubes of cheese down the feed tube into the spinning blade, but I've had better luck (and no harm done to the blade) by pulsing 2 cups of cubes 4 to 5 times (this produces very coarsely grated cheese), then running the motor non-stop until the cheese is as fine as I like, 10 to 15 seconds for fairly finely grated cheese; 20 seconds or more for feathery-fine.

Tip: I like to have a big jar of freshly grated Parmesan in the refrigerator, so I churn the cheese in 2-cup batches until I have 3 to 4 cups. Stored in a tightly capped preserving jar, it remains amazingly fresh for 4 to 6 weeks.

Tool to use for slicing semi-hard cheeses: Medium slicing disk.

Technique: Stand a block of cheese in the feed tube, then pulse through the slicing disk, exerting only as much pressure as needed.

Note: Inevitably, some pieces will flatten onto the spinning disk. Once the slicing is done and the machine has been snapped off, salvage these and, if possible, hand-cut to match. Otherwise, wrap in plastic wrap and save for other cooking jobs.

Tool to use for shredding semi-hard cheeses: Medium shredding disk.

Technique: The same as for slicing semi-hard cheeses.

CHICKEN, TURKEY (COOKED) Prep: Remove the bones, fat, and gristle, and cut into 1-inch cubes.

Tool to use for chopping/mincing/grinding: Metal chopping blade.

Technique: Place up to 2 cups chicken or turkey cubes in the food processor, and pulse quickly 2 to 3 times for a coarse chop; 4 to 5 for medium; 6 to 8 for fairly fine; and 8 to10 for fine. The danger here is churning the meat to paste, so watch closely and pulse only until you've achieved the desired texture.

CHICKEN, TURKEY (RAW) First of all, chicken and turkey cutlets are the only parts of the bird that I commit to the food processor, and then only to slice or sliver for stir-fries. I don't recommend shredding or grinding raw chicken or turkey in the processor.

Prep: Trim the cutlets of all fat and connective tissue, cut in columns the height and width of the feed tube, then wrap each piece in plastic food wrap, lay directly on the freezing surface of a 0°F freezer, and freeze until almost firm—35 to 45 minutes should do it if you turn the slices over at half-time.

Tool to use for slicing/slivering: Medium slicing disk.

Technique: Stack as many slices on end in the feed tube as you can for a snug fit, then with staccato pulses, push the meat through the slicing disk, exerting moderate pressure on the pusher. Repeat until all the chicken or turkey has been slivered.

CITRUS ZEST (LEMON, LIME, ORANGE, GRAPEFRUIT) Prep: Strip the zest (colored part of the rind) from the fruit with a swivel-bladed vegetable peeler.

Tool to use for grating: Metal chopping blade.

Technique: Place the zest in the work bowl along with some or all of the sugar (granulated, brown, or confectioners') from the recipe, unless the amount of sugar is more than 2 cups. I usually add from ¼ to 1 cup sugar depending on the amount of zest. Churn for 5 seconds, then using a plastic spatula and carefully skirting the blade, scrape the work bowl and stir. Churn 15 seconds longer, until the zest is finely grated. If large bits of zest remain, quickly pulse them out.

Note: If the recipe contains salt, I usually add it along with the sugar. This additional abrasiveness accelerates the process and helps keep the zest from reducing to paste. I've successfully grated zest with dry bread crumbs as well as with other gritty ingredients. Always look for gritty ingredients whenever a recipe calls for grated citrus zest.

COCONUT Prep: Pierce two of the coconut "eyes" with a screwdriver or icepick and drain out all liquid. Tap the coconut firmly all over with a hammer (to loosen the meat from the shell). Bake uncovered in a preheated 350°F oven for 15 minutes (to crack the coconut). Wrap the hot coconut in a dishtowel and break into small pieces with the hammer. If the meat doesn't separate easily, pry it from the shell with a screwdriver or sturdy table knife. With a vegetable peeler, strip off the brown skin. Rinse the coconut and pat dry on paper toweling. If the coconut is to be grated, cut into 1-inch chunks. If it is to be shredded, cut into columns to fit the feed tube.

Tool to use for grating: Metal chopping blade.

Technique: Place up to 2 cups coconut chunks in the work bowl. For coarsely grated coconut, churn for 10 seconds; for moderately finely grated, use two 10-second churnings, scraping the work bowl in between; and for finely grated, use three 10-second churnings, again scraping the work bowl between churnings.

Note: Inspect the coconut carefully after each churning and stop grating the minute you achieve the texture you want.

Tool to use for shredding: Medium shredding disk.

Technique: Stand as many columns of coconut in the feed tube as will fit, then exerting firm pressure on the pusher, pulse through the shredding disk. Repeat until all the coconut is shredded.

Note: I don't recommend shredding coconut unless you have a powerful processor with an unusually sharp shredding disk. Many coconuts are so hard they can dull the disk and stall the motor. A second method that is slower but easier on the machine is to pulse the columns one by one down the small inner feed tube.

COOKIE CRUMBS See Crumbs.

CORN Prep for cream-style corn: Cut the kernels from the cobs, or if you prefer, use frozen whole-kernel corn, either thawed and drained or solidly frozen.

Tool to use for making cream-style corn: Metal chopping blade.

Technique: Place up to 2 cups corn kernels in the work bowl. Fresh or thawed frozen corn will take three to four 1-second churnings; solidly frozen corn two to three 5-second churnings.

CRACKER CRUMBS See Crumbs.

CRANBERRIES Prep: Sort, wash, and stem.

Tool to use for chopping: Metal chopping blade.

Technique: Add up to 2 cups berries to the work bowl, and for a moderately coarse chop, pulse 2 to 3 times. For a finer chop—and there's some risk here of reducing the berries to mush—pulse once or twice more.

CREAM, HEAVY Prep: Have the cream refrigerator-cold; avoid using ultra-pasteurized, which is harder to whip.

Tool to use for whipping: Metal chopping blade or whip attachment (some new models have them).

Technique: Pour 1 to 2 cups cream into the work bowl (for smaller amounts, I use the mini food processor). If using the metal chopping blade, whip 5 seconds, then using a plastic spatula and minding the blade, scrape the work bowl and stir. Whip 5 to 6 seconds longer until the cream begins to stiffen. Using 1-second pulses, continue whipping until the cream mounds softly.

Caution: Watch closely lest you churn the cream to butter.

Note: I've found that I get the best results in the standard processor if I whip between 1½ and 2 cups of cream—1 cup isn't quite enough for the standard processor, but it's too much for some minis. To use the whip attachment, follow the manufacturer's directions—the design, size, and action of the beaters vary from brand to brand.

CRUMBS: Prep: None necessary unless you want to trim the crusts from the bread.

Tool to use for crumbing: Metal chopping blade.

DRY BREAD CRUMBS Technique: Break brittle-stale bread (or better yet, crisp dry toast) into 1- to 1½-inch chunks directly into the work bowl. For coarse crumbs, pulse 4 to 6 times; for moderately fine, 8 to 10; and for very fine, 12 to 15. Also see Fine Dry Bread Crumbs (page 67) for how to oven-toast bread until crisp and the color of pale caramel.

SOFT BREAD CRUMBS Technique: Tear 4 to 6 slices of firm-textured white bread into 1- to 1½-inch pieces, letting them drop into the work bowl. For crumbs of moderate texture, pulse 5 to 6 times; for fine crumbs use two to three 5-second churnings.

Note: You can chop as much as 1 cup of parsley while you crumb the bread. Just make sure that the parsley is good and dry. You can also mix in dried herbs and spices at the same time—a good thing to know when you're making meatloaf or a crumb topping.

COOKIE CRUMBS Technique: Crumble crisp dry vanilla wafers or gingersnaps (no more than 18 at a time) or 12 thin chocolate wafers into the processor work bowl. Churn 10 to 15 seconds for fairly coarse crumbs; 20 to 25 for crumbs of medium texture; and 30 seconds for fine. If any large pieces remain, quickly pulse them out. Repeat until you have as many crumbs as you need.

GRAHAM CRACKER CRUMBS Technique: Crumble twelve 2⅜-inch-square graham crackers into the work bowl. For coarse crumbs, churn 15 seconds; for moderately fine, 20 to 25; and for fine, 30 seconds. If large pieces remain, quickly pulse them out. Repeat until you have as many crumbs as you need.

SODA CRACKER CRUMBS Technique: Crumble up to two dozen 2-inch-square soda crackers into the work bowl. For moderately coarse crumbs, churn 8 to 10 seconds; for moderately fine, 15 to 20 seconds; and for very fine, 25 to 30 seconds. Repeat until you have as many crumbs as you need.

CUCUMBERS The best cucumbers to chop or slice in the processor are either Kirbys (small pickling cucumbers) or seedless (English hothouse) cucumbers, which come shrink-wrapped. Both are slim enough to fit in the smaller inner feed tube—essential if you want perfect slices. Both, moreover, are firm and less likely to have been waxed, meaning they don't always have to be peeled.

Prep: Peel the cucumbers if they've been waxed or if you prefer them that way. Or stripe them by running the vegetable peeler the length of the cucumbers at ½-inch intervals. Seed the cucumbers or not—it's your choice. To seed, halve the cucumbers lengthwise, and scoop out the seeds using a melon baller or teaspoon. If the cucumbers will be chopped, cut into 1-inch chunks; if sliced, cut in lengths to fit the small inner feed tube.

Tool to use for chopping: Metal chopping blade.

Technique: Drop up to 2 cups cucumber chunks into the work bowl and pulse in 1-second bursts to the desired texture. For a rough-chop, 2 to 3 pulses is usually sufficient. For a moderately fine one, 4 to 6. Be careful not to over process, or you'll liquefy the cucumbers.

Tool to use for slicing: Medium or thin slicing disk.

Technique: If perfect slices are your aim, pulse the cucumbers one by one down the smaller inner feed tube, exerting moderate pressure on the pusher. If the cucumbers have been seeded, reassemble the halves, then stand them in the inner feed tube (these slices will be crescents). If the recipe does not call for "camera-ready" slices, use the large feed tube, standing in it as many cucumbers as will fit snugly. Repeat until you have all the sliced cucumbers you need.

Tool for shredding cucumbers: Medium or coarse shredding disk.

Technique: Stand the cucumbers in the large feed tube, adding as many as you can for a tight fit. Exerting moderate pressure on the pusher, pulse through the shredding disk. Repeat until you have as much shredded cucumber as you need.

EGGPLANT The smaller the better. And if you can get them skinny enough to fit whole into the large feed tube, that's better still. Some species are so slim they will fit into the small inner feed tube.

Prep: Trim off both ends, then peel or stripe the eggplant, using a vegetable peeler. If the eggplant is to be chopped, cut into 1-inch cubes; if it is to be sliced, cut in lengths to fit the feed tube. If the eggplant is too plump to fit into the feed tube, halve it lengthwise.

Tool to use for chopping: Metal chopping blade.

Technique: Place up to 2 cups eggplant cubes in the processor work bowl and pulse briskly to the desired texture. Easy does it! I find that 2 to 3 pulses are enough for a rough chop; and 5 to 6 for one of moderate texture. I don't recommend going for a fine chop.

Tool to use for slicing: Medium or thick slicing disk.

Technique: Stand eggplant pieces in either the inner or outer feed tube, adding just enough for a snug fit. Exerting moderate pressure on the pusher, pulse them through the slicing disk. Repeat until all of the eggplant has been sliced.

EGGS, HARD-COOKED Prep: Peel the eggs and halve lengthwise, then crosswise.

Tool to use for chopping: Metal chopping blade.

Technique: Place up to 12 hard-cooked eggs in the processor work bowl, distributing evenly. Pulse quickly 5 times, scrape down the work bowl, then pulse 5 times more or until as coarse or fine as you like.

Note: For me, it is easier to slice hard-cooked eggs by hand or to use the little manual egg slicer. With the processor I can never get the eggs to stand just so in the feed tube, even though I halve them crosswise and lay them cut-sides down. I always seem to end up with ragged slices. But perhaps you will do better than I.

EGGS, RAW Some of the fancier new processors have whip or whisk attachments with which you can beat eggs and even egg whites. I personally find it easier to use an electric hand mixer, and if I'm making an angel food cake, a standing electric mixer with a whip attachment. If your food processor has the whip attachment and you want to use it for beating eggs or egg whites, follow the directions in the user's manual. There are too many variables to include helpful directions here.

FENNEL (FINOCCHIO) Prep: Trim the stalks and feathery tops from the bulbs (the tops can be minced and used to bolster flavor or to garnish, see below). Remove the coarse outer layers from the finocchio bulbs. If they're to be chopped, cut in 1-inch chunks; if sliced, halve the bulbs lengthwise unless they're slim enough to fit into the feed tube whole.

Tool to use for chopping: Metal chopping blade.

Technique: Drop the chunks of fennel (but no more than 2 cups at a time) into the work bowl. For a coarse chop, churn 5 seconds; for a moderate one, 6 to 8 seconds; and for a fine one, 8 to 10. Repeat until all the fennel is chopped.

Tool to use for slicing: Medium slicing disk.

Technique: Stand the fennel halves in the feed tube, as many as you can for a snug fit, then exerting firm pressure on the pusher, pulse through the slicing disk.

To chop the feathery fennel tops: This is a good job for a mini food processor or the mini insert of a standard model because you're not likely to need more than ½ to 1 cup of minced fennel tops. Tip the fennel into a fine sieve, rinse under cold running water, then wring as dry as possible in paper toweling. Add to a food processor fitted with the metal chopping blade and for coarsely chopped fennel tops, pulse briskly 3 to 5 times. If a finer chop is your aim, scrape the work bowl and pulse 4 to 6 times more or until as fine as you like.

Note: You can chop fresh dill exactly the same way.

FISH AND SHELLFISH To tell the truth, I rarely use the food processor for preparing fish and shellfish. They are so delicate that the machine's action is often too brutal for them. There are a few exceptions, however, and those techniques are best demonstrated in Spicy Potted Shrimp (page 100) and Tuna Salad with Lime and Fresh Herbs (page 154).

GARLIC Prep: Peel and if the cloves are large, halve.

Tool to use for chopping: Metal chopping blade.

Technique: I use two different techniques. If a lone clove of garlic is to be chopped, I usually snap the motor on, and drop the garlic down the feed tube into the spinning blade. The drawback here is that the blade throws the bits of garlic against the sides of the work bowl and it takes a fair amount of scraping to get them off. If more cloves are to be chopped, or if there's another food that can be chopped along with the single clove (fresh ginger, for example, or scallions), I usually place them in the work bowl and churn until finely minced, usually 5 to 10 seconds. Sometimes I simply pulse the garlic until it is as fine as I want. If the recipe I'm preparing doesn't call for other chopped ingredients, I'll chop the garlic in a mini. Giving specific churning times or number of pulses is difficult because these vary according to the job. You will find, however, that I am most specific in each recipe that calls for garlic.

Tool to use for slicing: Medium or thin slicing disk plus a food processor with a small inner feed tube. Without it, there's no point in trying to processor-slice garlic because the cloves will slither about the large feed tube.

Technique: Stand the garlic cloves in the smaller inner feed tube, arranging as needed for a snug fit, then exerting moderate pressure on the pusher, briskly pulse through the slicing disk.

FRESH GINGER Prep: Peel, and if the ginger is to be chopped, cut into 1-inch chunks; if sliced, cut into columns to fit the processor feed tube, or if only a small amount is to be sliced, the small inner feed tube.

Tool to use for chopping: Metal chopping blade.

Tool to use for slicing: Thin or medium slicing disk.

Techniques: The same as for garlic, which precedes.

HAM See Meat, cooked.

HAZELNUTS (FILBERTS) Prep: Spread the hazelnuts in an ungreased jelly-roll pan, set uncovered on the middle rack of a preheated 350°F oven, and toast until richly browned, 15 to 20 minutes. Cool the nuts until easy to handle, bundle in a clean dry dish towel, and rub briskly to remove the skins. Don't worry about recalcitrant bits of skin—they'll add color and texture.

Tool to use for chopping/grinding: Metal chopping blade.

Technique: Drop up to 2 cups hazelnuts in the work bowl and churn for 3 seconds. Tip the nuts into a pie pan, return any whole nuts and large chunks to the processor work bowl, and churn 3 seconds more. Repeat this sorting and churning until all hazelnuts are coarsely chopped. For finer chops, return all the nuts to the processor and with staccato pulses, process to the desired texture. To grind hazelnuts, churn 10 to 15 seconds until uniformly fine.

Note: If the recipe is a sweet, I like to chop the hazelnuts with some of the sugar—¼ to ½ cup, usually, but it depends on the amount of nuts. When grinding hazelnuts, I always include some, if not all, of the sugar from a recipe (see Toasted Hazelnut Biscotti, page 262).

HERBS, FRESH LEAFY (BASIL, CILANTRO, CHERVIL, MINT, PARSLEY, WATERCRESS) I use two different methods of chopping fresh herbs and it all depends on what I'm preparing (my recipes all specify which technique to use). The best sequence is to process a recipe's dry ingredients before moving on to the wet. This way there's no need to wash or dry the processor parts between steps. Sequence is doubly important with fresh herbs because if they are wet, they tend to purée instead of chop. For the most part, I chop the herbs in the processor, then wash them. But if a particular recipe makes this impractical (when I'm crumbing bread and chopping parsley simultaneously, for example), I wash the herbs and wring bone-dry in paper toweling before adding to the processor.

Prep: Discard coarse stems, then wash the herbs or not as individual recipes direct (see above).

Tool to use for chopping: Metal chopping blade.

Technique for chopping unwashed herbs: Place 1 to 2 cups fresh herbs in the work bowl (for smaller amounts, I use a mini processor). For a coarse chop, churn 3 to 5 seconds. For a finer chop, scrape the work bowl and churn 2 to 3 seconds more, or, if you prefer, pulse quickly to the desired texture. Tip the chopped herbs into a large fine sieve, then rinse the work bowl and blade in cool water running water directly over the sieve so that all stray bits fall into it. Next rinse the herbs well by holding the sieve under the cold tap. Tap the herbs onto to several thicknesses of paper toweling, and wring dry, transferring, if necessary, to fresh dry toweling, and wringing again. Roll up in the toweling and set aside until needed.

To chop washed herbs: The process is simply the reverse, that is rinse the herbs first in the sieve under the cold water tap, then wring in several changes of paper toweling until absolutely dry. For a coarse chop, use 2 to 3 staccato pulses; for a moderate one, 4 to 5; and for a fairly fine one, 6 to 8. Tap the chopped herbs onto paper toweling and reserve until needed.

Note: If a recipe calls for both parsley and cilantro or basil, or parsley and a small leafed herb like marjoram or oregano, chop the two together.

HORSERADISH Prep: Trim, peel, and cut into 1-inch chunks.

Tool to use for grating: Metal chopping blade.

Technique: Drop 1 cup horseradish chunks into the work bowl and churn 10 seconds. This will give you fairly finely grated horseradish—because of its pungency, you're not likely to want coarser texture. If I have less than 1 cup to grate, I'll use the mini processor.

Note: I don't recommend shredding horseradish in the processor. It is so tough and fibrous, it may stall the machine or deform the blade.

ICE Caution: Check your processor user's manual to see if it recommends crushing ice. Some machines aren't powerful enough.

Tool to use for crushing ice: Metal chopping blade.

Technique: If you merely want to crush ice—not mix it into a frozen cocktail or jiffy sorbet—turn the motor on, and drop the ice cubes one by one in rapid succession down the feed tube into the spinning blade (but no more than 12 in all). The minute the ice is the desired degree of fineness, stop the machine.

If you are mixing frozen daiquiris and such, you'll have to alter the procedure somewhat so that the ice does not go slushy the minute you add the alcohol and other ingredients. What works best, I've found, is to place the ice cubes in the work bowl, grind furiously for about 30 seconds, then pour the liquor and various flavorings down the feed tube with the motor running. The ice seems to hold up better this way. And my chopping blade hasn't suffered.

JICAMA Prep: Peel and if the jicama is to be chopped, cut into 1- to 1½-inch chunks. If it's to be sliced or shredded, cut in columns to fit the small inner feed tube.

Tool to use for chopping: Metal chopping blade.

Technique: Place up to 2 cups jicama chunks in the work bowl, and pulse in 1-second bursts to the desired texture. For a rough-chop, 2 to 3 pulses is usually sufficient. For a moderately fine one, 4 to 6. Easy does it.

Tool to use for slicing: Medium or thin slicing disk.

Technique: For precise slices, pulse the columns of jicama one by one down the small inner feed tube. Otherwise, stand as many columns in the large feed tube as will fit, then pulse them through the slicing disk, exerting moderate pressure on the pusher. Repeat until you have as much sliced jicama as you need.

Tool for shredding jicama: Medium or coarse shredding disk.

Technique: The same as for slicing.

LAMB See Meat, cooked.

LEEKS Prep: Because they are grown in sandy soil, leeks must be carefully washed. Trim off the tops and roots; also peel away coarse outer layers. Next make several cuts the length of each leek, from the top to within ½ inch of the root end. Hold the leeks under a cool tap, spreading the layers gently, so that the water flushes out the grit. If the leeks are to be chopped, cut into 1-inch chunks; if sliced, cut in lengths to fit the feed tube (the small inner feed tube, if your machine has one). The leeks can be pulsed down one by one, producing uniform slices.

Tool to use for chopping: Metal chopping blade.

Technique: Add up to 2 cups leek chunks to the work bowl and for a coarse chop (best for most recipes), pulse quickly 4 to 6 times. For finer texture, continue pulsing until just the right texture. Repeat until all leeks are chopped. As you will see in the recipes in this book, I often chop leeks with another ingredient of like texture—celery, for example—thereby doing two jobs at once.

Tool to use for slicing: Medium slicing disk.

Technique: Working with one leek at a time, stand root end down in the small inner feed tube. Exerting gentle pressure on the pusher, pulse through the slicing disk. If you have a big batch of leeks to slice and appearance is unimportant, stand root ends down in the large feed tube, fitting in as many leeks as you can—a snug fit is important. Exerting moderate pressure on the pusher, pulse the leeks through the slicing disk. Repeat until all leeks are sliced.

LEMONS, LIMES, ORANGES To be honest, if I have only a few citrus fruits to slice, I find it easier to do the job by hand. Certainly there's less clean-up.

Tip: Choose "seedless" varieties and fruits slim enough to fit into the feed tube.

Prep: Peel if recipes call for peeled lemons, limes, or oranges. Slice both ends off of the fruits so that they will stand square in the feed tube and won't wobble as you guide them through the slicing disk. If the oranges are too big to fit in the feed tube, halve them from stem end to blossom end.

Tool to use for slicing: Thin or medium slicing disk.

Technique: Stand as many lemons, limes, or oranges in the feed tube as will fit, then exerting moderate pressure on the pusher, pulse through the slicing disk.

Note: Tiny citrus fruits like kumquats and calamondins can be pulsed down the small inner feed tube. They should not be peeled.

Tool to use for juicing: Many new food processors now have attachments for juicing citrus fruits and they are wonderful when you have a load of lemons, limes, or oranges to juice.

Technique: These juicer attachments all operate a little differently so the best plan is to follow the directions in the user's manual.

MEAT, COOKED (BEEF, VEAL, LAMB, PORK, HAM) Because these are firm, they are much more suited to the food processor than raw meats. Still, I use the processor more for chopping or grinding them than for slicing. Cooked meats don't slice very neatly in a food processor without a serrated slicing disk (an optional extra with some brands). As for shredding cooked meats, forget it.

Prep: Remove all bones, sinew, and fat, then cut the meat into 1-inch chunks. If the meat is to be sliced, cut into blocks to fit the wide feed tube.

Tool to use for chopping/grinding: Metal chopping blade.

Technique: Place up to 2 cups (3 or 4 if your work bowl has a capacity of 14 cups [3½ quarts] or more). For a coarse chop, pulse the machine 3 to 4 times, for a medium chop, 5 to 6 times, and for a fine one, 7 to 8. For a moderately fine grind—good for meatloaves, croquettes, casseroles, and the like—use three 5-second churnings. For a coarser grind, use three 2-second churnings.

Tool to use for slicing: Medium serrated slicing disk.

Technique: Stand the block of meat in the feed tube, then exerting moderate pressure on the pusher, pulse through the serrated slicing disk. Repeat until all meat is sliced.

MEAT, RAW (BEEF, VEAL, LAMB, PORK)

I frankly find it more trouble than it's worth to try to grind, mince, chop, or slice raw meats in a food processor (my only exceptions are thin, boneless cutlets slivered for stir-fries, which can be dealt with exactly like chicken cutlets; see page 14). First, meats must be boned and trimmed of all fat and connective tissue, which can tangle in the blade. They must then be cubed or cut into columns to fit the food processor feed tube, and finally they must be partially frozen so that they offer some resistance to the blade. Even thus, the food processor doesn't do a very good job. Most supermarkets are now staffed with capable butchers, and I find it faster and more efficient to put them to good use.

MUSHROOMS

Prep: Remove the stems and wipe the caps clean (if a recipe calls only for caps, save the stems to use in soups and stews). If the mushrooms are to be chopped, halve or quarter the larger ones. Small mushrooms can go into the work bowl whole. In the case of portabellas or other oversize mushrooms, cut into 1- to 1½-inch chunks. If the mushrooms are to be sliced, only portabellas and other large mushrooms need special treatment. Usually quartering or halving them is sufficient, but occasionally they may need to be cut in columns to fit the processor feed tube.

Tool to use for chopping: Metal chopping blade.

Technique: Because mushrooms are so fragile, I've been able to chop a pound of them at a time. For that quantity and a coarse chop, pulse 4 to 5 times; for a moderately coarse chop, 6 to 8 times; for a moderately fine chop, 8 to 10; and for a fine one (really a grind), pulse 12 to 15 times. Small quantities require fewer pulses. Keep your eye on the work bowl, scrape as needed, and stop pulsing the minute the mushrooms are the texture you want.

Tool to use for slicing: Medium slicing disk.

Technique: Stand whole mushrooms on end in the processor feed tube, concave sides facing the same way, until you have a snug fit. Exerting the gentlest of pressures on the pusher, pulse the mushrooms through the slicing disk. For portabella quarters or halves, stand on end in the feed tube, again arranging for a tight fit. Pulse through the slicing disk as directed for whole mushrooms. Continue until all mushrooms are sliced.

OKRA Choose pods of approximately the same length so that the okra will slice uniformly.

Note: I do not processor-chop okra because it turns to mucilage.

Prep: Trim off caps.

Tool to use for slicing: Medium or thick slicing disk.

Technique: Stand the okra pods in the feed tube, alternating the directions for a tighter fit—one pod point down, the next point up, and so on. Exerting light pressure on the pusher, pulse the okra through the slicing disk. Repeat until all okra is sliced.

OLIVES I use the food processor to chop olives, nothing more. If they must be sliced, I do it by hand, which is easier than trying to arrange dozens of olives in the feed tube. They are slippery and slither about no matter how hard you try to anchor them with the pusher.

Prep: Pat the olives dry and pit. The fast way to pit them is to lay the olives on their sides on a cutting board and whack 3 to 4 at a time with a cutlet bat or broad side of a large chef's knife. Discard the pits. This mashes the olives somewhat, it's true. But does this matter when they're only going to be chopped?

Technique: Place 1 cup pitted ripe, green, or pimiento-stuffed olives in the work bowl. For a coarse chop, pulse briskly 2 to 3 times; for a moderate one, 4 to 5 times; and for a fine one, 6 to 8 times. Empty the work bowl, then repeat if more chopped olives are needed.

ONIONS Prep: Cut the tops and bottoms off the onions, halve from stem end to root end, then strip off the skin. Lay each half cut side down and if the onions are to be chopped, small onions need nothing more. If the onions are medium-size, either cut each half into slim wedges or quarter, crisscross fashion. Using the same technique, cut large onions into slim wedges or 1- to 1½-inch chunks. Giant onions—the faun-skinned Spanish onions and white Bermudas—should be cut into 1-inch chunks. If the onions are to be sliced, small ones can be peeled and left whole, but medium and large onions should be peeled and halved lengthwise from stem end to root end. The giants should be cut in columns the height and width of the feed tube, again from stem end to root end.

Tool to use for chopping: Metal chopping blade.

Technique: For best results, place no more than 2 cups of onion chunks in the work bowl. For a coarse chop use one to two 5-second churnings or, if you prefer, simply pulse to the desired texture. A moderate chop will require about three 5-second churnings; and a moderately fine one, four. For finely chopped, churn 8 to 10 to 12 seconds, scraping the work bowl at half time. If any large pieces remain, quickly pulse them out. Repeat until all the onions have been chopped.

Note: If a recipe calls for both bell peppers and onions, I often chop the two together, using the times suggested above.

Tool to use for slicing: Thin, medium, or thick slicing disk.

Technique: Place as many onions or pieces of onion in the feed tube as will fit, arranging them so the disk will slice across the rings. Exerting moderate pressure on the pusher, pulse the onions through the slicing disk. Repeat until all onions have been sliced.

PARMESAN CHEESE See Cheeses.

PARSLEY See Herbs.

PARSNIPS They are chopped, sliced, and shredded exactly like carrots (see pages 11–12).

PEACHES, APRICOTS, AND OTHER SOFT, FLESHY FRUITS Prep: Blanch the fruits 20 to 30 seconds in boiling water, drain, and slip off the skins. Halve and remove the pits. The fruits are now ready to slice. If they are to be chopped, halve each half crosswise, or if the fruits are large, cut in 1- to 1½-inch chunks.

Tool to use for chopping: Metal chopping blade.

Technique: Place up to 2 cups chunked fruit in the work bowl, sprinkle 1 tablespoon fresh lemon or lime juice evenly over all (to prevent darkening). Pulse once or twice for a coarse chop (perfect for shortcakes); 3 to 4 times for a finer chop (ideal for ice cream or cake topping).

Caution: Easy does it with these fragile fruits. Too many pulses or ones that are too long will mean fruit purée. For the proper way to purée fruits, see Purées, in this section.

Tool to use for slicing: Medium or thick slicing disk.

Technique: Stand the fruit halves on end in the processor feed tube, concave sides all facing the same way. Exerting light pressure on the pusher, pulse through the slicing disk. Repeat until all the fruit has been sliced. Sprinkle with 1 tablespoon fresh lemon or lime juice and toss lightly. This will retard browning.

PEANUTS Prep: The best nuts are raw ones, still in their skins. But they must be absolutely fresh. To blanch, immerse in boiling water for 20 to 30 seconds, drain, and slip off the skins. Spread the peanuts on several thicknesses of paper toweling and allow to dry for about an hour, replenishing the toweling as it dampens. Next, spread the peanuts in a large shallow baking pan, set uncovered on the middle rack of a preheated 300°F oven, and toast just until golden brown and irresistible smelling, about 20 minutes. Shake the pan several times as the peanuts toast.

Note: You can skip all of the above if you use cocktail peanuts, but they will never taste as fresh. If they are salted, you should reduce the amount of salt in the recipe by about ½ teaspoon.

Tool to use for chopping: Metal chopping blade.

Technique: Place no more than 2 cups of peanuts in the work bowl. For a coarse chop, use two 5-second churnings, for finer chops, simply pulse to the desired texture.

About making peanut butter: The first thing I wanted to do when I got a food processor was to make peanut butter. I managed it in the end, but not without adding considerable peanut oil and butter—not what this calorie-counter needed. I frankly think commercial peanut butters are better than homemade. The difference? Food companies grind peanuts under pressure, which of course home cooks cannot do. Some food processor user's manuals give directions for making peanut butter, and by all means give it a try. Perhaps you'll have better luck than I did.

PEARS Choose firm-ripe fruits.

Prep: Stem the pears, then depending upon size, halve or quarter lengthwise. Peel and scoop out the cores with a teaspoon or melon baller. The pears are now ready to slice. If they are to be chopped, cut in 1- to 1½-inch chunks.

Tool to use for chopping: Metal chopping blade.

Technique: Place up to 2 cups chunked pears in the work bowl and sprinkle with 1 tablespoon fresh lemon or lime juice to prevent darkening. Pulse once or twice for a coarse chop; 3 to 4 times for a finer chop. Use a light touch on the pulse button lest you reduce the pears to purée. For the proper way to purée fruits, see Purées, in this section.

Tool to use for slicing: Medium or thick slicing disk.

Technique: Stand the pear halves or quarters on end in the feed tube, arranging them for a snug fit. Exerting gentle pressure on the pusher, pulse through the slicing disk. Repeat until all the pears have been sliced. Sprinkle with 1 to 2 tablespoons fresh lemon or lime juice and toss lightly.

PECANS, WALNUTS Prep: None needed if the nuts are shelled.

Tool to use for chopping/grinding: Metal chopping blade.

Technique: Place up to 2 cups nuts in the processor work bowl and, if possible, add ¼ to ½ cup sugar from the recipe you are preparing. If not, add a tablespoon or two of flour from the recipe, even a bit of salt—as little as ½ teaspoon will help keep the nuts from churning to paste. For a coarse chop, pulse 2 to 3 times, then using a plastic spatula and minding the blade, stir. If large chunks remain, pulse once or twice more. For a medium chop, pulse 4 to 5 times; for a fine one, 6 to 8. To grind the nuts, let the machine run nonstop for 10 to 15 seconds.

PEPPERONI AND OTHER HARD SAUSAGES Prep: Cut the sausage in lengths to fit the feed tube, preferably the small inner feed tube, which will hold the sausage in place, ensuring clean-cut rounds.

Note: You also put less stress on the processor motor and slicing disk if you slice the sausages one by one instead of filling the wide feed tube.

Tool to use for slicing: Medium slicing disk, preferably a serrated one (an extra attachment available for some machines).

Technique: Stand a length of sausage in the small inner feed tube, then exerting firm, steady pressure on the pusher, pulse through the slicing disk. If you must use the wide feed tube, stand as many lengths of sausage in the feed tube as you can, then force through the slicing disk with the pusher, pulsing all the while. The noise can be deafening.

PEPPERS, SWEET AND HOT Bell peppers and chiles are handled the same way whether they're to be chopped or sliced.

Caution: Wear rubber gloves when handling the hottest chiles, and avoid rubbing your eyes. The hottest part of a chile, by the way, is the pithy part holding the seeds in place. The seeds, too, pack plenty of heat.

Prep: Core, quarter, and seed the bell peppers (small chiles only need to be halved). The fastest way to core, quarter, and seed a bell pepper is to slice off the stem end, stand the pepper upside-down, then cut straight down, following the pepper's natural convolutions so that you miss the core and seeds altogether. Also trim and use any fleshy parts around the stem. The peppers are now ready to slice. If they are to be chopped, cut into 1- to 1½-inch chunks. If small chiles are to be chopped, simply halve each half crosswise.

Tool to use for chopping: Metal chopping blade.

Technique: Place up to 2 cups pepper chunks in the work bowl. For a coarse chop, pulse quickly 2 to 3 times. For a chop of medium texture, pulse 4 to 5 times. For a fine chop, use three 3-second churnings.

Note: For amounts of less than 1 cup, I use the mini food processor. Whenever recipes call for both bell peppers (or even chiles) and onions or scallions, I chop the two together, saving myself a step. As long as you don't try to chop more than 2 cups at a time, it works beautifully. The chopping times remain the same as those above because onions and peppers are so similar in texture.

Tool to use for slicing: Medium slicing disk.

Technique: Stand the bell pepper quarters on end, concave sides facing the same way (just as you would stack spoons), fitting as many in the feed tube as you can—you need a snug fit if the peppers are to slice cleanly. Now with the quickest and gentlest of pulses, ease the peppers through the slicing disk with the pusher. Repeat until all the peppers have been sliced.

Note: Small chiles should be reassembled, that is, the two halves put back together so that you have a "hollow pepper," then pulsed one by one down the small inner feed tube.

PINEAPPLE Prep: Slice the top and bottom off the pineapple, then stand it on a cutting board, and cut straight down from top to bottom, removing all the prickly skin. Any remaining "eyes" can be dug out with the point of a vegetable peeler. Quarter the pineapple lengthwise and cut off the tough core at the point of each quarter. Now, halve each quarter lengthwise so that you have 8 long wedges. If the pineapple is to be sliced, cut in lengths to fit the feed tube. If chopped, cut each wedge into 1-inch chunks.

Tool to use for chopping: Metal chopping blade.

Technique: Place up to 2 cups pineapple chunks in the processor work bowl. For a coarse chop, use two 3-second bursts of speed, for a finer one, three to four 3-second pulses.

Tool to use for slicing: Medium slicing disk.

Technique: If the columns of pineapple will fit in the small inner feed tube, pulse them one by one through the slicing disk. If you must use the wide feed tube, stand the pineapple columns in it, reversing the directions so that the narrow side faces one way one time and the opposite way the next. You'll get a tighter fit. Exerting firm pressure on the pusher, pulse the pineapple through the slicing disk. Repeat until all pineapple has been sliced.

PINE NUTS (PIGNOLI, PIÑONS) Prep: None needed if the nuts have been shelled.

Tool to use for chopping: Metal chopping blade.

Technique: Place up to 2 cups pine nuts in the work bowl and if the recipe you're preparing contains sugar, add 2 to 4 tablespoons of it to the nuts. For a coarse chop, use two 3-second churnings; for medium, three 3-second churnings, and for fine, four or five. If there are several churnings, scrape the work bowl in between with a plastic spatula and stir, keeping your eye on the blade at all times. Repeat until you have all the chopped pine nuts you need.

PISTACHIO NUTS Prep: Shell, if necessary. If the nuts haven't been blanched, immerse in boiling water for 20 to 30 seconds. Drain well, then bundle, 1 cup at a time, in a dry dish towel, and rub briskly to take off the skins. Spread the pistachios on several thicknesses of paper toweling and dry for 1 to 2 hours, replenishing the toweling as it dampens.

Tool to use for chopping/grinding: Metal chopping blade.

Technique: Place up to 2 cups blanched pistachios in the work bowl and if the recipe you're preparing contains sugar, add ¼ to ½ cup of it to the nuts. For a coarse chop, pulse 2 to 3 times; for a medium chop, 4 to 5 times; and for a fine one, 6 to 8 times. For ground pistachios (popular in Greek and Turkish recipes), let the motor run nonstop for about 15 seconds.

PORK See Meat, cooked.

POTATOES, IRISH OR SWEET You'll save prep time if you buy potatoes the size and shape of the feed tube—especially important if they'll be sliced or shredded.

Prep: Peel the potatoes, removing all green patches and dark spots. If the potatoes are to be shredded or sliced and are too chunky for the feed tube, halve them lengthwise, then cut in lengths to fit it. If they're to be chopped or grated, cut in 1- to 1½-inch chunks.

Tool to use for chopping/grating: Metal chopping blade.

Technique: Place up to 2 cups potato chunks in the processor work bowl. For a coarse chop, pulse 3 to 4 times (perfect for hashes and such). For grated potatoes, churn 5 seconds, then with a plastic spatula, scrape the work bowl and stir, pushing large chunks to the bottom—mind the blade. Repeat the 5-second churning/scraping/stirring sequence 4 to 5 times until the potatoes are the texture of cooked oatmeal. If any large lumps remain, quickly pulse them out.

Tool to use for slicing: Thin or medium slicing disk.

Technique: Stand as many potatoes (or half potatoes) in the feed tube as you can for a tight fit, then exerting moderate pressure on the pusher, pulse through the slicing disk. Repeat until all potatoes have been sliced.

Tool to use for shredding: Fine, medium, or coarse shredding disk.

Technique: The same as for slicing potatoes.

Tool to use for mashing sweet potatoes: Metal chopping blade.

Technique: Place up to 4 cups peeled, chunked, cooked sweet potatoes in the work bowl, add a tablespoon of butter or a couple of tablespoons of milk or cream, and churn 5 seconds. Using a plastic spatula and minding the blade, scrape the work bowl and stir. Repeat once or twice until the potatoes are as smooth as you like.

Note: I've tried many different ways of mashing Irish potatoes, and I have to say it's faster and easier to mash them by hand, given all the steps you must take for a not very good approximation of Grandma's mashed potatoes. What does work magnificently, however, is puréeing mixtures of potatoes and other cooked vegetables. See Purée of Potato, Carrots, and Leek (page 178), also Potato and Celery Root Purée (page 179).

PURÉES The technique is similar whether you are puréeing soups, cooked vegetables, or raw or cooked fruits.

Tool to use for puréeing: Metal chopping blade.

Prep for berries and other fruits: Stem, wash, pit, and peel—whatever the particular fruit requires. Cut large fruits into 1- to 1½-inch chunks; peaches, plums, and other small round fruits can be cut into slim wedges. Cooked fruits should be peeled and pitted, if necessary. If they are large, they should also be chunked unless they're unusually soft.

Technique: Place up to 2 cups berries or fruit chunks in the processor work bowl. If you are puréeing apples, peaches, pears, and other fruits that darken, sprinkle with 1 to 2 tablespoons fresh lemon, lime, or orange juice. Churn in 5-second increments, scraping the work bowl and stirring as needed with a plastic spatula—mind the blade. Inspect the texture of the fruit after each churning and stop the instant it's velvety.

Note: Because of their many seeds, raspberry and blackberry purées should be sieved before they're served or used in recipes.

Prep for cooked vegetables: The vegetables that purée most successfully are those with high water content: asparagus, beets, broccoli, carrots, cauliflower, celery root, green beans and peas, mushrooms, onions, roasted bell peppers, turnips, winter squash, and of course, all leafy greens. If the vegetables are large, cut in 1- to 1½-inch chunks.

Technique: Except for leafy greens, which need no additional liquid, I customarily add 2 to 6 tablespoons of the cooking water—whatever it takes for a silky purée. Place up to 4 cups of the vegetable in the processor work bowl, and snap the motor on. Add the cooking liquid down the feed tube, tablespoon by tablespoon, until the consistency seems just right. Using a plastic spatula and skirting the blade, scrape the work bowl, and stir the purée. Continue churning until absolutely smooth.

Tip: For a richer purée, drop a pat of butter down the feed tube along with the cooking liquid.

Prep for soups: First of all, cool the soup for at least 15 minutes; if you don't, the pressure will build up inside the processor and the steaming soup will whoosh out of the work bowl (you can get a nasty burn). Second, remove all bones, skin, whole bay leaves, peppercorns, and other whole herbs or spices.

Technique: Purée the soup in 2- to 4-cup batches depending on the size of your work bowl, always including some of the liquid with the solids. Churn each batch for 20 to 30 seconds or however long it takes to achieve a smooth mixture. As each batch is puréed, pour back into the pan if the soup is to be served hot. If it's a cold soup, pour into a large bowl, cover, and refrigerate until ready to serve.

RADISHES If possible, choose radishes about the circumference of the small inner feed tube if you intend to slice or shred them. As for daikons—the big, white, mild Japanese radishes—choose firm, nicely shaped specimens. They'll be easier to trim for the feed tube.

Prep: Cut off the root and stem ends so that the radishes will stand without wobbling. If the radishes are to be chopped and they are large, cut into 1- to 1½-inch chunks. If daikons are to be sliced or shredded, cut in columns to fit the smaller inner feed tube (this will give you dainty slices or shreds).

Tool to use for chopping: Metal chopping blade.

Technique: If I'm chopping only a few radishes, I use the mini food processor. For bigger batches, place up to 2 cups radishes or radish chunks in the work bowl, then pulse in 1-second bursts until you get the desired texture. For a rough-chop, 2 to 3 pulses is usually sufficient. For a moderate one, 4 to 5. That's about as far as you can go without making pap of the radishes.

Tool to use for slicing: Medium or thin slicing disk.

Technique: If the radishes are the size of the inner feed tube, stack them up to within about an inch of the top, and pulse them through the slicing disk, exerting moderate pressure on the pusher. For daikons, either pulse the columns one by one down the inner feed tube (if uniform slices are needed), or if you're in a hurry and appearance doesn't matter, stand as many columns in the large feed tube as will fit snugly, and pulse the same way. Repeat until you have as many radish slices as you need.

Tool for shredding radishes: Medium or coarse shredding disk.

Technique: The same as for slicing.

RHUBARB Prep: The roots and leaves of rhubarb are poisonous, so trim the stalks carefully. If rhubarb is to be chopped, cut the stalks into 1-inch chunks; if they are to be sliced, cut in lengths to fit the processor feed tube.

To chop and slice: See Celery, in this section. The techniques for chopping and slicing rhubarb are the same.

RUTABAGA, TURNIP Prep: Cut off the tops and bottoms, then peel. If rutabaga is to be chopped, cut into 1-inch chunks; if sliced or shredded, cut in columns to fit the large feed tube. If turnips are to be chopped, small ones can simply be halved, larger ones quartered or cut into slim wedges. To ready turnips for slicing and shredding, trim them as needed to fit into the large feed tube.

Tool to use for chopping: Metal chopping blade.

Technique: Place up to 2 cups rutabaga or turnip chunks in the work bowl. For a coarse chop, use one to two 3-second churnings; for a moderate one, three or four 3-second churnings; and for fine, switch to the pulse button and zap 6 to 8 times or until as finely chopped as you like.

Tool to use for slicing: Medium slicing disk.

Technique: Stand as many pieces of rutabaga or as many turnips in the feed tube as you can for a tight fit, then pressing firmly on the pusher, pulse through the slicing disk. Repeat until all are sliced.

Tool to use for shredding: Medium shredding disk.

Technique: The same as for slicing.

SCALLIONS The chunkier the scallions, the better. Pencil-slim ones are spindly and difficult to handle, especially when it comes to slicing.

Prep: Bunch the scallions, and with one whack of the chef's knife, cut off all the roots. Realign the scallions, and in another single cut, remove all but 1 inch of the tops. Remove any withering outer layers and discard. If the scallions are to be chopped, cut into 1-inch chunks, if sliced, rebunch and cut in lengths to fit the small inner feed tube.

Tool to use for chopping: Metal chopping blade.

Technique: For 1 cup of scallion chunks or less, the mini is preferable; for larger amounts—but no more than 2 cups at a time—a full-size processor is the one to use. Place the scallions in the work bowl. For a coarse chop, pulse 2 to 3 times; for moderate, 4 to 6; for fine, pulse 8 to 10; and for very fine, churn 8 to 10 seconds.

Note: I often chop garlic and/or fresh ginger along with the scallions. It depends on the recipe.

Tool to use for slicing: Thin or medium slicing disk.

Technique: Bunch enough prepped scallions to fit snugly in the small inner feed tube and insert root ends down. Exerting gentle pressure on the pusher, pulse through the slicing disk. Repeat until all the scallions have been sliced.

SHALLOTS See Garlic. The technique is the same.

SHRIMP See Fish and shellfish.

SQUASH, SUMMER To simplify slicing and shredding, choose slim, straight young yellow squash or zucchini.

Prep: Cut off the stem and root ends. If the squash are to be sliced or shredded, cut in lengths to fit either the small inner feed tube (for perfect slices) or the large outer feed tube. If they're to be chopped, halve each squash lengthwise, then cut each half into1-inch chunks.

Tool to use for chopping: Metal chopping blade.

Technique: Place up to 2 cups squash chunks in the work bowl. For a coarse chop, use two to three 1-second pulses; for a moderate one, four or five 1-second pulses, and for a moderately fine one, pulse briskly 6 to 8 times. Scrape the work bowl sides and pulse 6 to 8 times more. Resist the temptation to chop the squash any finer because it will liquefy.

Tool to use for slicing: Medium or thick slicing disk.

Technique: For penny-perfect slices, pulse the pieces of squash one by one down the small inner feed tube, exerting moderate pressure on the pusher. Otherwise, stand as many pieces of squash in the large feed tube as needed for a snug fit, then exerting steady pressure on the pusher, pulse through the slicing disk. Continue until all of the squash has been sliced.

Tool to use for shredding: Medium or coarse shredding disk.

Technique: The same as for slicing.

SQUASH, WINTER See Purées.

STRAWBERRIES I find it completely impractical to slice strawberries in a food processor because they're misshapen and fragile. But I definitely use the processor to purée them (see Purées in this section), also to rough-chop them (just the thing for shortcake).

Prep: Sort the berries, wash, hull, and pat dry. Halve or quarter any berries that are large.

Tool to use for chopping: Metal chopping blade.

Technique: Place 2 to 4 cups strawberries in the work bowl (up to 6 cups if your machine is large) and pulse briskly 4 to 5 times. Scrape the work bowl and pulse 3 times more until coarsely chopped—no longer or you'll liquidize the berries.

TOMATOES Some food processor user's manuals describe how to slice tomatoes, but I find nothing daunting about hand-slicing them, and quite honestly, unless the tomatoes are really firm (read tasteless), the human hand does a better job. Yes, you can slice green tomatoes in the processor (cut off the tops and bottoms, stand cut-side down in the wide feed tube, then pulse through the medium slicing disk). But ripe, flavorful tomatoes are far too soft to slice cleanly. I do, however, rough-chop them in the processor, purée them (see Purées, in this section), and juice them. Choose sun-ripened tomatoes with a bit of residual firmness if you're going to chop them. For juice, they should be dead-ripe, indeed soft approaching mushy.

Prep: Peel the tomatoes or not as you wish. Core, and if the tomatoes are small to medium, cut into slim wedges; if large, cut in 1- to 1½-inch chunks.

Tool to use for chopping/juicing: Metal chopping blade.

Technique: Depending on the capacity of your work bowl, add 2 to 4 cups prepped tomatoes. For a rough-chop, pulse quickly 2 to 3 times. Using a plastic spatula and skirting the blade, scrape the work bowl and carefully stir the tomatoes up from the bottom. Pulse 2 to 3 times more until they reach the texture of salsa.

To juice: Use two to three 20-second churnings, scraping the work bowl and stirring in between. Put through a fine sieve to remove seeds and bits of skin.

TURNIPS See Rutabaga, turnip.

VEAL See Meat, raw and/or Meat, cooked.

WALNUTS See Pecans, walnuts.

WATERCRESS See Herbs.

ZUCCHINI See Squash, summer.

WHAT FOOD PROCESSORS DO NOT DO WELL

Things have changed significantly since the first food processors were introduced nearly thirty years ago. The new machines, most of them completely redesigned, are far more versatile than their predecessors, which now seem as obsolete as T-model Fords. Even so, the newest, fanciest machines can't do everything. At least not well. They don't, for example:

■ Grind spices to powder. The one exception is Cuisinart's Mini-Prep Plus, a tiny dynamo with reversible action plus a double-edged blade—dull for grinding spices, coffee beans, and such; sharp for mincing garlic, fresh herbs, and small amounts of onion and bell pepper. Even so, I was only able to grind cinnamon sticks to coarse crumbs, not to powder.

■ Mill whole grains into flour.

■ Whip egg whites to great heights unless the machine has a whip attachment (LeChef and top-of-the-line Cuisinarts and KitchenAids do).

■ Shred raw meat, even if it's been firmed up in the freezer.

■ Mash, slice, or shred cooked all-purpose potatoes (Maine or Eastern), new potatoes, redskins, or other waxy species. They become gluey. Even dry, mealy russets (Idahos or baking potatoes) fair poorly.

■ Chop candied or glacéed fruits, even if they've been hardened in the freezer. They're quickly puréed to gum.

■ Chop dates. They, too, are churned to a sticky paste.

SOME USEFUL EQUIVALENTS

The information here is designed to help you adapt your own recipe favorites to processor preparation. Because many recipes call for ingredients by the cup rather than by the piece or the pound—½ cup chopped onion, for example, 1 cup fine dry bread crumbs, or 2 cups leftover ground ham—it's useful to know how much onion you must processor-chop to equal ½ cup, how many slices of bread it takes for 1 cup of crumbs, and how many ounces of leftover ham will, when ground, amount to 2 cups.

The following table is arranged alphabetically, food by food. The equivalents, it should be stressed, can only be approximate because of the subtle differences that exist from processor to processor, from food to food (one bunch of leeks or scallions may require more trimming than another one of the same weight), and finally, from cook to cook. No two cooks will have identical techniques.

Note: Amounts for sliced and shredded foods were calculated using the medium slicing and medium shredding disks, standard equipment for most food processors.

FOOD AND AMOUNT	HOW PROCESSED	EQUIVALENT YIELD
ALMONDS		
1 cup whole, blanched	Coarsely chopped	1 cup
	Finely chopped	1¼ cups
APPLES		
1 medium	Coarsely chopped	½ cup
	Finely chopped	⅓ to ½ cup
	Sliced	¾ cup
AVOCADOS		
1 medium	Coarsely chopped	1¼ cups
	Sliced	1½ to 2 cups
	Puréed	¾ to 1 cup
BANANAS		
1 medium	Sliced	1 cup
	Mashed or puréed	⅔ cup
BEANS, GREEN OR WAX		
1 cup, cooked	Puréed	½ cup
BEETS		
1 medium	Sliced	⅔ cup
	Shredded	½ cup
	Puréed (cooked)	⅓ cup
BREAD		
2 slices with crusts	Crumbed	1 cup
BROCCOLI		
1 cup florets, cooked	Puréed	½ cup
CABBAGE		
1 medium, trimmed and cored	Coarsely chopped for slaw	8 cups
	Sliced for slaw	10 cups
CARROTS		
1 medium	Coarsely or finely chopped	½ cup
	Sliced	½ cup
	Shredded	½ cup
	Puréed (cooked)	¼ cup

FOOD AND AMOUNT	HOW PROCESSED	EQUIVALENT YIELD
CAULIFLOWER		
1 cup florets, cooked	Puréed	½ cup
CELERY		
2 medium ribs	Coarsely or finely chopped	⅔ cup
	Sliced	¾ cup
CELERY ROOT		
1 medium	Sliced	¾ cup
	Shredded	¾ cup
	Puréed (cooked)	⅓ to ½ cup
CHEESES		
Parmesan, Romano, 8 ounces	Grated	1¾ cups
Cheddar, Jack, 8 ounces	Shredded	2 cups
Gruyère, Swiss, 8 ounces	Shredded	2 cups
CHICKEN, TURKEY		
Raw cutlets, 8 ounces	Slivered for stir-fries	2 cups
Cooked, 8 ounces, boned and trimmed	Coarsely ground or chopped	1½ cups
COCONUT		
1 medium	Grated (chopped)	5 cups
	Shredded	7 cups
CORN		
1 cup kernels	Chopped cream-style	½ cup
CRANBERRIES		
1 cup	Coarsely chopped	¾ to 1 cup
CUCUMBERS		
1 medium, peeled and seeded	Coarsely chopped	1 cup
	Sliced	1¼ cups
	Shredded	1 to 1¼ cups
CRUMBS, FINE		
Soda crackers, 28 (2-inch) squares	Crumbed	1 cup
Graham crackers, 15 (2⅜-inch) squares	Crumbed	1 cup
Vanilla wafers, gingersnaps, 24	Crumbed	1 cup
Chocolate wafers, 16 (2-inch)	Crumbed	1 cup

FOOD AND AMOUNT	HOW PROCESSED	EQUIVALENT YIELD
GARLIC		
1 medium clove	Coarsely or finely chopped	1 to 1½ teaspoons
HAZELNUTS (FILBERTS)		
1 cup, skinned	Coarsely chopped	1 cup
	Finely chopped	1¼ cups
HERBS, FRESH LEAFY		
Basil, cilantro, chervil, mint, parsley, watercress 1 cup lightly packed	Coarsely chopped	½ cup
	Finely chopped	⅓ cup
ICE CUBES		
3 standard	Crushed	¾ to 1 cup
LEEKS		
2 medium, trimmed	Coarsely or finely chopped	1 cup
	Sliced	1 cup
MEAT, COOKED		
8 ounces boned and trimmed beef, veal, lamb, pork, ham	Coarsely chopped or ground	1 to 1½ cups
	Sliced	1½ cups
MUSHROOMS		
4 ounces, trimmed	Coarsely chopped	1¼ cups
	Finely chopped	¾ to 1 cup
	Sliced	1½ cups
ONIONS, YELLOW OR RED		
1 medium	Coarsely chopped	½ cup
	Finely chopped	⅓ cup
	Sliced	½ to ¾ cup
PEACHES		
1 medium	Coarsely chopped	½ to ⅔ cup
	Sliced	⅔ to 1 cup
PEANUTS		
1 cup, blanched	Coarsely or finely chopped	1 cup
PEARS		
1 medium	Coarsely chopped	½ to ¾ cup
	Sliced	¾ to 1 cup

FOOD AND AMOUNT	HOW PROCESSED	EQUIVALENT YIELD
PECANS		
1 cup broken meats	Coarsely chopped	1 cup
	Finely chopped	1¼ cups
PEPPERS, BELL		
1 medium green,	Coarsely chopped	1 cup
red, yellow, orange, or purple	Finely chopped	¾ cup
	Sliced	1¼ cups
PINEAPPLE		
1 medium, trimmed and cored	Coarsely chopped	3½ cups
	Sliced	4 cups
PINE NUTS, PISTACHIOS		
1 cup	Coarsely or finely chopped	1 cup
POTATOES		
1 medium Irish or sweet	Coarsely chopped	¾ cup
	Sliced	¾ cup
	Shredded	½ to ⅔ cup
PURÉES		
1 cup cooked, drained vegetable	Puréed	½ cup
1 cup cooked, drained, pitted fruit	Puréed	½ cup
1 cup prepped raw berries or other fruit	Puréed	½ cup
RADISHES		
6 medium, trimmed	Coarsely chopped	½ to ¾ cup
RUTABAGA		
1 cup peeled chunks	Coarsely chopped	1 cup
	Sliced	1 to 1¼ cups
SCALLIONS		
6 medium, trimmed	Coarsely chopped	⅓ cup
	Finely chopped	¼ cup
SHALLOTS		
6 medium	Coarsely chopped	⅓ cup
	Finely chopped	¼ cup

FOOD AND AMOUNT	HOW PROCESSED	EQUIVALENT YIELD
SQUASH, SUMMER		
1 medium yellow, pattypan, zucchini	Coarsely chopped	1¼ cups
	Finely chopped	1 cup
	Sliced	1½ cups
	Shredded	1 cup
SQUASH, WINTER (ACORN, BUTTERNUT, ETC.) See Purées.		
TOMATOES		
1 medium	Coarsely chopped	1 cup
TURKEY		
See Chicken, turkey.		
TURNIP		
1 medium	Coarsely chopped	⅔ cup
	Finely chopped	½ to ⅔ cup
	Sliced	¾ cup
	Shredded	½ to ¾ cup
WALNUTS		
1 cup broken meats	Coarsely chopped	1 cup
	Finely chopped	1¼ cups
WATERCRESS See Herbs		
ZUCCHINI See Squash, summer		

Basic Recipes

Condiments, Crumb Crusts, Pastry Dough, Salsas, Salad Dressings, Sauces and Such

I'M NOT A CHEF, but from friends who are I've learned that the fastest way to jump-start a meal is to have freezer and refrigerator stocked with the basics: crumbs and crumb toppings, for example, salsas, sauces, and salad dressings plus a variety of stocks and flavored butters.

Before the food processor revolutionized my life, I frankly never bothered because the prep was always so daunting. Consider, for example, the endless slicing, mincing, and chopping needed to make beef stock the old-fashioned way. The processor does it all on fast-forward.

And it churns out flavored butters even faster. I roll them into logs, foil-wrap them, and freeze them so that all I need do is slice off a pat or two whenever I need them and return the balance to the freezer. Is there an easier way to dress up grilled steaks, chops, chicken, fish, or steamed vegetables? I don't think so.

I dislike commercially grated Parmesan (to me it tastes of nothing but salt), so I'll buy a couple of pounds of Parmigiano-Reggiano, chunk it, and grate it in a processor fitted with the metal chopping blade. Stored in a tightly capped jar in the refrigerator, it tastes freshly grated for weeks. Ditto bread crumbs and crumb toppings.

In the pages that follow you'll find recipes for the make-aheads I like to keep on hand. All prove what a whiz the food processor is and how much time and energy it can spare you.

Chicken Stock

If you've poached a hen or capon, save the stock and substitute for some of the liquid called for here. Also add the carcass to the kettle and use three pounds of chicken wings and backs instead of four. For maximum flavor, I processor-slice the vegetables instead of chunking or dicing.

MAKES ABOUT 4 QUARTS

4 pounds chicken wings and backs

4 quarts cold water

1 large yellow onion, peeled and cut in columns to fit the processor feed tube

2 medium carrots, peeled and cut in lengths to fit the processor feed tube

2 medium ribs celery, trimmed and cut in lengths to fit the processor feed tube (reserve tops)

4 large branches Italian parsley

1 large whole bay leaf

8 peppercorns

2 teaspoons salt

1. Place the chicken wings and backs in a large heavy soup kettle and add the water. Set aside while you prepare the vegetables.

2. Equip the food processor with the medium slicing disk, stand the pieces of onion in the feed tube arranging so that they fit snugly, then exerting gentle but steady pressure on the pusher, pulse through the slicing disk.

3. Now slice the carrots and celery the same way, each time fitting as many pieces in the feed tube as possible.

4. Add the sliced vegetables to the kettle along with the parsley, bay leaf, peppercorns, salt, and reserved celery tops. Bring to a boil over moderately high heat and skim off any scum that rises to the top. Adjust the heat so the liquid bubbles lazily, cover, and simmer until the stock has developed rich chicken flavor—about 2 hours. Skim off fat, then taste for salt, and adjust as needed.

5. Line a large colander with several thicknesses of cheesecloth, set over a large heatproof bowl, pour in the stock, and let it drip through undisturbed. Reserve what chicken meat you can to use in soups, salads, casseroles, pot pies, and the like. Discard all bones, skin, vegetables, and other solids.

6. Chill the chicken stock until the fat solidifies on top. Scoop off the fat and blot up loose bits. The stock is now ready to use in soups, sauces, stews, and other recipes.

7. To store, ladle into 1-pint or 1-quart freezer containers leaving ½-inch head space, snap on the lids, label, date, and set in a 0°F freezer. Use within 6 months.

Note: If refrigerated, the stock will keep for about a week.

Beef Stock

As with the Chicken Stock that precedes, I processor-slice the vegetables so that they release more flavor. As for the beef bones, have the butcher crack them.

MAKES ABOUT 3 QUARTS

5 pounds mixed beef bones, cracked (marrow, shin, rib, etc.)

2 large yellow onions, peeled and cut in columns to fit the processor feed tube

4 large leeks, trimmed, washed carefully, and cut in lengths to fit the processor feed tube

3 medium carrots, peeled and cut in lengths to fit the processor feed tube

3 medium ribs celery, trimmed and cut in lengths to fit the processor feed tube

4 large branches Italian parsley

2 large whole bay leaves

8 peppercorns

5 quarts cold water

1 tablespoon salt

1. Trim a little fat from the bones, dice it, then melt in a large heavy soup kettle over high heat. Add the bones and turn in the drippings until nicely browned on all sides. Reduce the heat to low and let the bones continue cooking.

2. Equip the food processor with the medium slicing disk, stand as many pieces of onion in the feed tube as will fit snugly, then pulse through the slicing disk. Repeat until both onions are sliced; add to the kettle.

3. Now slice the leeks, carrots, and celery the same way, each time fitting as many into the feed tube as possible.

4. Add to the kettle along with the parsley, bay leaves, peppercorns, water, and salt. Bring to a boil over moderately high heat, skim off the scum that rises to the top, then adjust the heat so the liquid barely trembles. Cover and simmer slowly until the stock has rich beefy flavor, 4½ to 5 hours. Skim off as much fat as possible.

5. Line a large colander with several thicknesses of cheesecloth, set over a second large kettle, pour in the stock, and let it drip through undisturbed. Discard all solids.

6. Cool the stock to room temperature, then chill until the fat solidifies on top. Lift off the fat and blot up any loose bits. The stock is now ready to use in soups, sauces, and stews.

7. To store, ladle into 1-pint or 1-quart freezer containers, leaving ½-inch head space, snap on the lids, label, date, and set in a 0°F freezer. Use within 6 months. If refrigerated, the stock will keep for about 1 week.

Glace de Viande

Boil 1 cup Beef Stock uncovered in a small saucepan over moderate heat until reduced by two-thirds. Just a tablespoon or two of this rich brown glaze will heighten the color and flavor of gravies, sauces, soups, and stews. Stored in a tightly capped jar in the refrigerator, Glace de Viande keeps for about a month. Makes ⅓ cup.

Fish Stock

Here's another handy stock to have on hand. Use it in seafood soups, mousses, soufflés, and sauces served with fish. To extract as much flavor from the vegetables as possible, I slice them.

Note: I personally prefer to use the bones and trimmings of lean white fish for stock because oily fish make it unpleasantly "fishy."

MAKES ABOUT 2½ QUARTS

1 pound trimmings, heads, and bones from a mixture of fish (cod, haddock, flounder, etc.) (see note)

2 quarts cold water

2 cups dry white wine

1 large yellow onion, peeled and cut in columns to fit the processor feed tube

1 large carrot, peeled and cut in lengths to fit the processor feed tube

1 large rib celery, trimmed and cut in lengths to fit the processor feed tube (reserve tops)

3 large branches Italian parsley

1 large sprig fresh lemon thyme or ½ teaspoon dried leaf thyme, crumbled

8 peppercorns

1 teaspoon salt

1. Place the fish trimmings, heads, and bones in a large heavy soup kettle, add the water and wine, and set aside while you prepare the vegetables.

2. Equip the food processor with the medium slicing disk, stand the pieces of onion in the feed tube so that they fit snugly, then exerting gentle but steady pressure on the pusher, pulse through the slicing disk.

3. Slice the carrot and celery the same way, each time fitting as many pieces in the feed tube as possible.

4. Add the sliced vegetables to the kettle along with the parsley, thyme, peppercorns, salt, and reserved celery tops. Bring to a boil over moderately high heat and skim off any scum that rises to the surface. Adjust the heat so the liquid bubbles gently, cover, and simmer slowly until the stock has developed delicate but well balanced fish flavor—about 1 hour. Taste for salt and adjust as needed.

5. Line a large colander with several thicknesses of cheesecloth, set over a large heatproof bowl, pour in the stock, and let it drip through undisturbed. Discard all solids. The stock is now ready to use in soups, sauces, and other seafood recipes.

6. To store, ladle into 1-pint or 1-quart freezer containers leaving ½-inch head space, snap on the lids, label, date, and set in a 0°F freezer. Use within 6 months.

Note: If refrigerated, the stock will keep for about a week.

Vegetable Stock

I load my vegetable stocks with a variety of vegetables. Onions go into the pot, as do leeks, celery, carrots, even turnips, tomatoes, and mushrooms. The processor chops them so fine this stock's as rich as beef broth. Well, almost. It's perfect for any vegetarian recipe that requires stock.

MAKES ABOUT 2 QUARTS

4 quarts cold water

2 large yellow onions, peeled and cut in 1-inch chunks

4 large leeks, trimmed, washed carefully, and cut in 1-inch chunks

4 large ribs celery, trimmed and cut in 1-inch chunks (reserve tops)

4 large carrots, peeled and cut in 1-inch chunks

2 medium white turnips, peeled and cut in 1-inch chunks

2 large fully ripe tomatoes, cored and cut into slim wedges (no need to peel)

½ pound medium mushrooms, wiped clean, stemmed, and quartered (reserve stems)

6 large branches Italian parsley

2 large whole bay leaves (preferably fresh)

8 peppercorns

1 tablespoon salt

1. Place the water in a large nonreactive kettle and set aside while you prepare the vegetables.

2. Finely chop the onions by churning 8 to 10 seconds in a food processor fitted with the metal chopping blade—no matter if a few large pieces remain. Scoop the onions into the kettle.

3. Add the leeks and celery to the processor and chop fine by churning 10 to 12 seconds. Add to the kettle with the reserved celery tops.

4. Now finely chop the carrots and turnips by churning 12 to 15 seconds. Add to the kettle.

5. Add the tomatoes to the processor and reduce to juice by whizzing 3 to 5 seconds; pour into the kettle.

6. Finally, mince the mushroom caps and stems very fine by churning about 5 seconds. Add to the kettle along with the parsley, bay leaves, peppercorns, and salt.

7. Bring all to a boil over moderately high heat, adjust the heat so the mixture bubbles gently, cover, and simmer until the stock develops rich vegetable flavor, about 3 hours.

8. Line a large colander with several thicknesses of cheesecloth, set over a second large kettle, pour in the stock, and let it drip through undisturbed. Discard all solids.

9. Set the kettle of stock over moderate heat and boil uncovered until reduced to 2 quarts. Taste for salt and adjust as needed. The stock is now ready to use in soups, sauces, and vegetarian recipes that call for stock.

10. To store, ladle into 1-pint or 1-quart freezer containers leaving ½-inch head space, snap on the lids, label, date, and set in a 0°F freezer. Use within 6 months.

Note: If refrigerated, the stock will keep for about 2 weeks.

Lemon Sauce

I've broken some classic sauce-making rules here because I wanted to see if the processor could shortcut the preparation of this starch-and-egg-thickened sauce. My aim was to combine everything by processor, then cook it. And it worked. In fact this tart lemon sauce is silkier than any I've made the old-fashioned way. I serve it with Salmon Loaf with Fresh Dill and Sweet Red Pepper (page 149), also with grilled or poached fish and such vegetables as asparagus, broccoli, carrots, and cauliflower. I even like it with grilled chicken.

Note: The same technique will also work with Béchamel and white sauces both thick and thin. However, if your processor sauces are to be smooth, the butter, liquids, and egg, if used, must all be at room temperature.

MAKES ABOUT 2 CUPS

2 tablespoons cornstarch

3 tablespoons butter, cut into pats, at room temperature

1 to 2 teaspoons sugar

½ teaspoon salt

¼ teaspoon freshly ground white or black pepper

3 tablespoons fresh lemon juice, at room temperature

1 large egg yolk, at room temperature

2 cups chicken or vegetable broth or fish stock, at room temperature

1. Place the cornstarch, butter, 1 teaspoon of the sugar, the salt, pepper, lemon juice, and egg yolk in a food processor fitted with the metal chopping blade and with two to three 5-second churnings, process until smooth. Using a plastic spatula, scrape the work bowl between churnings and stir. At first the mixture will look curdled, but with subsequent churnings it will become creamy.

2. With the motor running, slowly drizzle the broth down the feed tube. Scrape the work bowl and lid well, then pulse quickly 3 to 5 times until smooth.

3. Pour the mixture into a small, heavy nonreactive saucepan, set over moderate heat, and cook, stirring constantly, just until the mixture bubbles up and thickens slightly, 3 to 4 minutes. Do not allow the sauce to boil actively because it may curdle.

4. Taste and if too tart, mix in the second tablespoon of sugar. Also adjust the salt and pepper as needed. Serve warm as an accompaniment to fish or vegetables.

Lemon-Caper Sauce

Prepare the Lemon Sauce as directed but omit the salt. Just before serving mix in 2 to 4 tablespoons well drained small capers. Serve with grilled fish (especially salmon or tuna) or grilled chicken.

Marinara Sauce

For years I'd slip a little brown sugar into my marinara sauce to mellow the tartness of the tomatoes. Then an Italian friend said, "No! Add a chopped carrot instead." I must say that it produces a better marinara sauce as well as a more nutritious one.

Note: Unless sun-ripened, home-grown tomatoes are available, use canned plum tomatoes.

MAKES ABOUT 3½ CUPS, ENOUGH TO DRESS 1 POUND OF PASTA

1 large whole clove garlic, peeled

1 small carrot, peeled and cut into 1-inch chunks

1 large yellow onion, peeled and cut into slim wedges

1 teaspoon dried leaf basil

1 teaspoon dried leaf oregano or marjoram

3 tablespoons olive oil

2 large whole bay leaves (preferably fresh)

½ cup dry white wine such as a Pinot Grigio

6 medium dead-ripe tomatoes (about 2½ pounds), peeled, cored, and cut into slim wedges, or one 28-ounce can plum tomatoes with their liquid

3 tablespoons tomato paste

1 teaspoon salt

¼ teaspoon freshly ground black pepper

1. Churn the garlic and carrot in a food processor fitted with the metal chopping blade for 5 seconds. Scrape the work bowl. Add the onion, basil, and oregano, and pulse 5 to 6 times until moderately coarsely chopped.

2. Heat the olive oil in a very large, heavy nonreactive skillet over moderate heat 1 minute. Add the chopped vegetables and bay leaves, reduce the heat to low, and cook slowly, stirring now and then, until the vegetables are soft but not brown, 10 to 15 minutes. Add the wine and allow to simmer uncovered while you chop the tomatoes.

3. If using fresh tomatoes, rough-chop in two batches in the food processor (no need to wash the work bowl or blade) using 8 to 10 staccato pulses. As each batch is chopped, add to the skillet. If using canned tomatoes, empty into the processor and pulse quickly several times to break up the tomatoes.

4. When all the tomatoes are in the skillet, mix in the tomato paste, salt, and pepper. Bring to a boil, adjust the heat so that the mixture bubbles gently. Partially cover and simmer just until the flavors mellow and the sauce is a good consistency for ladling over pasta, 20 to 25 minutes. Discard the bay leaves.

5. Taste for salt and pepper and adjust as needed. Serve hot over freshly cooked pasta.

Arrabbiata Sauce

Prepare the Marinara Sauce as directed, tripling the garlic and adding ½ teaspoon red pepper flakes in Step 4 along with the other ingredients.

Note: Arrabbiata is Italian for "angry" and there's no denying that this sauce is "heated."

Puttanesca Sauce

Prepare the Marinara Sauce as directed but triple the amount of garlic. Also chop ⅓ cup pitted ripe olives and 2 tablespoons well drained capers along with the onion, basil, and oregano in Step 1. In Step 4, omit the salt and smooth in 2 tablespoons anchovy paste.

Note: Legend has it that this spicy sauce was a favorite among Neapolitan streetwalkers—they could make it as fast as they could turn a trick.

Pesto

If pesto is to be mellow, you must use young, tender basil. Over-the-hill leaves will surely make it bitter. Many Italian cooks insist that bush basil, with its tiny aromatic leaves, is best of all for pesto. That's not widely available so I call for the big-leafed, bright green variety now stocked by every farmer's market and supermarket (you'll need two huge bunches). The pasta traditionally served with pesto is trenette, flat strands similar to—but thinner than—fettuccine (thin spaghetti works well, too). When dressing pasta, add only enough pesto to coat each strand lightly, thinning as needed with a little of the hot pasta cooking water. Pesto's terrific, too, spread on sliced ripe tomatoes.

MAKES ABOUT 1¼ CUPS, ENOUGH TO DRESS 1½ TO 2 POUNDS PASTA

2 quarts loosely packed tender young basil leaves, washed, spun dry in a salad spinner, and patted dry on paper toweling

⅓ cup pine nuts

2 large whole cloves garlic, peeled

2 tablespoons freshly grated Parmesan cheese

¾ teaspoon salt

¼ teaspoon freshly ground black pepper

⅓ to ½ cup olive oil

1. Place all ingredients except the olive oil in a food processor fitted with the metal chopping blade and churn 30 seconds. Scrape down the work bowl sides and churn 30 seconds longer to form a thick paste.

2. With the motor running, drizzle the olive oil down the feed tube, adding only enough to give the pesto the consistency of prepared mustard.

3. Scoop into a small bowl, press plastic food wrap flat on top (to keep the pesto from darkening), and refrigerate until needed. Bring to room temperature and stir well before using.

Sour Cream Mustard-Dill Sauce

This is such an easy sauce and a versatile one, too. Serve with Ham and Sausage Loaf with Capers and Lemon (page 140), with cold baked ham, cold roast beef, or cold poached salmon.

MAKES ABOUT 2½ CUPS

½ cup lightly packed fresh dill sprigs (just the feathery tips), washed and wrung dry on paper toweling

1½ cups sour cream (use reduced-fat, if you like)

½ cup mayonnaise (use light, if you like)

3 tablespoons Dijon mustard

2 tablespoons prepared horseradish

2 tablespoons milk

3 tablespoons well drained small capers

1. Churn the dill sprigs 5 seconds in a food processor fitted with the metal chopping blade.

2. Add the sour cream, mayonnaise, mustard, horseradish, and milk and pulse quickly to combine. Add the capers and pulse once or twice—no more.

3. Transfer to a small bowl, cover, and refrigerate several hours before serving.

Mustard-Caper Sauce
Prepare as directed but increase both the mustard and the capers to ¼ cup. Also reduce the horseradish to 1 tablespoon. Good with ham loaf, boiled or baked ham.

Sweet-Sour Mustard Sauce
Prepare as directed using 1 cup each sour cream and mayonnaise. Omit the horseradish, milk, and capers, and at the end, pulse in ⅓ cup drained India relish. Good with ham loaf, baked ham, boiled shrimp, or broiled salmon.

Cucumber Sour Cream Sauce

It's important that you salt and sugar the chopped cucumbers and let them drain for about an hour before combining them with the sour cream because if you don't, they will water down the sauce. For me, this sauce is the perfect choice for Salmon Loaf with Fresh Dill and Sweet Red Pepper (page 149). I like it, too, with cold baked ham, ham loaf, and cold poached salmon.

Note: The best cucumbers to use here are Kirbys (pickling cucumbers) or English hothouse cucumbers, also sometimes called "seedless cucumbers" although they do have seeds (these are the long, skinny cucumbers that arrive at the supermarket shrink-wrapped). English hothouse cucumbers weigh about a pound apiece, so for this recipe you will need one-half cucumber. If you opt for Kirbys, you'll need two to three.

Tip: The fastest way to seed cucumbers is to halve them lengthwise, then scoop out the seeds with a melon baller or teaspoon.

MAKES ABOUT 2 CUPS

½ pound cucumbers, peeled, seeded, and cut into 1-inch chunks (see tip)

1 teaspoon salt

1 teaspoon sugar

1¼ cups sour cream (use light, if you like)

¼ cup milk

¼ teaspoon freshly ground black pepper

1. Coarsely chop the cucumbers with the salt and sugar by pulsing briskly 3 to 5 times in a food processor fitted with the metal chopping blade. Using a plastic spatula and minding the blade, scrape down the work bowl and stir the cucumbers, pushing larger chunks to the bottom. Pulse briskly until you get a fairly uniform coarse chop, 2 to 3 times more should do it.

Tip the cucumbers into a large fine sieve set over a large bowl, spread the cucumbers in the sieve, and allow to "drip-dry" for about an hour. Discard the cucumber liquid.

2. Add the sour cream, milk, and pepper to the processor work bowl (no need to have washed or rinsed it) and pulse quickly to blend.

3. Return the cucumbers to the processor and with staccato pulses, combine with the sour cream mixture. Easy does it! You don't want to purée the cucumbers. Taste for salt and pepper and adjust as needed.

4. Serve with cold cooked fish or shellfish, cold ham loaf, or cold baked ham. Stored tightly covered in the refrigerator, this sauce keeps well for about 5 days.

Tartar Sauce

Nice and tart and delicious with almost any fish or shellfish.

Note: You'll probably fare better if you buzz this up in a mini food processor instead of in a larger model because the quantities to be chopped are so small.

MAKES ABOUT 1¾ CUPS

One 2-inch piece dill pickle, cut into 1-inch chunks, or 4 gherkins, halved

3 medium shallots, peeled, or 3 medium scallions, trimmed and cut into 1-inch chunks (include some green tops)

¼ cup lightly packed curly parsley sprigs, washed and wrung dry in paper toweling

2 tablespoons fresh tarragon leaves, washed and wrung dry in paper toweling, or 1 teaspoon dried leaf tarragon

1 teaspoon sugar

1¼ cups mayonnaise (use light, if you like)

3 tablespoons red or white wine vinegar

2 teaspoons Dijon mustard

3 tablespoons well drained small capers

1. Place the pickle, shallots, parsley, tarragon, and sugar in a food processor fitted with the metal chopping blade and pulse 4 to 6 times until coarsely chopped. Scrape the work bowl.

2. Add the mayonnaise, vinegar, mustard, and capers and pulse quickly 2 to 3 times to incorporate.

3. Spoon the sauce into a small bowl, cover with plastic wrap, and refrigerate an hour or two before serving. If the sauce seems thick, thin with a little milk.

Processor Hollandaise

If you have a mini food processor, use it to whip up this two-minute Hollandaise. You'll find that the sauce emulsifies faster in a smaller space because the ingredients don't fly all over the place and require so much bowl-scraping.

Note: Only recently have pasteurized eggs come to the supermarket and that's good news for all of us who like to make our own Hollandaise, Béarnaise, mayonnaise, and other sauces containing raw eggs. With salmonella ever present, using unpasteurized eggs may be risky.

MAKES ABOUT 1½ CUPS

2 tablespoons fresh lemon juice

1 pasteurized extra-large or jumbo egg (see note)

¼ teaspoon salt

¼ teaspoon freshly ground black pepper

½ cup (1 stick) melted unsalted butter

½ cup vegetable oil (preferably corn or peanut) or olive oil

1. Blend the lemon juice, egg, salt, and pepper by pulsing 4 to 5 times in a food processor fitted with the metal chopping blade.

2. With the motor running, drizzle first the melted butter, then the vegetable oil, down the feed tube in a stream as fine as thread. This is important; if you add the melted butter and oil too fast, the sauce will not emulsify. When all of the butter and oil have been incorporated, run the machine for 30 seconds.

3. Serve the Hollandaise at once with steamed artichokes, asparagus, broccoli, cauliflower, or green beans.

Mustard Hollandaise

Prepare the Hollandaise as directed, but in Step 1, add 2 tablespoons Dijon mustard. Delicious with grilled fish and every vegetable suggested for Hollandaise.

Maltaise Sauce

Prepare the Hollandaise as directed, but in Step 1, churn one 3-inch strip orange zest (removed from the orange with a vegetable peeler) with the salt and pepper about 10 seconds until finely grated. Scrape the work bowl, add the lemon juice and egg and proceed as directed in Steps 1 and 2. Delicious with grilled fish, shellfish, and chicken in addition to all of the vegetables suggested for Hollandaise.

Mousseline Sauce

Fold ½ cup softly whipped cream into the finished Hollandaise. Serve with fish or shellfish as well as any vegetable suggested for Hollandaise. Makes about 2 cups.

Figaro Sauce

Fold 2 tablespoons each tomato purée and coarsely chopped Italian parsley into the finished Hollandaise. Serve with grilled chicken, fish, or shellfish.

Faux Hollandaise

When I need Hollandaise in a hurry and don't have pasteurized eggs on hand, I put my mini processor to use by rustling up this superfast Faux Hollandaise.

MAKES ABOUT 1½ CUPS

1½ cups mayonnaise (use light, if you like)

3 tablespoons fresh lemon juice

⅛ teaspoon hot red pepper sauce

⅓ cup melted unsalted butter

1. Blend the mayonnaise, lemon juice, and red pepper sauce in a mini food processor fitted with the metal chopping blade by churning 2 to 3 seconds. Scrape the work bowl.

2. With the machine running, drizzle the melted butter down the feed tube or through the hole in the lid in a threadlike stream. When all the butter has been incorporated, churn for another second or two.

3. Transfer to a small sauceboat and serve.

Aïoli (Provençal Garlic Mayonnaise)

The French spoon aïoli over steamed salt cod and stir it into bourride, a Provençal seafood soup. *Note:* This recipe contains raw egg yolks, so for safety's sake, use only pasteurized eggs.

MAKES ABOUT 1½ CUPS

1 slice firm-textured white bread, trimmed of crusts and torn into small pieces

5 medium whole cloves garlic, peeled

2 pasteurized large egg yolks (see note)

3 tablespoons fresh lemon juice

¼ teaspoon salt

⅛ teaspoon freshly ground white pepper

1 cup olive oil (the fruitiest you can find)

3 to 4 tablespoons light cream or half-and-half

1. Churn the bread, garlic, egg yolks, lemon juice, salt, and pepper 10 seconds in a food processor fitted with the metal chopping blade. Scrape the sides of the work bowl and churn 5 seconds longer to form a smooth paste.

2. With the motor running, drizzle the olive oil down the feed tube in a threadlike stream, then continue churning for 5 seconds after all of the oil is incorporated. Pulse in 3 tablespoons of the cream and if the mixture is thicker than mayonnaise, pulse in the remaining 1 tablespoon cream.

3. Spoon the aïoli into a small bowl, cover with plastic food wrap, and refrigerate. About a half hour before serving, remove the aïoli from the refrigerator and let stand at room temperature.

Processor Béarnaise

The classic French sauce for grilled steaks.

Note: There is no longer any reason to substitute dried herbs for fresh because little packets of fresh herbs are now sold in nearly every upscale grocery. Many people, moreover, are growing their own herbs, even on big-city windowsills. The egg you use for this sauce should be pasteurized. Most supermarkets now sell them.

Tip: Because the quantities here are so small, you'll have better luck with this sauce if you use a mini food processor or the mini bowl and blade that are now standard accessories for one major brand.

MAKES ABOUT 1½ CUPS

2 tablespoons fresh tarragon leaves

2 tablespoons fresh chervil leaves (if unavailable, double the amount of tarragon)

1 large shallot, peeled and halved

¼ cup tarragon vinegar

2 tablespoons dry white wine

¼ teaspoon salt

¼ teaspoon freshly ground black pepper

1 pasteurized extra-large or jumbo egg

½ cup (1 stick) unsalted butter, melted

½ cup corn oil

1. Place the tarragon and chervil in a mini food processor equipped with the metal chopping blade and churn 2 to 3 seconds. Scrape the work bowl and pulse quickly until coarsely chopped.

2. Tip the herbs into a small fine sieve, set under cool running water, and rinse well. Also rinse the work bowl and blade under the cold tap, letting stray bits of herb fall into the sieve. Upend the sieve on several thicknesses of paper toweling and rap several times until all the herbs fall onto the toweling. Roll up, wring dry, and set aside.

3. Quickly dry the work bowl and blade and reassemble. Add the shallot to the processor along with the vinegar, wine, salt, and pepper. Pulse quickly several times until the shallot is finely chopped.

4. Transfer the shallot mixture to a very small nonreactive pan or butter warmer, add the reserved chopped herbs, and set uncovered over moderate heat. Boil until the liquid is reduced to 2 tablespoons. This will only take a few minutes so "watch the pot."

5. Scrape all back into the processor and cool for 5 minutes. Break the egg into the work bowl and pulse quickly 2 to 3 times to combine.

6. Now with the motor running, drizzle first the butter, then the corn oil down the feed tube in the finest of streams. In the beginning the stream should be as fine as thread but as the sauce begins to emulsify (resemble mayonnaise), you can add the butter and oil a bit faster. When both have been incorporated, churn the sauce for 20 seconds nonstop.

7. Serve the Béarnaise warm with broiled or grilled steaks, chops, chicken, and such strong-flavored, firm-fleshed fish as salmon and tuna. I even like Béarnaise with steamed lobster.

One-Minute Mayonnaise

As with all processor sauces containing raw eggs, this one should be made with pasteurized eggs only. Fortunately, they're widely available. You'll find this mayonnaise somewhat thinner than commercial varieties, but then it contains no stabilizers, thickeners, or emulsifiers.

Note: Stored tightly covered in the refrigerator, this mayonnaise keeps well for about five days.

MAKES ABOUT 2 CUPS

2 pasteurized large egg yolks (see headnote)

1 pasteurized jumbo egg

¼ cup fresh lemon juice

2 tablespoons white wine vinegar

½ teaspoon dry mustard

½ teaspoon salt

¼ teaspoon freshly ground white pepper

1 cup olive oil (the fruitiest you can find)

1 cup corn, peanut, or vegetable oil

1. Equip the food processor with the metal chopping blade, add the egg yolks, egg, lemon juice, vinegar, mustard, salt, and pepper, and pulse 2 to 3 times to combine.

2. Combine the olive oil and corn oil in a spouted 2-cup measure, then with the processor motor running, drizzle down the feed tube in the finest of streams.

3. When all of the oil has been incorporated, churn 15 to 20 seconds nonstop until smooth and pale yellow.

4. Spoon the mayonnaise into a 1-pint jar, screw the lid down tight, and store in the refrigerator.

Curry Mayonnaise

This quick mayonnaise is perfectly delicious with baked ham, grilled chicken, roasted asparagus, steamed broccoli or cauliflower, cold poached fish, or shellfish. Use it, too, when making deviled eggs—simply substitute for plain mayonnaise, adding only enough to give the mashed yolks a good consistency.

Note: This sauce is made with raw eggs, so play it safe and use the pasteurized. A mini food processor is the best choice here. Tightly covered and refrigerated, this mayo will keep for about 5 days.

MAKES ABOUT 1¼ CUPS

2 tablespoons unsalted butter

2 large scallions, trimmed, washed, and cut into 1-inch chunks (white part only)

1 tablespoon curry powder

1 pasteurized large egg yolk

1 pasteurized large egg

3 tablespoons fresh lemon juice

1 tablespoon tarragon vinegar

¼ teaspoon dry mustard

¼ teaspoon salt

¼ teaspoon hot red pepper sauce

1 cup corn, peanut, or vegetable oil

1 to 2 tablespoons half-and-half cream (if needed to thin the mayonnaise)

1. Melt the butter in a very small heavy skillet over moderate heat; set off the heat and keep warm.

2. Coarsely chop the scallions by pulsing 3 to 5 times in a mini food processor fitted with the metal chopping blade.

3. Add to the skillet, return to moderate heat, and cook, stirring now and then, until the scallions are limp but not brown—3 to 5 minutes. Blend in the curry powder, and cook and stir until no raw curry taste remains—2 to 3 minutes.

4. Scrape the scallion mixture back into the food processor and cool for 5 minutes. Add the egg yolk, egg, lemon juice, vinegar, mustard, salt, and hot pepper sauce, and pulse 2 to 3 times to incorporate.

5. With the motor running, drizzle the oil down the feed tube in a threadlike stream, and when all of the oil is incorporated, continue churning until fluffy-smooth, 3 to 4 seconds. If the mayonnaise seems thick, pulse in 1 to 2 tablespoons half-and-half.

6. Spoon the mayonnaise into a small bowl, cover with plastic food wrap, and refrigerate. About a half hour before serving, remove from the refrigerator and let stand at room temperature. This gives the flavors a chance to mellow and also means that you won't be spooning a refrigerator-cold sauce over hot meats or vegetables.

Vinaigrette

I like to keep this French dressing on hand to use when tossing salads. It is thick and creamy and extremely tart, the way I like it. If you prefer a mellower dressing, add the optional tablespoon of sugar.

Note: This dressing tends to spatter as you add the olive oil, so drizzle it down the smaller inner feed tube instead of the big wide-open one. Stored tightly covered in a glass jar in the refrigerator, this vinaigrette keeps well for seven to ten days.

MAKES ABOUT 1⅓ CUPS

⅓ cup red wine vinegar or cider vinegar or ¼ cup fresh lemon juice

3 tablespoons Dijon mustard

1 tablespoon sugar, optional
(see headnote)

½ teaspoon salt

½ teaspoon freshly ground black pepper

1 cup olive oil, the fruitiest you can find

1. Churn the vinegar, mustard, sugar if desired, salt, and pepper in a food processor fitted with the metal chopping blade until well blended, about 10 seconds. Scrape down the work bowl sides and lid.

2. With the motor running, drizzle the olive oil down the small inner feed tube in the finest of streams. After the first ½ cup, you can add the oil a little faster but keep the machine running full tilt all the while.

3. Transfer the dressing to a 1-pint preserving jar, screw the lid down tight, and store in the refrigerator. Shake well before using.

Roquefort Dressing
Prepare the Vinaigrette as directed but omit the salt. At the end of Step 2, crumble 4 ounces Roquefort or other blue cheese into the dressing and pulse 4 to 6 times until as lumpy or smooth as you like. Store as directed in Step 3. Makes about 1½ cups.

Tarragon Dressing
Begin the Vinaigrette as directed but in Step 1 add ⅓ cup lightly packed fresh tarragon leaves, which have been washed and wrung dry in paper toweling, along with the other ingredients. Also substitute tarragon vinegar for red wine vinegar, or if you prefer, a half-and-half mix of tarragon vinegar and white balsamic vinegar. Proceed as directed in Steps 1, 2, and 3. Makes about 1⅓ cups.

Thousand Island Dressing

A "retro" recipe that's come round again. It's said to have been created in the early 1900s by the chef at the Drake Hotel in Chicago—but it was his wife who named it. When she saw this lumpy dressing, she said it reminded her of the Thousand Islands, which she had just visited. Originally spooned over wedges of iceberg lettuce, Thousand Island can also be tossed with mixed greens.

Note: Use a mini processor to make the dressing, if you have one. It does a better job than a full-size machine. Stored tightly covered in the fridge, Thousand Island keeps well for about five days.

MAKES ABOUT 1½ CUPS

Two 1-inch squares green bell pepper

1 medium scallion, trimmed and cut into 1-inch chunks (include some green tops)

6 pimiento-stuffed green olives, well drained

1 large hard-cooked egg, peeled and quartered

1 cup mayonnaise (use light, if you like)

¼ cup chili sauce or ketchup

¼ teaspoon hot red pepper sauce

1. Coarsely chop the green pepper and scallion by pulsing briskly 3 to 5 times in a food processor fitted with the metal chopping blade. Scrape the work bowl.

2. Add the olives and pulse 3 to 5 times until coarsely chopped. Add the egg and pulse briskly just until the egg is very coarsely chopped—a couple of zaps should do it.

3. Add the mayonnaise, chili sauce, and red pepper sauce and pulse 2 to 4 times to combine.

4. Transfer the dressing to a 1-pint preserving jar, screw the lid down tight, and mellow in the refrigerator for at least an hour. Stir well before using.

Green Goddess Dressing

Although I usually chop fresh herbs in the processor before I wash them, I make an exception here because it doesn't matter if the herbs aren't bone dry. Green Goddess Dressing, a particular favorite of mine, is an American classic that dates back to the 1920s. It was created at the Palace Hotel in San Francisco to honor actor George Arliss, who stayed there while starring in a play called *The Green Goddess*. The Palace chef tossed this creamy dressing with chunks of romaine. I also like it with such bitter greens as arugula, dandelion, watercress, and radicchio—either singly or mixed. And I often add a few nasturtium leaves and blossoms.

Note: Stored tightly covered in the refrigerator, Green Goddess dressing keeps for about a week.

Tip: The most efficient way to snip fresh chives is to cut straight across the bundle with scissors.

MAKES ABOUT 2½ CUPS

1 cup lightly packed fresh curly parsley sprigs, washed and patted dry on paper toweling

⅓ cup fresh tarragon leaves, washed and patted dry on paper toweling

¼ cup snipped fresh chives (see tip)

2 medium scallions, trimmed and cut into 1-inch chunks (include some green tops)

1 medium whole clove garlic, peeled

1½ cups mayonnaise

½ cup sour cream

¼ cup tarragon vinegar

2 tablespoons anchovy paste

¼ teaspoon freshly ground black pepper

2 to 3 tablespoons buttermilk (as needed to thin the dressing)

1. Churn all ingredients together in a food processor fitted with the metal chopping blade for 5 seconds. Scrape the work bowl, then churn 5 seconds longer or until smooth.

2. If the dressing seems thick (it should be about the consistency of milk gravy), pulse in 2 to 3 tablespoons buttermilk.

3. Transfer the dressing to a 1-quart preserving jar, screw the lid down tight, and allow to mellow in the refrigerator for at least an hour. Shake well before using.

Green Mayonnaise

Just the dressing for cold poached salmon, cold boiled lobster or shrimp, and cooked vegetable salads. Tedious to make when all the chopping had to be done by hand, green mayo is a snap with the food processor.

Note: As with Green Goddess Dressing (which precedes), I wash the herbs before I add them to the food processor. Refrigerated and tightly covered, green mayonnaise will keep for three to five days—but I'll bet that it's gone before then.

MAKES ABOUT 1½ CUPS

1 cup lightly packed fresh curly parsley sprigs, washed and patted dry on paper toweling

1 cup fresh watercress leaves, washed and patted dry on paper toweling

¼ cup lightly packed fresh dill sprigs, washed and patted dry on paper toweling

¼ cup snipped fresh chives

1¼ cups mayonnaise (use light, if you like)

1 tablespoon fresh lemon juice

¼ teaspoon salt

¼ teaspoon hot red pepper sauce

1. Churn all ingredients together in a food processor fitted with the metal chopping blade for 5 seconds. Scrape the work bowl, then churn 5 seconds longer or until herbs are finely chopped and the mixture is smooth.

2. Spoon into a small bowl, cover, and refrigerate for several hours before serving.

Green Mayonnaise with Spinach
Prepare as directed but substitute tender young spinach leaves for half or all of the watercress, and fresh tarragon or chervil for the dill.

Creamy Buttermilk Dressing

Ranch Dressing is a trademarked name and cannot be used. Moreover, the exact recipe remains secret. This easy buttermilk dressing is definitely similar and can be tossed with any salad greens.

Note: Stored tightly covered in the refrigerator, this dressing keeps well for about a week.

MAKES ABOUT 1 QUART

⅓ cup lightly packed fresh curly parsley sprigs, washed and patted dry on paper toweling

4 medium scallions, trimmed and cut into 1-inch chunks (include some green tops)

2 medium whole cloves garlic, peeled

½ teaspoon salt

½ teaspoon freshly ground black pepper

2 cups buttermilk

1 cup sour cream (use light, if you like)

½ cup mayonnaise (use light, if you like)

⅓ cup cider vinegar

1. Churn the parsley, scallions, and garlic with the salt and pepper in a food processor fitted with the metal chopping blade for 5 seconds. Scrape the work bowl.

2. Add the buttermilk, sour cream, mayonnaise, and vinegar and churn for 5 seconds. Scrape the work bowl, then churn 5 seconds longer until smooth.

3. Transfer the dressing to a 1-quart preserving jar, screw the lid down tight, and allow to mellow in the refrigerator for at least an hour. Shake well before using.

Roasted Roma and Red Onion Salsa

As salsas go, this one is pretty tepid. To turn up the heat, double the number of jalapeños or if you have an asbestos palate, use one habanero (or maybe one-half habanero) and no jalapeños.

Note: I do not roast all the tomatoes because I like the firm texture and fresh taste of the raw.

MAKES ABOUT 2 CUPS

½ cup lightly packed fresh cilantro leaves

1½ pounds firm, sun-ripened Roma (Italian plum) tomatoes, halved and seeded

1 large red onion, peeled, quartered, and the individual layers separated

2 medium-large jalapeño peppers, halved and seeded

4 large cloves garlic, peeled and halved

1 teaspoon salt

1 tablespoon fresh lime juice

1 tablespoon olive oil or corn oil

1. Preheat the oven to 450°F.

2. Coarsely chop the cilantro in a food processor fitted with the metal chopping blade using 4 to 5 fairly long pulses. Tip into a large fine sieve and rinse under cold running water for a few seconds. Also rinse the bowl and blade under the cold tap, letting stray bits of cilantro fall into the sieve. Drain the cilantro on several thicknesses of paper toweling, roll up, and wring as dry as possible; set aside. Invert the work bowl on a clean dry dish towel, set the blade beside it, and allow both to drip-dry while you proceed.

3. Place all but two of the tomatoes, all of the onion, jalapeños, and garlic on an ungreased 15½ × 10½ × 1-inch jelly roll pan, toss well, then spread evenly.

4. Set uncovered on the middle oven rack and roast for 15 minutes. Stir well, again spread evenly, and roast 15 minutes more until the vegetables are soft and nicely browned. Remove from the oven and cool 15 minutes.

5. Meanwhile, cut the 2 raw tomatoes into 1-inch chunks, drop into the reassembled food processor, add the salt, and pulse quickly 5 times until coarsely chopped.

6. Scrape the roasted vegetables into the work bowl, being sure to include all browned bits, add the lime juice, olive oil, and reserved cilantro and give them 5 to 6 staccato pulses. With a plastic spatula and minding the blade, scrape the work bowl and stir. Give the salsa another 5 to 6 staccato pulses until coarsely but uniformly chopped.

7. Scoop the salsa into a nonreactive bowl and let stand at room temperature about half an hour before serving. I find this salsa especially good with grilled chicken, tuna, and salmon.

Tomatillo Salsa with Peppers Sweet and Hot

What a long way we have come. Ten years ago few of us beyond the reach of big cities had ever heard of tomatillos. Today nearly every high-end supermarket carries them. Sometimes called "Mexican tomatoes," they are cherry tomato–sized green fruits wrapped in papery husks much like Chinese lanterns. According to Rick Bayless, Chicago restaurateur, cookbook author, and my guru for all things Mexican, tomatillos are indeed related to Chinese lanterns, also to ground cherries, which grow wild in many southeastern states.

Note: This salsa is hotter than Roasted Roma and Red Onion Salsa (which precedes). Still, you could hardly call it incendiary. This bright red and green salsa goes well with roast pork or chicken, and with almost anything grilled, including red meat, fish, and fowl.

MAKES ABOUT 3 CUPS

½ cup lightly packed fresh cilantro leaves

¾ pound tomatillos, husked

1 large red bell pepper, cored, seeded, quartered, and each quarter halved crosswise

1 large green bell pepper, cored, seeded, quartered, and each quarter halved crosswise

6 large scallions, trimmed and cut into 1-inch chunks (include some green tops)

4 medium-large jalapeño peppers, halved and seeded

5 large cloves garlic, peeled and halved

4 large (8 to 10 ounces each) firm, sun-ripened Roma (Italian plum) tomatoes, halved, seeded, and cut into 1-inch chunks

1 teaspoon salt

1 tablespoon light brown sugar

1 tablespoon fresh lime juice

1 tablespoon olive oil or corn oil

1. Preheat the oven to 450°F.

2. Coarsely chop the cilantro in a food processor fitted with the metal chopping blade using 4 to 5 fairly long pulses. Tip into a large fine sieve and rinse under cold running water for a few seconds. Also rinse the bowl and blade under the cold tap, letting stray bits of cilantro fall into the sieve. Drain the cilantro on several thicknesses of paper toweling, roll up, and wring as dry as possible; set aside. Invert the work bowl on a clean dry dish towel, set the blade beside it, and allow both to drip-dry while you proceed.

3. Place the tomatillos, red and green bell peppers, scallions, jalapeños, and garlic on an ungreased 15½ × 10½ × 1-inch jelly roll pan, toss well, then spread evenly.

4. Set uncovered on the middle oven rack and roast for 15 minutes. Stir well, again spread evenly, and roast 15 minutes more until the vegetables are soft and nicely browned. Remove from the oven and cool 15 minutes.

5. Meanwhile, pulse the tomatoes with the salt in the reassembled food processor 5 to 6 times until coarsely chopped.

6. Scrape the roasted vegetables into the work bowl, being sure to include all browned bits, add the brown sugar, lime juice, olive oil, and reserved cilantro and give them 5 to 6 staccato pulses. With a plastic spatula and minding the blade, scrape the work bowl and stir. Give the salsa another 5 to 6 staccato pulses until coarsely but uniformly chopped.

7. Scoop the salsa into a non-reactive bowl and let stand at room temperature for about half an hour before serving.

Easy Red Onion Pickle with Honey and Lime

Better on burgers than a slice of yellow onion and delicious, too, with barbecue, grilled meat, fish, or fowl. I like to keep this jiffy sweet-sour pickled onion on hand in the refrigerator and to tell you the truth, I can just spoon it up and eat it.

Note: Use fresh lime juice only for this recipe.

MAKES ABOUT 4 CUPS

⅓ cup fresh lime juice

3 tablespoons light honey

½ teaspoon salt

¼ teaspoon hot red pepper sauce (more, if you like it hot)

1 large red onion (about 1 pound), peeled and cut into 6 slim wedges

1. Whiz the lime juice, honey, salt, and red pepper sauce in a food processor fitted with the metal chopping blade for 2 seconds. Using a plastic spatula and steering clear of the blade, scrape the work bowl, and stir the mixture. Remove the chopping blade and set aside. Insert the slicing disk, preferably the thin-slicing disk.

2. Stand as many onion wedges on end in the feed tube as will fit, then exerting moderate pressure on the pusher, pulse through the slicing disk, letting the onion slices fall directly into the lime mixture.

3. Transfer all to a nonreactive bowl, toss well, cover, and refrigerate for at least 2 hours. Toss well again before serving.

Sweet-Sour Mango Salsa

I find this sweet-sour fruit salsa particularly good with grilled chicken, salmon, and tuna. It's delicious, too, with spit-roasted pork or lamb. If this salsa is to have any texture, you must choose a firm mango. The processor will reduce soft ones to mush.

Note: Mangoes are tricky to pit because the flesh seems glued to the fuzzy seed. Here's how to go about it: stand the mango on its butt end, then cut straight down along each side of the pit, more or less dividing the fruit in half. To skin, place each half skin-side down on a cutting board, slide the knife underneath the skin at one end, then holding the knife at about a twenty-degree angle, pull the skin toward you, separating it from the flesh. It's the same technique you use when skinning a fish or a chicken breast.

MAKES ABOUT 2 CUPS

¼ cup lightly packed fresh mint leaves

¼ cup lightly packed fresh cilantro leaves

One 2-inch strip lemon or lime zest, removed with a vegetable peeler

1 large clove garlic, peeled and halved

1 tablespoon sugar

½ teaspoon salt

2 large scallions, trimmed and cut into 1-inch chunks (include some green tops)

1 large red bell pepper, cored, seeded, quartered, and each quarter halved crosswise

1 small jalapeño pepper, halved, seeded, and each half cut in two crosswise

1 large firm-ripe mango (about 1 pound), pitted, peeled, and cut in 1-inch chunks (see note)

1 tablespoon fresh lime or lemon juice

1 tablespoon olive oil or corn oil

1. Coarsely chop the mint and cilantro in a food processor fitted with the metal chopping blade using 4 to 5 fairly long pulses. Tip into a large fine sieve and rinse under cold running water for a few seconds. Also rinse the bowl and blade under the cold tap, letting stray bits of mint and cilantro fall into the sieve. Drain the herbs on several thicknesses of paper toweling, roll up, and wring as dry as possible; set aside.

2. Dry the work bowl and blade and reassemble. Place the lemon zest, garlic, sugar, and salt in the processor and grind very fine—two 10-second churnings should do it. Scrape the work bowl between churnings with a plastic spatula and stir, pushing larger bits to the bottom. Mind the blade at all times.

3. Add the scallions and with 5 to 6 quick pulses, chop fairly fine. Add the bell pepper and jalapeño and coarsely chop with 8 to 10 staccato pulses. Scrape the work bowl and stir.

4. Add the mango, lime juice, olive oil, and reserved chopped herbs and pulse 3 to 4 times. Scrape the work bowl and stir, then pulse 3 to 4 times more until coarsely chopped.

5. Scoop the salsa into a nonreactive bowl and let stand at room temperature for about half an hour before serving.

Fine Dry Bread Crumbs

I like to keep a supply of homemade dry bread crumbs in the fridge or freezer not only because so many recipes call for them, but also because those I've made myself are so superior to the commercially packaged. Certainly they taste fresher. With a food processor, reducing bread or crisp toast to crumbs can be done in seconds.

MAKES ABOUT 2 CUPS

16 slices firm-textured white sandwich bread

1. Preheat the oven to 300°F.

2. Arrange the slices of bread, not touching, on an ungreased large baking sheet, set uncovered on the middle oven shelf, and toast until the color of light caramel, 20 to 25 minutes.

3. Remove the toast from the oven, cool to room temperature, then break into 1 to 1½-inch chunks.

4. Drop the chunks into a food processor fitted with the metal chopping blade and pulse 12 to 15 times until uniformly fine.

5. Transfer the crumbs to a 1-pint preserving jar, screw the lid down tight, then label, and date. Store in the refrigerator or freezer. If refrigerated, use within 1 month; if frozen, within 3 months.

Bread Crumb Topping

Like cracker crumbs, soft bread crumbs (white, whole-wheat, even light rye) can be buzzed up with melted butter, then stored in the refrigerator for about two weeks. They're as much a time-saver as store-bought toppings, and these, at least, always taste *fresh*.

MAKES ABOUT 2 CUPS, ENOUGH TO TOP FOUR AVERAGE-SIZE CASSEROLES

4 slices firm-textured white, whole-wheat, or light rye bread

2 tablespoons (¼ stick) unsalted butter, melted

1. Tear the bread into small pieces, letting them drop directly into the work bowl of a food processor fitted with the metal chopping blade. Reduce to moderately coarse crumbs by pulsing quickly 3 to 4 times.

2. Drizzle the melted butter evenly over the crumbs and pulse briskly 2 to 3 times until evenly distributed.

3. Empty the crumb topping into a 1-pint preserving jar and screw the lid down tight. Label, date, and store in the refrigerator.

Italian-Style Bread Crumb Topping

Use firm-textured white bread and after dropping the torn pieces into the work bowl, add 3 tablespoons freshly grated Parmesan or Romano cheese, ½ teaspoon dried leaf oregano or marjoram, and ¼ teaspoon each dried leaf basil and freshly ground black pepper. Reduce to crumbs as directed, substituting 2 tablespoons top-quality olive oil for melted butter. Store in an air-tight jar in the refrigerator.

Cracker Crumb Topping

If you make casseroles often, you'll be happy to have a supply of this crumb topping at the ready. Stored in a tightly capped jar in the refrigerator, it will keep for about two weeks.

MAKES ABOUT 2 CUPS, ENOUGH TO TOP 4 AVERAGE-SIZE CASSEROLES

4 dozen 2-inch-square soda crackers

¼ cup (½ stick) unsalted butter, melted

1. Place half the crackers in a food processor fitted with the metal chopping blade and reduce to moderately coarse crumbs by churning 8 to 10 seconds.

2. With the motor running, drizzle 2 tablespoons of the melted butter down the feed tube, then pulse quickly 3 to 4 times to incorporate. Empty into a 1-pint preserving jar.

3. Crumb the remaining crackers and incorporate the remaining melted butter exactly the same way. Add to the crumbs in the jar.

4. Screw the lid down tight, label, date, and store in the refrigerator.

Cheese-Crumb Topping

Prepare as directed, pulsing 2 tablespoons freshly grated Parmesan cheese into each batch of crumbs after the melted butter has been incorporated.

Herbed Crumb Topping

Prepare as directed, crumbing each batch of crackers with ½ teaspoon crumbled dried leaf thyme, marjoram, oregano, or sage.

Flavored Butters

I keep a variety of flavored butters in the refrigerator or freezer to dress up steaks and chops, grilled chicken or fish, even vegetables and breads. All are ideal candidates for the mini food processor and all are made more or less the same way. Directions for shaping, storing, and using these flavored butters appear following the recipes.

EACH RECIPE MAKES ¾ CUP

Maître d'Hôtel Butter

Finely chop ½ cup lightly packed, washed and dried curly parsley sprigs by churning 5 to 10 seconds in a mini food processor fitted with the metal chopping blade; scrape the work bowl. Add ¾ cup (1½ sticks) room-temperature unsalted butter, 2 tablespoons lemon juice, ½ teaspoon salt, and ⅛ teaspoon freshly ground black or white pepper, and churn 5 to 10 seconds until smooth. Shape and store as directed below.

Note: This classic French butter can be used to season steaks, chops, chicken, fish, beets, broccoli, carrots, and green beans.

Garlic-Parmesan Butter

Place 1 large peeled clove garlic, ¼ cup freshly grated Parmesan cheese, ¼ teaspoon salt, and ⅛ teaspoon freshly ground black pepper in a mini food processor fitted with the metal chopping blade, and churn 5 to 10 seconds until the garlic is finely chopped; scrape the work bowl. Add ¾ cup (1½ sticks) room-temperature unsalted butter and churn 5 to 10 seconds more until smooth. Shape and store as directed below. Use in making garlic bread, or serve with broiled chops, chicken, steamed broccoli or green beans.

Anchovy Butter

Churn ¾ cup (1½ sticks) room-temperature unsalted butter, 2 tablespoons anchovy paste, 1 teaspoon lemon juice, and ⅛ teaspoon ground hot red pepper (cayenne) in a mini food processor fitted with the metal chopping blade until smooth—5 to 10 seconds. Shape and store as directed below. Spread on broiled steaks, chops, or fish. I like it, too, on toasted baguette slices.

Horseradish Butter

Place ¾ cup (1½ sticks) room-temperature unsalted butter in a mini food processor fitted with the metal chopping blade. Add 2 tablespoons prepared horseradish, ½ teaspoon salt, and ¼ teaspoon freshly ground black pepper, and churn 5 to 10 seconds until smooth. Shape and store as directed below. Serve with boiled beef, boiled beets, broiled steaks, chops, or shrimp.

Mustard Butter

Churn ¾ cup (1½ sticks) room-temperature unsalted butter and 2 tablespoons Dijon mustard in a mini food processor fitted with the metal chopping blade until smooth, 5 to 10 seconds. Shape and store as directed below. Use to jazz up broiled steaks, chops, fish, or chicken, and such steamed vegetables as asparagus, broccoli, carrots, cauliflower, and green beans.

To Shape and Store Flavored Butters: Shape each into a log about 1½ inches in diameter, place on a square of aluminum foil, fold the ends of the foil over the log, then roll up in the foil, and seal. Label, date, and store in a 0°F freezer or in the fridge. Maximum freezer storage time: 3 months. Maximum refrigerator storage time: 2 weeks.

To Use Flavored Butters: Slice as many ½-inch pats from the frozen or ice-cold roll as you need (each recipe suggests the best "go-withs"). I usually allow one pat per steak, chop, chicken breast, fish steak or fillet, and one-half pat per portion of vegetables or slice of bread.

Processor Pastry for Tarts and Pies

I'd tried making processor pie dough many times but it wasn't until I saw Pastry Chef Karen Barker demonstrate her version on national TV that I saw the light. Karen, a supremely gifted pastry chef and owner, with husband Ben Barker, of Durham, North Carolina's award-winning Magnolia Grill, also happens to be a friend. I adore Karen and Ben and get to their benchmark restaurant as often as I can. I'm forever counting calories but Karen's desserts are always worth a splurge. This pastry recipe was inspired by one of hers in *Not Afraid of Flavor*, the cookbook she and Ben loaded with Magnolia Grill's very best.

Tip: To dice butter, halve the stick lengthwise, give it a quarter-turn, and halve lengthwise again. Next, cut into pats just as if you were dividing into tablespoons.

Note: If making a double-crust pie, it's best to do two batches of this recipe instead of one big one because the longer processing needed to mix it may toughen the pastry.

MAKES ENOUGH FOR ONE 9-, 10- OR 10½-INCH PIE OR TART SHELL

1½ cups sifted all-purpose flour

1 tablespoon sugar

¼ teaspoon salt

½ cup (1 stick) refrigerator-cold unsalted butter, diced (see tip)

1 large egg yolk whisked with 2 tablespoons heavy cream, half-and-half, or milk

1. Place the flour, sugar, and salt in a food processor fitted with the metal chopping blade and pulse 4 to 6 times to combine.

2. Scatter the bits of butter evenly over all and cut in with three 3-second churnings. Scrape the work bowl between churnings with a plastic spatula and stir, pushing bits of butter to the bottom. Now pulse 4 to 6 times until the mixture is the texture of coarse meal.

3. Drizzle the yolk mixture evenly over all and pulse 8 to 10 times until the dough begins to come together. Remove the chopping blade and set aside.

4. Scoop the dough onto a large piece of plastic food wrap, shape into a ball, then flatten into a disk about 6 inches across and ½ inch thick.

5. Wrap in plastic wrap and refrigerate for several hours before rolling. This relaxes the gluten and makes the pastry much easier to handle.

6. Roll or shape the pastry as individual recipes direct.

Note: I've made this pastry dough as much as three days ahead of time with great success. For best results, I let it stand at room temperature 10 to 15 minutes before rolling—no longer or it will become too soft to work.

Crumb Crusts

Because the techniques used to make crumb crust mixtures are similar, I group them together here, and tell how to fit them into pans, and bake them at the end. Again, the same techniques apply.

EACH MAKES ONE 9-INCH PIE SHELL

Graham Cracker Crumb Crust

Crumble twelve 2⅜-inch-square graham crackers into the work bowl of a food processor fitted with the metal chopping blade. Add ⅓ cup sugar, a pinch each of ground cinnamon and nutmeg, and reduce to fine crumbs by churning 30 seconds. If any large pieces remain, churn 30 seconds more. Crumble another 12 graham crackers into the work bowl and churn to crumbs the same way. With the motor running, drizzle ⅓ cup melted unsalted butter down the feed tube. Using a plastic spatula and minding the blade, scrape the work bowl and stir the crumb mixture. Pulse briskly 5 to 10 times until the butter is evenly distributed and the mixture is the texture of cornmeal. Fit the crumb mixture into the pan and bake as directed below.

Vanilla Wafer Crumb Crust

Place 18 vanilla wafers, 1 tablespoon light brown sugar, and a pinch of ground nutmeg in a food processor fitted with the metal chopping blade, and reduce to fine crumbs by churning about 30 seconds. Add another 18 vanilla wafers to the processor and churn to crumbs the same way. With the motor running, drizzle ⅓ cup melted unsalted butter down the feed tube. Using a plastic spatula and minding the blade, scrape the work bowl, and stir the crumb mixture. Now pulse briskly 5 to 10 times until the butter is evenly distributed and the mixture is the texture of cornmeal. Fit the crumb mixture into the pan and bake as directed below.

Gingersnap Crumb Crust

Prepare the Vanilla Wafer Crumb Crust as directed, substituting 36 gingersnaps for vanilla wafers and adding pinches of ground ginger and cinnamon along with the nutmeg. Fit the crumb mixture into the pan and bake as directed below.

Nut-Crumb Crust

Place ½ cup pecans, walnuts, or slivered almonds in the work bowl of a food processor fitted with the metal chopping blade. Crumble in 24 vanilla wafers, add a pinch of salt, and using three or four 5-second churnings, reduce to fine crumbs. With the motor running, drizzle ¼ cup melted unsalted butter down the feed tube. Using a plastic spatula and minding the blade, scrape the work bowl, and stir the crumb mixture. Now pulse briskly 5 to 10 times until the butter is evenly distributed and the mixture is the texture of cornmeal. Fit the crumb mixture into the pan and bake as directed below.

Chocolate Crumb Crust

Crumble 12 thin, 2-inch-round chocolate wafers into the work bowl of a food processor fitted with the metal chopping blade. Add 1 tablespoon sugar and a pinch of salt, and reduce to fine crumbs by churning 30 seconds. If any large pieces remain, churn 30 seconds more. Crumble another 12 chocolate wafers into the work bowl, add another tablespoon of sugar, and churn to crumbs the same way. With the motor running, drizzle ⅓ cup melted unsalted butter down the feed tube. Using a plastic spatula and minding the blade, scrape the work bowl, and stir the crumb mixture. Now pulse briskly 5 to 10 times until the butter is evenly distributed and the mixture is the texture of cornmeal. Fit the crumb mixture into the pan and bake as directed below.

Chocolate-Nut Crumb Crust

Crumble 18 thin 2-inch-round chocolate wafers into the work bowl of a food processor fitted with the metal chopping blade, add ½ cup pecans, walnuts, or slivered almonds, 2 table-spoons sugar, and a pinch of salt. Using three or four 5-second churnings, reduce to fine crumbs. With the motor running, drizzle ¼ cup melted unsalted butter down the feed tube. Using a plastic spatula and minding the blade, scrape the work bowl, and stir the crumb mixture. Now pulse briskly 5 to 10 times until the butter is evenly distributed and the mixture is the texture of cornmeal. Fit the crumb mixture into the pan and bake as directed below.

To Fit Crumb Crusts Into Pans: Spoon the crumb mixture into a 9-inch pie pan (a sturdy metal pan, not a flimsy foil one) or into a 9-inch springform pan, and pat firmly over the bottom and up the sides, using your hands or the back of a large spoon.

Note: If the recipe calls for an unbaked crumb crust, fill straight away, and proceed as the recipe directs.

To Bake Crumb Crusts: Set uncovered on the middle rack of a preheated 350°F oven and bake for 10 minutes. Cool to room temperature before filling.

Starters and Snacks

Hors d'Oeuvre, Savory Cheesecake and Flan, Dips, Sandwich Spreads, and Cocktail Wafers

THANKS TO THE stunning speed with which a food processor can whip up pâtés, terrines, and savory mousses, we can graduate from gloppy cocktail dunks to something far more sophisticated and elegant.

I must admit that before I had a processor to streamline the prep of such long-winded appetizers, I didn't serve them often. Nor, even though I was mad-keen for it, would I bother to make *brandade de morue,* that fluffy south-of-France salt cod spread that required no end of elbow grease. Ditto baba ghanouj, the smoky Middle Eastern appetizer compounded of roughly chopped roasted eggplant; and Liptauer, a paprika-blushed Austro-Hungarian cheese spread with capers and scallions.

Certainly I didn't often make my own pimiento cheese if I had to hand-grate the Cheddar, and I rarely potted shrimp because it had to be minced to velvet. Was I lazy? Maybe. But I like to think that it was a matter of priorities. I rationalized that if I pulled out all the stops for soups, main courses, vegetables, and desserts, no one would notice that I'd short-shrifted the hors d'oeuvre.

Now I have three food processors—mini, medium, and large—and no excuse for not treating my party guests to something special during the cocktail hour. The recipes that follow are for the most part adapted from dishes I've enjoyed on my travels, streamlined from top to bottom so that the food processor does most of the work.

Two-Pepper Parmesan Wafers

Is there anyone who doesn't love nippy cheese wafers? If so, I've never met him. This recipe couldn't be quicker because the processor does all the work. Would you believe these cocktail nibbles are ready to serve in less than 30 minutes? It's true.

Note: Use Parmigiano-Reggiano only for this recipe and make sure that its trimmed weight (minus the rind) is 8 ounces exactly. The fastest way to cut or break it into chunks is with a cheese wedger. If you like "white hot" cheese wafers, increase the amount of red pepper to 1 teaspoon.

MAKES ABOUT 6 DOZEN

8 ounces Parmesan cheese, cut into 1½-inch chunks (see note)

2½ cups sifted all-purpose flour

½ teaspoon salt

½ teaspoon ground hot red pepper (cayenne)

½ teaspoon freshly ground black pepper

½ pound (2 sticks) refrigerator-cold unsalted butter, cut into pats (use the wrapper markings)

1. Preheat the oven to 350°F.

2. Place the cheese in a food processor fitted with the metal chopping blade and churn 15 to 20 seconds nonstop or until finely grated.

3. Add the flour, salt, red and black peppers and pulse 3 to 4 times to combine.

4. Scatter the butter pats evenly over the surface and churn 10 seconds nonstop. Scrape down the work bowl sides and churn until a dough forms and rides up on the blade, 10 to 15 seconds more.

5. Pinch off small pieces of dough, roll into ¾-inch balls, and space 2 inches apart on ungreased baking sheets. Flatten each ball to a thickness of ⅜ inch with the tines of a table fork.

6. Bake until lightly browned and irresistible smelling, 12 to 14 minutes.

Note: If you don't want to bake the cheese wafers right away (or don't want to bake all of them), divide the dough in half, wrap snugly in aluminum foil, label and date, then set in the refrigerator or freezer. The dough will keep fresh for about a week in the fridge, three months in the freezer.

7. Transfer at once to wire racks to cool, then serve with cocktails.

Tomato Granité with Fresh Tarragon

I can think of no first course more refreshing than this fluffy tomato granité. Or one easier to make. Fresh tarragon is my herb of choice but I sometimes substitute fresh dill, basil, or mint, all of which complement tomatoes.

Note: If you have metal ice cube trays, use them for freezing the granité because it's sometimes more difficult to remove from plastic trays.

SERVES 4 TO 6

1½ cups tomato juice or tomato-vegetable juice

1½ cups beef, chicken, or vegetable broth

One ¼-ounce envelope plain gelatin

1 tablespoon fresh lime or lemon juice

1 tablespoon sugar

Four 4-inch sprigs fresh tarragon, washed, patted dry, and lightly wrung with your hands (this releases flavor)

2 large whole bay leaves (preferably fresh)

¼ teaspoon freshly ground black pepper

OPTIONAL GARNISHES
4 to 6 small sprigs fresh tarragon

4 to 6 thin slices lime

1. Place the tomato juice and broth in a medium-size, heavy nonreactive saucepan and sprinkle the gelatin evenly on top. Let stand 5 minutes.

2. Add all remaining ingredients, set over moderate heat, and cook, stirring often, until the gelatin dissolves completely, about 5 min-utes. Reduce the heat to its lowest point, cover, and let the mixture steep for 5 minutes.

3. Pour through a fine sieve set over a large heatproof bowl. Discard the solids and cool the tomato mixture for 30 minutes.

4. Divide the tomato mixture between two ice cube trays and freeze until firm, 2 to 3 hours.

5. Equip the food processor with the metal chopping blade, snap the motor on, and drop one tray of frozen granité cubes down the feed tube one by one into the spinning blade. Con-tinue churning until fluffy, 3 to 5 seconds. Scoop into a 1-quart freezer container and set in the freezer.

6. Buzz up the remaining granité cubes the same way, add to the freezer container, snap on the lid, and freeze until icy but still soft enough to spoon up, 30 minutes to 1 hour. Don't leave the gran-ité in the freezer for more than 1 hour because it will freeze solid and be difficult to serve.

7. Spoon the tomato granité into stemmed goblets and garnish each porition, if you like, with a sprig of tarragon and slice of lime.

Chicken Liver and Red Onion Jam Pâté

If you want a quick and easy pâté, this is the recipe to try. The most time-consuming part is caramelizing the onion, but that takes just ten minutes.

Note: If you cool the chicken liver mixture thoroughly before you add the cream cheese, and if you have the cheese refrigerator-cold, you can serve this pâté straight away. But I prefer the recipe as written and think the pâté better when allowed to mellow in the refrigerator for several hours.

SERVES 6

1 large red onion, peeled and cut into 1-inch chunks

½ teaspoon freshly grated nutmeg

½ teaspoon dried leaf thyme

¼ teaspoon freshly ground black pepper

4 tablespoons unsalted butter

½ pound chicken livers, halved at the natural separation, and trimmed of fat and connective tissue

½ teaspoon salt

⅓ cup sweet Madeira wine (Malmsey or Bual)

One 8-ounce package cream cheese, cubed and brought to room temperature

1. Coarsely chop the onion with the nutmeg, thyme, and pepper by churning 3 seconds in a food processor fitted with the metal chopping blade. Scrape the work bowl and churn 3 seconds longer until uniformly fine.

2. Melt 3 tablespoons of the butter in a medium skillet over moderate heat, add the onion mixture, stir well to coat with butter, then reduce the heat to low, and allow the onion to caramelize slowly. This will take about 10 minutes and you must stir often. Your aim is onion that it is lightly golden, translucent, and about the consistency of jam.

3. Add the remaining tablespoon of butter to the skillet and when it melts, add the chicken livers and salt and cook, stirring often over moderate heat, until the livers are no longer pink. Reduce the heat to low and cook the livers, stirring now and then, about 10 minutes more or until well done. Scoop the skillet mixture onto a plate and reserve.

4. With the skillet off the heat, add the wine. Set over moderate heat and boil, stirring often, for 2 to 3 minutes until only a glaze remains on the skillet bottom. Return the chicken liver mixture and any accumulated drippings to the skillet, and turn to coat with the glaze.

5. Transfer all to the food processor, still fitted with the metal chopping blade, and churn 5 seconds. Scrape the sides of the work bowl and churn 5 seconds more.

6. With the motor running, drop half the cream cheese down the feed tube, cube by cube. Scrape the work bowl, then snap the motor on, and add the remaining cream cheese the same way. Scrape the work bowl once again, then churn 10 to 15 seconds until the pâté is absolutely smooth.

7. Scoop into a small bowl, press plastic wrap flat on top, and refrigerate for several hours.

8. Let the pâté stand at room temperature for 30 minutes, fluff the surface with a spoon, and serve with melbas or crisp crackers.

Leek and Sweet Red Pepper Flan

One of the loveliest appetizers I've ever eaten is the silky red pepper flan served at 11 Madison, Danny Meyer's delightful restaurant overlooking New York's Madison Square Park. This is my interpretation of that dish and the processor does it to perfection. Serve at the start of an elegant meal, or as the entrée of a light lunch, accompanied by Focaccia (page 221) or yeast rolls fresh from the oven.

Note: The only pesky parts of this recipe: washing the leeks, skinning the peppers, and sieving the flan mixture (you can skip this but your flan won't be silky). A chinois, available at any good kitchen shop, will speed the sieving.

Tip: The fastest way to core, quarter, and seed a bell pepper is to slice off the stem end, stand the pepper upside-down, then cut straight down, following the pepper's natural convolutions so that you miss the core and seeds altogether. Also trim and use any fleshy parts around the stem. As for washing leeks, cut off roots and coarse green tops, then beginning at the top, make several slashes the length of each leek, cutting to within about ½ inch of the root end. Hold the leeks under cold running water, one by one, spreading the layers so all grit is flushed out.

SERVES 6

6 large red bell peppers (about 2¾ pounds), cored, quartered, and seeded (see tip)

6 medium leeks (about 2 pounds), trimmed, washed, and sliced ½-inch thick (see tip)

4 large whole cloves garlic, peeled

Two 2-inch sprigs fresh lemon thyme or ½ teaspoon dried leaf thyme, crumbled

One 3-inch sprig fresh rosemary or ½ teaspoon dried leaf rosemary, crumbled

2 tablespoons olive oil

¾ cup chicken broth

¼ cup heavy cream

2 large eggs

4 large egg yolks

1 teaspoon salt

¼ teaspoon freshly ground black pepper

3 cups mesclun, lightly dressed with a good vinaigrette

1. Preheat the oven to 375°F.

2. Place the bell peppers, leeks, garlic, thyme and rosemary sprigs in an ungreased large shallow roasting pan. Drizzle the olive oil over all, toss well, then spread the mixture evenly in the pan. Roast uncovered until the peppers and leeks are soft and begin to caramelize, 1 to 1¼ hours.

3. Remove the pepper mixture from the oven, discarding the thyme and rosemary sprigs, then cool until easy to handle. Meanwhile, reduce the oven temperature to 350°F. Also coat six 4-ounce ramekins with nonstick spray and set aside.

4. Slip the skins off the peppers and discard. This should be easy—don't worry about any recalcitrant bits of skin because they will be sieved out.

5. Transfer the pepper mixture to a food processor fitted with the metal chopping blade and churn 10 seconds nonstop. Scrape down the work bowl sides, then continue churning until reduced to a thick purée, 10 to 15 seconds more. Add the chicken broth, cream, eggs, egg yolks, salt, and black pepper and pulse 3 to 4 times until smooth.

6. Pour the mixture into a large fine sieve set over a large bowl (or better yet into a chinois) and with the bowl of a ladle or the back of a wooden spoon, force the mixture through the sieve. This takes patience and elbow grease—I won't pretend otherwise. Keep at it, however, until only a tablespoon or so of dry pulp remains in the sieve.

7. Divide the pepper mixture among the six prepared ramekins, set—not touching—in a large shallow baking pan, and add enough hot water to the pan to come halfway up the ramekins. Do not cover.

8. Bake for about 1 hour or until set like custard—a toothpick inserted in the center of a flan should come out clean.

9. Remove the flans from the oven, lift from the hot water bath, and cool on a wire rack to room temperature.

10. Using a thin-blade spatula dipped into hot water, loosen the flans around the edge and invert on salad plates. Wreathe with mesclun and serve.

Pesto Cheesecake

This recipe demonstrates the importance of sequence in food processor prep—that is, working from dry ingredients to wet so that there's no need to wash the work bowl and blade between stages. This recipe was e-mailed to me by Janet Jackson-Ledermann of Raleigh, North Carolina. My two nieces, Linda and Kim, had tasted her pesto cheesecake at a party and couldn't stop raving about it. Janet says she's had the recipe so long she can't remember where she originally got it—"it's one of the hand-written ones in my recipe box." She adds that she's taken the pesto cheesecake "to parties and it's always the number one hit!" Janet doesn't make her pesto cheesecake by food processor—this is my all-processor variation. It's also a lower-fat, lower-calorie version because I've substituted low-fat cream cheese and part-skim ricotta for the "fully loaded," which Janet uses.

MAKES ONE 9-INCH CHEESECAKE; SERVES 8 AS A FIRST COURSE OR LIGHT LUNCHEON ENTRÉE,
16 TO 18 AS A COCKTAIL SPREAD

TOPPING
¼ cup pine nuts

CRUST
¼ cup Fine Dry Bread Crumbs (page 67)

2 tablespoons freshly grated
Parmesan cheese

1 tablespoon olive oil

FILLING
1½ cups firmly packed tender young basil leaves
(you'll need 1 large bunch)

½ cup plus 2 tablespoons freshly grated
Parmesan cheese

2 tablespoons pine nuts

2 tablespoons olive oil

1 large whole clove garlic, peeled

¼ teaspoon freshly ground black pepper

Two 8-ounce packages light cream cheese
(Neufchâtel), at room temperature

1 cup packed part-skim ricotta cheese

¼ teaspoon salt

¼ teaspoon hot red pepper sauce

3 large eggs

1. Preheat the oven to 325°F. Coat a 9-inch springform pan well with nonstick cooking spray and set aside.

2. Topping: Coarsely chop the pine nuts by pulsing 3 to 4 times in a food processor fitted with the metal chopping blade, tip onto a piece of wax paper, and reserve.

3. Crust: Pulse the bread crumbs, Parmesan, and oil 3 to 4 times in the food processor until uniformly crumbly. Tip into the prepared pan and tilt from side to side until bottom and sides are lightly and evenly coated; set aside.

4. Filling: Churn the basil, 2 tablespoons of the Parmesan, the pine nuts, oil, garlic, and black pepper 15 seconds in the food processor.

Scrape down the work bowl sides, and churn 15 seconds longer until thick and smooth. Transfer the mixture to a 1-quart measuring cup, scraping as much pesto from the work bowl and blade as possible.

5. Wipe the bowl and blade dry with paper toweling and reassemble the processor. Add the cream cheese, ricotta, ½ cup Parmesan, salt, and red pepper sauce and churn 15 seconds. Scrape down the work bowl and churn until smooth, about 15 seconds longer.

6. Drop the eggs, one by one, down the feed tube, pulsing each in well before adding the next. The mixture should be silky-smooth.

7. Pour ½ of the cheese mixture into the pesto and beat until smooth. Carefully spoon the pesto mixture into the prepared crust, taking care not to dislodge the crumbs.

8. Top the pesto layer with the remaining cheese mixture, again taking care not to dislodge the crumbs. Scatter the reserved pine nut topping evenly over all.

9. Bake on the middle oven rack 40 to 45 minutes or until the filling jiggles only slightly when you nudge the pan.

10. Remove the cheesecake from the oven and carefully run a thin-blade spatula around the edge of the pan. Cool the cheesecake in the upright pan on a wire rack to room temperature. It will shrink somewhat but that's okay. Cover with plastic food wrap and refrigerate several hours until firm.

11. Carefully loosen the cheesecake around the edge with a thin-blade spatula, release and remove the springform pan sides. Gently slide the spatula underneath the cheesecake, then ease it onto a round platter. Let stand about 30 minutes at room temperature before serving.

12. Cut the pesto cheesecake into eight wedges and serve as the main course of a light luncheon (you'll need only a tartly dressed green salad to accompany and fruit for dessert). Or make it the centerpiece of a party buffet, set a basket of crackers nearby, and let everyone dig in, spreading crackers as thickly or thinly as they like.

Terrine of Pork and Ham with Calvados and Juniper Berries

One of the blessings of the food processor is that it simplifies the making of messy pâtés and terrines. How much neater it is to mince raw liver in an enclosed work bowl than to squish it through a meat grinder. And how much faster it is to grind raw pork (many butchers, by the way, will not grind it for you). If you plan the sequence of chopping and mixing correctly, you won't have to wash the processor blade or bowl until the terrine is in the oven. Calvados is a fine apple "brandy" made in Normandy.

Note: You will find pork easier to grind if you set it in the freezer for 30 to 40 minutes. This partial freezing provides just the right amount of resistance and makes for a cleaner cut. Whenever I grind or mix raw pork in the food processor, I scald all parts of it before loading them into the dishwasher.

Tip: The easiest way to line a loaf pan with barding fat is to cut paper patterns for the bottom, sides, and ends—baking parchment works fine. Simply lay the pan on the paper, trace round the bottom, then one side, and one end. Place the paper patterns on the sheets of barding fat and cut with a sharp knife. You'll need one piece for the bottom and two each for the ends and sides.

MAKES ONE 9 × 5 × 3-INCH LOAF

5 large sheets of barding fat to line the pan (have your butcher cut these about ⅛ inch thick; the best barding fat surrounds the loin) (see tip)

½ cup loosely packed Italian parsley leaves

1 tablespoon fresh lemon thyme leaves or ½ teaspoon dried leaf thyme, crumbled

5 slices firm-textured white bread, broken into small chunks

½ teaspoon salt

½ teaspoon freshly ground black pepper

¼ teaspoon freshly grated nutmeg

⅛ teaspoon ground allspice

½ cup half-and-half cream

3 tablespoons bacon drippings

6 medium scallions, trimmed and cut into 1-inch chunks (include some green tops)

2 medium whole cloves garlic, peeled

4 juniper berries

1 pound calf's liver, trimmed of veins and sinew and cut into 1-inch chunks

1 pound boneless pork loin, trimmed of sinew but not excess fat, cut into 1-inch chunks, and partially frozen (see note)

½ pound boneless smoked ham, cut into 1-inch chunks

2 large eggs

¼ cup Calvados or brandy

1. Preheat the oven to 350°F. Lightly oil a 9 × 5 × 3-inch loaf pan, then line with the barding fat as described in the tip. Refrigerate until ready to use.

2. Place the parsley and fresh thyme in a fine sieve and rinse well under cold running water. Tip onto several thicknesses of paper toweling and wring as dry as possible. Tip onto fresh dry paper toweling and wring again. If fresh herbs are to chop cleanly in the food processor, they must be absolutely dry.

3. Place the parsley, thyme, bread, salt, pepper, nutmeg, and allspice in a food processor fitted with the metal chopping blade and with three 5-second churnings, chop fairly fine. Empty the crumb mixture into a large mixing bowl, drizzle the cream evenly over all, and toss lightly to mix; set aside.

4. Melt the bacon drippings in a small heavy skillet over moderate heat and while they melt, finely chop the scallions, garlic, and juniper berries in the food processor by churning 8 to 10 seconds. Scrape into the skillet, reduce the heat to low, and cook slowly, stirring now and then, until limp, about 5 minutes.

5. Meanwhile, finely mince the calf's liver, half of the total amount at a time, by churning 5 seconds in the food processor. Scoop into the bowl with the crumb mixture.

6. Grind the pork the same way in two batches, letting each churn about 10 seconds. Add to the mixing bowl. Now moderately coarsely grind all of the ham by churning 5 to 10 seconds, pausing every now and then to pulse. Scrape into the mixing bowl.

7. Add the skillet mixture to the bowl and mix all well with your hands or with a wooden spoon. Add the eggs and Calvados and mix well again.

8. Pack the mixture firmly into the prepared pan, cover with several thicknesses of aluminum foil, then set a brick on top to weight. Set in a large baking pan and add enough hot water to come about halfway up the sides of the terrine pan.

9. Bake on the middle oven rack until the terrine is firm to the touch and pulls from the sides of the pan, about 2½ hours.

10. Remove the terrine from the oven and from the water bath, lift off the weight and the foil, set on a wire rack, and cool in the upright pan to room temperature.

11. Once the terrine is cool, re-cover with foil, and refrigerate at for at least 12 hours.

12. To unmold, carefully loosen the terrine around the edge with a thin-blade spatula, lay a small platter on top, and invert. The terrine will drop out without further encouragement but this may take at least an hour because the barding fat must soften and separate from the sides of the pan.

13. Slice the terrine and serve as a first course with crisp slices of melba toast, gherkins, and whole grain mustard. Or spread on melbas or crackers and pass with cocktails.

Bruschetta with Tomatoes and Garlic

I saw Sara Moulton make a similar cocktail nibble one night on *Cooking Live,* her Food Network call-in show. She did everything by hand, but I decided to see if this couldn't be whizzed up by processor. Sara, a bud for 25 years, used canned tomatoes because "the fresh tomato season is so very short." I, too, used Roma (Italian plum) tomatoes for this recipe, a good Italian brand from my supermarket. They were water-packed whole Romas, not those put up in tomato sauce. I drained them well, then patted them dry between several thicknesses of paper toweling. This is important because the tomato mixture should not be soupy.

Note: I chiffonaded the basil by hand because it's just plain faster: Working with 5 or 6 large leaves at a time, stack them, roll up tight, then slice crosswise at ⅛-inch intervals with a sharp chef's knife.

MAKES ABOUT 1½ DOZEN

One 20- to 22-inch baguette (about ½-pound)

¼ cup olive oil

6 medium scallions, trimmed and cut into 1-inch chunks (include some green tops)

1 large whole clove garlic, peeled

¼ teaspoon salt

¼ teaspoon freshly ground black pepper

Two 14½-ounce cans water-packed Roma (Italian plum) tomatoes, drained well and patted dry on paper toweling (see headnote)

12 large fresh basil leaves, washed, patted dry on paper toweling, and cut into chiffonade (see note)

1. Preheat the oven to 300°F.

2. Slice the baguette on the bias, spacing the cuts about ½ inch apart. You should have about 18 slices. Arrange the slices on an ungreased baking sheet, then using 2 tablespoons of the olive oil, brush the tops of each. Set on the middle oven shelf and toast until lightly golden. This will take about 20 minutes.

3. Meanwhile, coarsely chop the scallions and garlic with the salt and pepper by churning 3 seconds in the food processor with the metal chopping blade. Scrape the work bowl sides, then churn about 3 seconds more or until fairly finely chopped.

4. Add the tomatoes and remaining 2 tablespoons olive oil and pulse quickly 2 to 3 times. Open the work bowl and with a plastic spatula, carefully stir the mixture up from the bottom—mind the blade! Now pulse 2 to 3 times more to rough-chop the tomatoes. The texture should be about like salsa.

5. Scoop the mixture into a small bowl and let stand at room temperature for about 1 hour to mellow the flavors.

6. When ready to serve, spread each piece of toast with a scant tablespoon of the tomato mixture, and sprinkle with the basil.

Brandade de Morue (Provençal Salt Cod Spread)

Few recipes are more tedious to prepare the old-fashioned way than this fluffy salt cod spread from the South of France. The preliminaries are easy enough—soaking stiff slabs of salt cod, then cooking them until tender. But the puréeing—still done in Provence with a mortar and pestle— is something else again. Imagine the elbow grease (not to mention the time) needed to pound them to velvet. Here again the food processor is a miracle worker.

Note: Brandade can be made several days ahead of time, refrigerated, then reheated just before serving in the top of a double boiler over simmering water. Fluff the brandade with a fork as it heats and, if necessary, soften by beating in 1 to 2 tablespoons milk. Brandade is delicious with aperitifs, but I like it, too, as the centerpiece of a light lunch. The perfect accompaniment? Mesclun or other mixed salad greens tossed with a tart vinaigrette.

MAKES ABOUT 3 CUPS

1 pound boneless dried salt cod

1 large whole clove garlic, peeled

Zest of ½ lemon, removed in strips with a vegetable peeler

3 tablespoons fresh lemon juice

½ cup plus 3 tablespoons heavy cream, at room temperature

½ cup plus 3 tablespoons olive oil

¼ teaspoon freshly ground white or black pepper (white is traditional but I prefer black)

1. Soak the cod overnight in the refrigerator in enough cold water to cover. Next day, drain and rinse well, then simmer in enough water to cover just until the cod flakes easily at the touch of a fork, about 15 minutes. Drain well, then pat dry on paper toweling.

2. Equip the food processor with the metal chopping blade, snap the motor on, and drop the garlic and lemon zest down the feed tube into the spinning blade. Continue churning for 5 to 10 seconds until the garlic and zest are finely minced. Scrape down the work bowl.

3. Break the cod into 1-inch chunks and add to the work bowl along with the lemon juice, ½ cup each of the cream and olive oil, and the pepper. Purée by churning 30 seconds.

4. With the machine still on, drizzle the remaining 3 tablespoons cream, then the remaining 3 tablespoons olive oil down the feed tube. Continue processing until the brandade is as fluffy as mashed potatoes, 10 to 15 seconds. Scrape down the work bowl and pulse once or twice.

5. Serve the brandade warm with toasted slices of French bread that have been lightly brushed with olive oil.

Guacamole

Before pulse buttons, before powerful braking action, it was nearly impossible to make a proper guacamole in a food processor—proper meaning "lumpy." Early models puréed the avocados no matter how fast you snapped the machine on and off. I learned several things while developing this processor guacamole: choreography is key, also chopping the cilantro *before* you wash it, and not only draining the canned diced tomatoes and green chiles well but also patting them absolutely dry on paper toweling. It's important, too, to choose firm-ripe avocados, those that barely yield when you press them. The variety I prefer because of its nutlike flavor is Hass, a small California avocado with pebbly dark green or black skin.

Note: Never feel guilty about eating avocados. They are powerhouses of potassium, good sources, too, of vitamins A, C, and niacin. Moreover, the fat they contain is mostly unsaturated, they are low in sodium and cholesterol-free. For the record, one small Hass avocado weighs in at about 240 calories, some 50 less than a cup of fruit yogurt made with whole milk. I often make this guacamole several hours, sometimes even a day, ahead of time and store in the refrigerator. I've discovered that if I press plastic food wrap flat over the surface of the guacamole, it will not darken.

MAKES ABOUT 4 CUPS; 12 TO 14 APPETIZER SERVINGS OR 6 SALAD SERVINGS

1 cup fresh cilantro leaves (do not pack) (see headnote)

One 10-ounce can diced tomatoes with green chiles (as mild or hot as you like), drained

8 medium scallions, trimmed and cut into 1-inch chunks (include some green tops)

1 large whole clove garlic, peeled

¾ teaspoon salt

2½ pounds firm-ripe Hass avocados (about 6 small; see note)

4 to 5 tablespoons fresh lime juice

1. Coarsely chop the cilantro in a food processor fitted with the metal chopping blade using 4 to 5 fairly long pulses. Tip into a small fine sieve and rinse under cold running water for a few seconds. Also rinse the bowl and blade under the cold tap, letting stray bits of cilantro fall into the sieve. Drain the cilantro on several thicknesses of paper toweling, roll up, and wring as dry as possible. Set aside.

2. Spread the drained tomatoes with green chiles on several thicknesses of paper toweling, cover with more paper toweling, and pat as dry as possible. If necessary, replenish the toweling. If the tomatoes and chiles aren't dry, they'll water down the guacamole.

3. Coarsely chop the scallions and garlic with the salt by churning 3 seconds in the food processor. Scrape the work bowl sides, then pulse once or twice.

4. Halve and pit the avocados, then working directly over the open work bowl, scoop the avocado flesh on top of the chopped scallion mixture. When half of the avocados have been added, drizzle evenly with 2 tablespoons of the lime juice. Add the remaining avocados and lime juice the same way.

5. Add the reserved cilantro and tomatoes with green chiles, distributing evenly on top of the avocados. Pulse briskly 3 times, then using a plastic spatula, stir the guacamole up from the bottom of the work bowl keeping your fingers far, far away from the chopping blade. Pulse 3 times more until uniformly lumpy—the guacamole should be slightly lumpier than large-curd cottage cheese.

6. Transfer the guacamole to a medium-size mixing bowl, stir well, then taste. If it's not tart enough to suit you, add the final tablespoon of lime juice. Also adjust the salt as needed.

7. Smooth a sheet of plastic food wrap flat on top of the guacamole, pressing it into all the nooks and crannies. Refrigerate until ready to serve.

8. Serve with tortilla chips as a cocktail dip. Or mound on crisply shredded iceberg lettuce, bracket with wedges of ripe plum tomatoes, and serve as a salad.

Black Olive Mayonnaise

Here's another idea I picked up while watching Sara Moulton on *Cooking Live*. Of all the shows on the Food Network, Sara's is the one I always watch because, despite my many years in the food business, she usually manages to teach me something. What I've done here is rework Sara's recipe, gearing it to the food processor. You'll find this a singularly versatile mayonnaise. Sara serves it as a dunk for deep-fried Vidalia onion rings, but it's also terrific with crudités. Or just spread it on melbas, or serve on the side with grilled chicken, salmon, or tuna.

MAKES ABOUT 1⅓ CUPS

⅓ cup oil-cured black olives, pitted and patted very dry on paper toweling

1 cup mayonnaise (use light, if you like)

1 to 2 tablespoons fresh lemon juice

¼ teaspoon hot red pepper sauce

1. Pulse the olives briskly 3 to 4 times in a food processor fitted with the metal chopping blade. Scrape down the work bowl, then pulse quickly once or twice.

2. Add the mayonnaise, 1 tablespoon of the lemon juice, and the red pepper sauce and pulse quickly to combine. Scrape down the work bowl, taste, and if the mayonnaise is not tart enough, pulse in the second tablespoon of lemon juice.

3. Mound in a colorful bowl and serve as a dip for raw zucchini or fennel sticks, cauliflower or broccoli florets.

Coyote Caviar

The traditional way to serve this Southwestern dip is on a plate spread with cream cheese—unnecessary calories, as far as I'm concerned. I also dispense with the garnishes, chopped hard-cooked eggs and salsa, because I don't think it needs any gussying up. I just put out a big bowl of tortilla chips, the round ones made especially for dipping.

Note: This recipe isn't likely to need any salt because of the saltiness of the olives—but taste and adjust before serving. The black olives you use should be the firm oil-cured ones, otherwise your "caviar" will be soupy.

Tip: The fastest way to pit olives is to lay 3 or 4 at a time on their sides and whack them with the broad side of a large chef's knife or a cutlet bat.

MAKES ABOUT 3 CUPS

½ cup firmly packed fresh cilantro leaves

1 large whole clove garlic, peeled

6 medium scallions, trimmed and cut into 1-inch chunks (include some green tops)

2 teaspoons chili powder

½ teaspoon ground cumin

½ teaspoon freshly ground black pepper

¼ teaspoon red pepper flakes

1 cup black olives, pitted (see note)

One 15-ounce can black beans, rinsed, drained, and patted dry on paper toweling

One 10-ounce can diced tomatoes with green chiles, drained and patted dry on paper toweling

2 tablespoons olive oil

2 tablespoons fresh lime juice

1. Coarsely chop the cilantro in a food processor fitted with the metal chopping blade using 4 to 5 fairly long pulses. Tip into a small fine sieve and rinse under cold running water for a few seconds. Also rinse the bowl and blade under the cold tap, letting stray bits of cilantro fall into the sieve. Drain the cilantro on several thicknesses of paper toweling, roll up, and wring as dry as possible. Set aside.

2. Churn the garlic, scallions, chili powder, cumin, black pepper, and red pepper flakes 5 seconds in a food processor fitted with the metal chopping blade. Scrape down the work bowl sides, churn 5 seconds more, then scrape the work bowl again.

3. Add the olives and pulse 5 times. Quickly scrape the work bowl, stirring up any large pieces of olive, and pulse 5 more times. A rough chop is what you want.

4. Place the beans, diced tomatoes with green chiles, olive oil, lime juice, and reserved chopped cilantro in a medium-size mixing bowl. Add the processor mixture and stir well.

5. Spoon into a colorful bowl and serve with tortilla chips. This dip will be even better if you make it several hours ahead and refrigerate until about ½ hour before serving.

Mushroom Caviar

If any recipe is tailor-made for the food processor, it's Mushroom Caviar. Any combination of mushrooms works well here, but the two I like best are portabellas (now available cleaned and sliced) and the standard white mushrooms. Just be sure that these are on the small side and absolutely fresh—if the caps have separated from the stems exposing the brown gills, the mushrooms are over the hill. I find Mushroom Caviar endlessly versatile. In addition to serving it as a cocktail spread, I use it to dress pasta (usually fettuccine or linguine). I also like to spread it on firm-textured white bread that's been toasted 20 to 25 minutes in a 300° F oven until the color of pale caramel. I top the mushroom-spread slices with freshly grated Parmesan cheese (about 1 tablespoon per slice), then broil eight inches from the heat for six to eight minutes, just until the cheese and is tipped with brown. One to two slices plus a crisp green salad make a fast and filling lunch.

MAKES ABOUT 3 CUPS

2 large yellow onions, peeled and cut into 1-inch chunks

1 tablespoon fresh lemon thyme leaves or 1 teaspoon dried leaf thyme, crumbled

½ teaspoon salt

½ teaspoon freshly ground black pepper

¼ cup olive oil

One 6-ounce package portabella slices, cut into 1-inch chunks

1½ pounds small white mushrooms, wiped clean, stemmed, and quartered

3 tablespoons fresh lemon juice

1 tablespoon unsalted butter, diced

1. Pulse the onions, thyme, salt, and pepper 10 to 12 times in a food processor fitted with the metal chopping blade, until finely chopped, scraping down the work bowl at half time.

2. Meanwhile, heat the olive oil in a very large heavy skillet over moderately high heat until ripples appear on the skillet bottom.

3. Add the chopped onion mixture to the skillet and cook uncovered, stirring now and then, until the onions are very soft and tipped with brown. This will take 20 to 25 minutes.

4. Add the portabella slices and white mushrooms to the processor (in two batches, if necessary) and pulse 12 to 15 times until finely chopped, scraping the work bowl at half time.

5. Add the mushrooms to the browned onions in the skillet, stir well, reduce heat to moderate, and cook uncovered, stirring occasionally, until the color and consistency of caviar, about an hour. You don't have to stand and stir—a quick stir every 20 minutes is enough.

6. Mix the lemon juice into the mushroom caviar, remove from the heat, and cool 10 minutes. Scatter the bits of butter over the mushroom caviar, and stir until incorporated.

7. Scoop the mushroom caviar into a 1-quart container, press plastic food wrap flat on top, snap on the lid, and store in the refrigerator. Serve within 3 to 4 days.

8. Mellow at room temperature for about 30 minutes, then serve as a cocktail spread.

Mushroom Pinwheels

If you should have Mushroom Caviar on hand, you can rustle up these elegant pinwheels. With frozen puff pastry, they're a snap. Serve with cocktails.

MAKES 18

1 sheet frozen puff pastry (from a 17.3-ounce package)

¼ cup freshly grated Parmesan

⅛ teaspoon ground hot red pepper (cayenne)

¾ cup packed Mushroom Caviar (page 90)

1. Thaw the frozen pastry just long enough to unfold it, spread on a lightly floured cloth, and thaw completely. This will take about 30 minutes. With a lightly floured rolling pin, roll the pastry into a rectangle 13 inches long and 11 inches wide, paying special attention to the seams where the pastry was folded and making sure that any splits are completely sealed. Brush these with a little water and pinch shut, if necessary.

2. Arrange the pastry sheet on the floured cloth so that an 11-inch side faces you. Sprinkle the pastry with 2 tablespoons of the grated Parmesan, leaving ½-inch margins on the bottom, left and right sides, and a ¾ inch margin at the top. Sprinkle the cayenne evenly over the Parmesan.

3. Spread a smooth, thin layer of Mushroom Caviar over the grated Parmesan, leaving the same margins as before. Scatter the remaining Parmesan evenly on top.

4. Roll the pastry up jelly-roll style, starting at the 11-inch end and rolling as tight as possible. Lifting the end of the pastry cloth will encourage the pastry to roll up on itself. Moisten the top edge of the pastry with water or milk, then press into the roll to seal.

5. Wrap the roll snugly in plastic food wrap and freeze several hours or until firm. Twirling the ends of the plastic wrap will make the roll even tighter—important if the pinwheels are to retain their shape as they bake.

6. About 20 minutes before you are ready to bake the pinwheels, preheat the oven to 400°F. Coat two baking sheets with nonstick cooking spray and set aside.

7. With a sharp knife, cut the frozen mushroom roll into slices ⅜ inch thick and space 2 inches apart on the prepared baking sheets.

8. Bake, one sheet at a time, on the lowest oven shelf until puffed and brown, 12 to 15 minutes. Let the pinwheels cool on the baking sheet 1 minute, then loosen with a pancake turner, and transfer to wire racks to cool. Serve at room temperature as an hors d'oeuvre.

Tapenade

The only olives to use for this Provençal recipe are oil-cured ones from the South of France. They're small, firm, and often cured with sprigs of thyme and/or rosemary. Many high-end groceries sell pitted Provençal olives but these, I've found, are not entirely pit-free so I check carefully before committing them to the food processor. Pitting small Provençal olives isn't a big deal, however. When I have dozens to do, I'll attack six or eight olives at a time. I cluster them on a chopping board, then give them a good whack with a cutlet bat. This splits the olives exposing the pits, which can be lifted right out. The French like to dunk fresh vegetables into tapenade—sticks of fennel or celery, for example, broccoli or cauliflower florets. I prefer to spread it on crisp crackers or toss it with hot pasta.

Note: True tapenade calls for anchovy fillets but I substitute anchovy paste, which has none of their "furriness." I also sometimes add two or three fresh rosemary leaves (not sprigs) and/or lemon thyme leaves (not sprigs) to the work bowl before whizzing everything up. The olives, anchovies, and capers in this recipe are all so salty no additional salt is needed. Tapenade, by the way, is a perfect candidate for a mini processor.

MAKES ABOUT 1¼ CUPS

4 medium whole cloves garlic, peeled

½ pound oil-cured black olives, pitted and patted very dry on paper toweling (see headnote)

¼ cup well drained small capers

1 tablespoon anchovy paste

½ teaspoon freshly ground black pepper

½ cup olive oil

1. Equip a food processor (a mini, if you have one) with the metal chopping blade, snap the motor on, and drop the garlic cloves down the feed tube into the spinning blade. Continue churning for 5 seconds, then scrape down the work bowl.

2. Add the olives, capers, anchovy paste, and pepper and churn 10 seconds. Scrape down the work bowl.

3. With the motor running, drizzle half the olive oil down the feed tube and continue churning for 5 seconds. Scrape down the work bowl and stir the mixture with a plastic spatula.

4. Snap the machine on, drizzle the remaining olive down the feed tube, then pulse 5 to 6 times until the tapenade is as coarse or fine as you like. I like mine the texture of fine black caviar.

5. Serve as a cocktail dip or spread or toss with a bowl of hot thin spaghetti. Stored in a tightly covered jar in the refrigerator, tapenade keeps for several weeks.

Olivada

For this caviar-rich spread, you will need brined Kalamata (Greek) or ripe Mediterranean olives with intense fruity flavor. Many specialty food shops sell them pitted, but you can't assume that they're totally pitless. To make sure, I press each olive firmly with the palm of my hand on several thicknesses of paper toweling, replenishing the toweling as needed. This also forces out excess brine so the olivada is neither too salty nor too soupy. Ten minutes should do the job.

MAKES ABOUT 1½ CUPS

3 cups (about 1 pound) pitted, brined Kalamata or other ripe Mediterranean olives, drained well and pressed dry on paper toweling

2 large whole cloves garlic, peeled

2 teaspoons fresh lemon thyme leaves or ½ teaspoon dried leaf thyme, crumbled

1 tablespoon olive oil

¼ teaspoon freshly ground black pepper

1. Churn all ingredients in a food processor fitted with the metal chopping blade 1 minute, scrape down the work bowl sides, and churn 1 to 1½ minutes longer to form a smooth, thick paste.

2. Spoon into a small bowl, press plastic food wrap gently on top, and let stand about 1 hour at room temperature.

3. Serve as a spread for crackers or chewy chunks of country bread. Also delicious as a dip for raw sticks of celery or fennel, even raw cauliflower or broccoli florets. Stored in an airtight jar in the refrigerator, olivada will keep as long as 10 days. Let come to room temperature before serving.

Hummus

Now that tahini (sesame seed paste) has come to the supermarket, there's no reason not to make this garlicky Middle Eastern appetizer. With a food processor, it's a whiz. Tahini doesn't exactly fly off the store shelves, so the tin you buy will probably have several inches of oil on top and a sludgy paste underneath. No problem. Simply scoop everything into the food processor and whiz for a minute or so—the tahini instantly re-emulsifies. Once open, tahini should be refrigerated. Stored in a tightly capped jar in the refrigerator, hummus will keep for about a week. Before using hummus in a falafel sandwich, thin with water until the consistency of gravy.

Note: The best way to avoid "soupy" hummus is to drain the chickpeas well and pat them dry on paper toweling. To give hummus nuttier flavor, spread the chickpeas in a small roasting pan lightly coated with nonstick spray, and set uncovered in a 400°F oven for 20 to 25 minutes.

MAKES ABOUT 2 CUPS

¼ cup lightly packed Italian parsley sprigs

2 large whole cloves garlic, peeled

1 teaspoon salt

¼ teaspoon freshly ground black pepper

One 15½-ounce can chickpeas, drained well and if desired, lightly roasted (see note)

1 cup tahini (see headnote)

½ cup fresh lemon juice

¾ cup cold water (about)

3 tablespoons olive oil

1. Drop the parsley into a food processor fitted with the metal chopping blade and give a couple of 5-second pulses until coarsely chopped. Transfer to a large fine sieve and set under cool running water for several seconds. Also rinse the bowl and blade under the cold tap, letting bits of parsley fall into the sieve. Tap the parsley onto several thicknesses of paper toweling, roll up, wring dry, and set aside.

2. Add the garlic, salt, and pepper to the processor, and mince by churning 5 seconds.

With a plastic spatula, scrape the work bowl, then pulse 2 to 3 times.

3. Add the chickpeas and churn until fairly smooth, about 5 seconds. Add the tahini and lemon juice and pulse 4 to 5 times to incorporate. Scrape the work bowl sides.

4. With the motor running, drizzle the water down the feed tube, adding only enough to make the hummus slightly creamier than peanut butter; stop and scrape the work bowl sides once or twice as you add the water. Taste for salt and pepper and adjust as needed.

5. Spoon the hummus into a serving bowl, press plastic wrap flat on top, and let stand at room temperature for 1 hour. Remove the plastic and with the back of a tablespoon, make a large shallow crater in the center of the hummus. Sprinkle the reserved parsley around the edge and spoon the olive oil into the crater.

6. Serve as a spread or dip for crisp triangles of pita bread or sesame crackers. Good, too, with raw zucchini sticks and broccoli florets.

Skordalia (Greek Garlic Spread)

Greeks are not afraid of garlic and this creamy spread contains enough to blow a safe. Potatoes are the usual foundation for skordalia, but we learned early on that processors churn them to glue. So I've taken considerable liberties with the classic Greek recipe, substituting cannellini (white kidney beans) for potatoes and adding just enough bread for proper consistency. Spread skordalia on crisp crackers, use as a dunk for raw vegetables (cucumber and zucchini sticks are especially good), or serve as an accompaniment to dried bean salad. I like to eat skordalia "straight up," just as I would mashed potatoes.

Note: You must drain the cannellini very well, then pat dry on several thicknesses of paper toweling, otherwise your skordalia will be more sauce than spread. I usually do this at the outset, sometimes an hour ahead of time. And I also replenish the paper toweling whenever it gets soggy. If you prefer whiter skordalia, use six slices of bread instead of four and trim off the crusts.

MAKES ABOUT 2 CUPS

4 medium whole cloves garlic, peeled

½ teaspoon salt

½ teaspoon freshly ground black pepper

4 slices firm-textured white bread, torn into 1-inch chunks (see note)

One 1-pound, 3-ounce can cannellini (white kidney beans), drained well and patted dry on paper toweling

¼ cup fresh lemon juice

¼ cup olive oil (I like to use a gutsy Greek olive oil)

1. Equip the food processor with the metal chopping blade, snap the machine on, and drop the garlic, salt, and pepper down the feed tube into the spinning blade. Churn 3 to 4 seconds, then scrape down the work bowl.

2. With the machine running, drop the pieces of bread down the feed tube and when all are in, churn for 5 seconds. Again scrape the work bowl.

3. Add the cannellini and churn 5 seconds. Scrape the work bowl, add the lemon juice, and whiz for another 5 seconds.

4. With the motor running, drizzle the olive oil down the feed tube, then continue processing for 60 seconds or until creamy and the color of pale ivory.

5. Mound in a colorful bowl and serve as a cocktail spread or dunk.

Baba Ghanouj

This eggplant dip doesn't get "A-plus for visuals," as my friend Sara Moulton would say. But oh my, the flavor. This is one of the few times I use a hickory-smoke seasoning and only because I have no grill to give the baba ghanouj the proper smokiness.

Note: Be sure the eggplants you choose are unwaxed, firm, and heavy for their size. If your tahini has separated, read the headnote for Hummus on page 94, which tells you how to re-emulsify it in the food processor. Incidentally, once you've done this you don't have to wash the processor bowl or blade.

MAKES ABOUT 1½ CUPS

2 small, firm eggplants (about 1½ pounds in all)

3 tablespoons olive oil blended with 2 teaspoons liquid hickory-smoke seasoning

1 large whole clove garlic, peeled

1 teaspoon salt

½ teaspoon freshly ground black pepper

2 tablespoons fresh lemon juice

2 tablespoons tahini

1. Preheat the broiler.

2. Trim the eggplants, then remove some of the peel by running a vegetable peeler the length of each eggplant at ½-inch intervals, leaving a striped effect. Halve each eggplant lengthwise, then halve each half lengthwise. Arrange the eggplant pieces on an ungreased baking sheet and brush each with the olive oil mixture.

3. Set in the broiler 4 inches from the flame and broil until the eggplant is dark brown, 5 to 6 minutes. Turn the pieces and brush the flip sides with the remaining olive oil mixture. Broil about 5 minutes longer until the eggplant is soft. Cool 5 minutes.

4. Meanwhile, churn the garlic with the salt and pepper in a food processor fitted with the metal chopping blade 5 seconds; scrape down the work bowl sides.

5. Scoop the eggplant into the processor, add the lemon juice and tahini, and churn 3 to 4 seconds. Scrape down the work bowl and if there are any large pieces of eggplant, pulse once or twice. The mixture should be lumpy.

6. Spoon the baba ghanouj into a colorful bowl and serve as a dip for crisp pieces of Arabic bread or pita bread, or for sesame crackers.

Liptauer Cheese

When I was growing up in Raleigh, North Carolina, my parents liked to take my brother and me to a little Austrian restaurant, partly, I think, to relive their early married days in Vienna, and partly because the food was so good. The specialty of the house was Liptauer and I ordered it whenever it appeared on the menu. Often it didn't, the explanation being that the chef hadn't had time to make it. Did he really make this pale pink cheese himself? And why was it so difficult? With a food processor, this sharp Austro-Hungarian spread is a one-minute production.

MAKES ABOUT 1½ CUPS

1 medium scallion, trimmed and cut into 1-inch chunks (white part only)

2 tablespoons snipped fresh chives (I snip across the bunch with sharp kitchen shears)

1 tablespoon well-drained small capers

1 tablespoon sweet paprika (preferably Hungarian sweet rose paprika)

1 teaspoon caraway seeds

1 teaspoon dry mustard

¼ teaspoon salt

¼ teaspoon freshly ground black pepper

One 8-ounce package light cream cheese (Neufchâtel), at room temperature

¼ cup (½ stick) unsalted butter, at room temperature

1. Churn the scallion, chives, capers, paprika, caraway seeds, mustard, salt, and pepper in a food processor fitted with the metal chopping blade until reduced to paste, about 15 seconds. Scrape the work bowl well.

2. Add the cream cheese and butter and let the motor run nonstop until the mixture is smooth and creamy, about 20 seconds. Scrape the work bowl well and churn 20 seconds longer.

3. Pack into a small bowl, cover, and mellow in the refrigerator for 1 to 2 hours.

4. Let stand at room temperature 30 minutes or until a good spreading consistency, then serve as an hors d'oeuvre with triangles of dark pumpernickel.

Pimiento Cheese

Using the processor to chop the onion, blend the seasonings, and shred the cheese makes this once tedious Southern classic a five-minute wonder. The only thing the machine won't do is dice pimientos neatly. I use bottled diced pimientos and pulse them in at the end so that they aren't reduced to paste. Choose a good sharp, orange Cheddar for this spread and add only enough milk to give it the consistency of cream-style cottage cheese. Although Southerners dote upon pimiento cheese sandwiches—two slices of white bread enclosing a thick slather of orange—they also pass pimiento cheese with cocktail crackers and stuff it into bite-size chunks of celery.

MAKES ABOUT 3 CUPS

1 small yellow onion, peeled and quartered

¾ cup mayonnaise (use light, if you like)

2 tablespoons ketchup

1 tablespoon spicy brown mustard

1 tablespoon cider vinegar

¼ teaspoon hot red pepper sauce

1 pound well-aged sharp Cheddar cheese, cut in chunks to fit the feed tube of your food processor

One 4-ounce jar diced pimientos, with their liquid

4 to 6 tablespoons milk or half-and-half cream

1. Pulse the onion in a food processor fitted with the metal chopping blade 5 to 6 times until coarsely chopped.

2. Add the mayonnaise, ketchup, mustard, vinegar, and red pepper sauce and churn 5 seconds. Scrape the work bowl sides. Lift out the chopping blade and set aside.

3. Equip the processor with the coarse shredding disk, fit the chunks of Cheddar in the feed tube, trimming as needed for a snug fit, then snap the machine on and push the cheese down the feed tube, letting the shreds fall directly into the mayonnaise mixture below.

4. Remove the shredding disk, rearrange the cheese shreds as needed to accommodate the chopping blade, then carefully push it into place. Pulse the machine 3 to 4 times to combine everything. Scrape the work bowl.

5. Add the pimientos and their liquid and pulse to incorporate—easy does it. Pulse in 4 tablespoons of the milk and if the mixture seems thick, pulse in the additional milk.

6. Scoop the pimiento cheese into a small bowl, cover with plastic wrap, and let season several hours in the refrigerator before serving.

Spicy Pimiento Cheese
Prepare as directed but substitute relish-style sandwich spread for mayonnaise. These spreads are usually a little thinner than mayonnaise so you may need less milk than that called for.

Jalapeño Cheese
Prepare as directed but increase the amount of mayonnaise to 1 cup and substitute one 4.5-ounce can diced jalapeños, well drained, for the pimientos. Save the can liquid, if you like, and use it instead of milk to thin the spread to the proper consistency.

Ham Salad Sandwich Spread

If you're as fond of ham salad as I am, you'll be happy to have a fast processor version (for best results, use a machine with a work bowl that holds 12 cups or more). This is a delicious sandwich filling, but also try it spread on fresh-baked biscuits or homemade cocktail melbas.

Note: The best ham to use is a deeply smoky one that hasn't been pumped full of water (read the label). If the ham isn't firm, the processor will reduce it to paste instead of grinding it. I don't always have fresh dill on hand, so I use dill weed in this recipe. You can substitute ¼ cup tightly packed tiny fresh dill sprigs for the dried as long as they've been washed in cool water and wrung bone dry in paper toweling. This recipe doesn't need salt—the ham, mustard, and capers all contribute their share.

MAKES ABOUT 4 CUPS

6 large scallions, trimmed and cut into 1-inch chunks (include some green tops)

1 medium rib celery, trimmed and cut into 1-inch chunks

1 teaspoon dill weed

½ teaspoon freshly ground black pepper

1 cup relish-style sandwich spread

2 tablespoons well-drained capers

1 tablespoon Dijon mustard

1 tablespoon prepared horseradish

2 tablespoons fresh lemon juice

1½ pounds fully cooked, boneless smoked ham trimmed of excess fat (1½ pounds trimmed weight is what you need), cut into 1-inch cubes

1 to 2 tablespoons milk, if needed to thin the ham salad

1. Coarsely chop the scallions and celery with the dill weed and pepper by pulsing 5 to 6 times in a food processor fitted with the metal chopping blade. Scrape down the work bowl.

2. Add the sandwich spread, capers, mustard, horseradish, and lemon juice and pulse quickly to combine. Again scrape the work bowl.

3. Add the ham, distributing it evenly over the relish mixture, and pulse 5 times. Scrape down the work bowl with a plastic spatula and, minding the blade, stir the mixture up from the bottom. Repeat twice more or until the ham salad is as coarse or fine as you like. If the mixture seems dry, pulse in 1 to 2 tablespoons milk.

4. Spoon the spread into a small bowl, cover tightly, and refrigerate until ready to use. This spread keeps well for 3 to 5 days in a tightly covered container in the refrigerator.

Spicy Potted Shrimp

Without a food processor, I'd never make this retro party pleaser. Can you imagine pounding or grinding shrimp to paste by hand?

Note: If you can sweet-talk your fishmonger into shelling and deveining raw shrimp for you, you're way ahead of the game. I call for no salt in this recipe because the shrimp and anchovy paste are both plenty salty. But taste before serving and adjust as needed.

MAKES ABOUT 2½ CUPS

1 pound shelled and deveined raw medium shrimp (see note)

½ cup (1 stick) unsalted butter, at room temperature

⅓ cup fresh lemon juice

2 tablespoons anchovy paste

½ teaspoon freshly ground black pepper

¼ teaspoon ground hot red pepper (cayenne)

¼ teaspoon ground cloves

1. Cook the shrimp in enough boiling water to cover in a large heavy saucepan over moderate heat just until pink, 3 to 4 minutes. Drain well, then pat dry on paper toweling.

2. Place the shrimp in a food processor fitted with the metal chopping blade and mince fairly fine by churning for 5 seconds. Scrape down the work bowl.

3. Add all remaining ingredients and purée until smooth by churning 30 seconds. Scrape down the work bowl and pulse quickly once or twice.

4. Pack the shrimp mixture into a crock or bowl, press plastic food wrap flat on top, and let season in the refrigerator for several hours.

5. Serve as a cocktail spread for homemade melbas. Or stuff into fresh snow pea pods, tiny marinated artichoke bottoms, or hollowed-out bite-size chunks of cucumber or zucchini. Stored in a tightly covered container in the refrigerator, potted shrimp will keep for 3 to 5 days.

Egg Salad

I wasn't sure if I could make a good egg salad in a food processor because I was afraid that it might churn the eggs to paste. It doesn't. Use as a cocktail spread for crisp homemade melbas or as sandwich filling. For fancier finger food, mound inside hollowed-out cherry tomatoes, zucchini, or cucumber logs.

MAKES ABOUT 4 CUPS

½ cup lightly packed Italian parsley leaves

12 large eggs

4 large scallions, trimmed and cut into 1-inch chunks (include some green tops)

1 small rib celery, trimmed and cut into 1-inch chunks

⅔ cup mayonnaise (use light, if you like)

¼ cup well-drained India relish

2 tablespoons well-drained capers

1 tablespoon Dijon mustard

½ teaspoon salt

½ teaspoon freshly ground black pepper

1 to 2 tablespoons milk, if needed to thin the egg salad

1. Drop the parsley into a food processor fitted with the metal chopping blade and give a couple of 5-second pulses until coarsely chopped. Transfer to a large fine sieve and set under cool running water for several seconds. Also rinse the bowl and blade under the cold water tap, letting bits of parsley fall into the sieve. Tap the parsley onto several thicknesses of paper toweling, roll up, wring dry, and set aside. Keep the parsley in the rolled-up toweling.

2. Place the eggs in a large heavy saucepan, add enough cold water to cover by 1 inch, then set over moderate heat and bring to a full rolling boil. The minute the water boils, set the pan off the heat, cover, and let stand for 15 minutes—no more, no less.

3. Drain the eggs, plunge immediately into an ice bath, and let stand 15 minutes (quick-chilling keeps that ugly dark green ring from forming between the yolk and the white).

4. While the eggs chill, add the scallions and celery to the processor and pulse 5 to 6 times. Add the mayonnaise, relish, capers, mustard, salt, and pepper and pulse quickly to combine. Let stand while you deal with the eggs.

5. Peel the hard-cooked eggs, halve lengthwise, then crosswise, and drop into the processor work bowl, distributing evenly. Pulse quickly 5 times, scrape down the work bowl, then pulse 5 times more or until as coarse or fine as you like.

6. Transfer the egg salad to a small bowl and if it seems dry, mix in 1 to 2 tablespoons milk. Also taste for salt and pepper, adjust as needed, and serve.

Even Easier Egg Salad

Prepare as directed but substitute 1 cup relish-style sandwich spread for the ⅔ cup mayonnaise and omit the parsley, relish, mustard, and capers.

Dilled Egg Salad

Prepare as directed but substitute ½ cup tiny dill fronds for the parsley. Omit the India relish and substitute two 1-inch chunks well drained dill pickle, chopping these along with the scallions and celery.

Egg Salad with Tarragon

Prepare as directed but use ¼ cup each fresh tarragon leaves and Italian parsley leaves instead of ½ cup parsley. Also add 1 tablespoon tarragon vinegar in Step 4 along with the mayonnaise and other ingredients.

Soups

Hot and Cold, Thick and Thin

WHENEVER I USE the processor to shortcut tedious soup-making jobs, I wonder what my Grandmother Johnson, soup maker par excellence, would think of my indispensable speed demon. She was an old-fashioned Illinois lady, a mostly meat-and-potatoes cook, who lived, indeed died, before electric appliances streamlined our lives. She'd be goggle-eyed watching a food processor slice, mince, chop, and purée at near orbital speed. But, oh my, how she would have appreciated the time and energy it saves.

And that's precisely the point. With the food processor to jump-start the preparation of so many long-winded soups, with greenmarkets putting farm-fresh fruits, vegetables, and herbs within easy reach, I'm proselytizing for back-to-scratch.

I do admit to using canned broths in many of my soups—how many people make their own chicken, beef, and vegetable stocks today? For those who do, I include processor recipes for them (see Basic Recipes, page 42). I also plead guilty to using canned tomatoes in certain soups because the tomato season is pitifully short and because canned tomatoes, picked at their bursting-with-flavor best and canned straight away, are far superior to the tasteless specimens most supermarkets stock month in and month out.

Instant Icy Avocado Soup

If there's a faster way to take the sizzle out of summer, I don't know it. This soup is plenty rich and if the courses to follow are substantial, the recipe will serve six. Otherwise, it will serve four.

Note: The chicken broth must be only partially frozen, about the texture of granité. Larger, icier lumps may nick or dent your chopping blade. I sometimes leave the can of broth in the freezer overnight, then thaw it for several hours. I open the can, dump the broth into a metal bowl, and attack any large chunks with an ice pick or cheese wedger.

SERVES 4 TO 6

2 large scallions, trimmed and cut into 1-inch chunks (include some green tops)

1 small jalapeño pepper, cored, seeded, and cut into 1-inch pieces

1 small whole clove garlic, peeled

½ teaspoon salt

¼ cup lightly packed fresh cilantro leaves, washed and wrung dry in paper toweling

4 small ripe Hass avocados (about 1¼ pounds), halved and pitted

2 tablespoons fresh lime juice

One 14½-ounce can chicken broth, partially frozen (see note)

1 cup half-and-half cream

¾ to 1 cup milk

1 lime, thinly sliced (optional garnish)

1. Churn the scallions, jalapeño, garlic, and salt in a food processor fitted with the metal chopping blade 5 seconds. Scrape the work bowl. Add the cilantro and churn 5 seconds more. Again scrape the work bowl.

2. Working directly over the work bowl, scoop the avocado flesh into the bowl, then drizzle the lime juice evenly over all. With two 5-second churnings, purée until smooth, pausing between churnings to scrape the work bowl and stir the mixture. Use a plastic spatula for scraping and stirring and steer clear of the chopping blade.

3. Add the chicken broth, churn 5 seconds, then scrape the bowl and stir. Repeat 3 to 4 times until the soup is absolutely smooth.

4. With the motor running, pour the cream, then ¾ cup of the milk down the feed tube. Scrape the work bowl and if the soup seems thick, pulse in the remaining ¼ cup milk.

5. Ladle into chilled soup bowls and if you like, float a slice of lime in each portion.

Tuscan White Bean Soup

If you're going to make a pot of soup, you might as well make a big one, especially if the soup's as good as this one. It keeps well in the refrigerator for as long as five days and for several months in the freezer

Note: Unless farm-fresh tomatoes are available—unlikely at the time of year I'm inclined to make this soup—I use canned crushed tomatoes.

SERVES 8

1 pound dried cannellini, navy, or great northern beans, washed, sorted, soaked overnight according to package directions, and drained

2 quarts water

1½ teaspoons salt

8 black peppercorns

½ cup lightly packed Italian parsley leaves

4 slices bacon, stacked and snipped crosswise at ½-inch intervals

2 tablespoons olive oil

2 large whole cloves garlic, peeled

2 large yellow onions, peeled and cut into slim wedges

2 medium carrots, peeled and cut into 1-inch chunks

Two 3-inch sprigs fresh sage or 1 teaspoon dried leaf sage, crumbled

Two 3-inch sprigs fresh thyme (preferably lemon thyme) or 1 teaspoon dried leaf thyme, crumbled

2 large whole bay leaves (preferably fresh)

One 14½-ounce can crushed tomatoes, with all liquid

1. Bring the beans, water, salt, and peppercorns to a boil in a large heavy kettle over moderate heat, adjust the heat so the water bubbles gently, cover, and cook until the beans are very soft, about 2 hours.

2. Meanwhile, coarsely chop the parsley in a food processor fitted with the metal chopping blade using two to three 5-second pulses. Scrape into a large fine sieve and rinse under cool running water. Also rinse the work bowl and blade, letting stray bits of parsley fall into the sieve. Tap the parsley onto several thicknesses of paper toweling, wring dry, roll up in the toweling, and refrigerate. Dry the processor blade and bowl and reassemble.

3. Sauté the bacon in a second large heavy kettle over moderately low heat until all the drippings cook out leaving crisp brown bits, about 10 minutes. Using a slotted spoon, lift the browned bacon bits to paper toweling and reserve. Add the olive oil to the drippings in the kettle.

4. Churn the garlic in the food processor 5 seconds, scrape the work bowl, then add the onions and coarsely chop with one to two 5-second churnings. Add to the kettle with the olive oil and bacon drippings and toss to glaze.

5. Now coarsely chop the carrots in the processor by churning 8 to 10 seconds. Add to the onions and garlic along with the sage, thyme, and bay leaves, and sauté over moderate heat, stirring now and then, until the onions are limp and golden, 8 to 10 minutes.

6. Mix in the tomatoes, turn the heat to its lowest point, and mellow while the beans finish cooking. If needed to prevent scorching, slide an insulator underneath the kettle.

7. When the beans are done, add 2 cups of them to the tomato mixture. Cool the remaining beans for 10 minutes, then purée with the cooking water, 2 cups at a time, by churning 10 to 15 seconds nonstop. As you purée the beans, add to the tomato mixture.

8. Mix in the reserved parsley and bacon, reduce the heat to low, and mellow the flavors by simmering uncovered for 15 to 20 minutes, stirring occasionally. Remove and discard the bay leaves, sage, and thyme sprigs. Taste for salt and pepper and adjust as needed.

9. Ladle into heated soup plates and accompany with a good country bread.

Cool Summer Soup of Roasted Beets and Cucumbers

The trouble with beets is that they stain everything in sight—countertop, sink, chopping board, hands. And those bright carmine spatters aren't so easy to remove. To minimize the problem, I wrap the beets in foil and roast them until soft. I then open the foil packets one by one, peel and quarter the beets right in the packets, then tip them into the food processor. While developing this recipe, only my hands turned beet-red and a couple of scrubbings took care of that. For me, this gazpacho-thick soup is a melding of summer's best—fresh beets, cucumbers, lime juice, and dill. Make no substitutions!

Note: The best cucumbers to use are either Kirbys (small pickling cucumbers) or the long, skinny English hothouse or "seedless" cucumbers sent to market in plastic wrappers.

Tip: Set the unopened can of chicken broth in the freezer the night before, then thaw just until you can hear a little liquid sloshing among the chunks of ice when you shake the can.

SERVES 4

2½ pounds untrimmed beets (about 6 medium) (save the tops and cook as you would turnip greens or collards)

1 tablespoon olive oil

1 large shallot, peeled and quartered

¼ cup lightly packed sprigs fresh dill, washed and patted dry on paper toweling

1 teaspoon salt

¼ teaspoon freshly ground black pepper

½ pound cucumbers, peeled, seeded, and cut into 1-inch chunks (see note)

One 14½-ounce can chicken broth, partially frozen (see tip)

2 tablespoons fresh lime juice

2 tablespoons white balsamic vinegar

4 tablespoons sour cream

4 sprigs fresh dill

1. Preheat the oven to 425°F.

2. Trim the beets of all but ½ inch of the tops and leave the root ends intact. Scrub the beets well, brush with olive oil, then wrap one by one in squares of heavy-duty aluminum foil. Place the foil-wrapped beets, not touching, in a 15½ × 10½ × 1-inch jelly roll pan, set on the middle oven rack, and roast until very soft, about 1½ hours. Remove the beets from the oven and cool to room temperature in their foil packets.

3. Meanwhile, finely chop the shallot and the ¼ cup dill with the salt and pepper in a food processor fitted with the metal chopping blade using two 5-second churnings; minding the blade, scrape the work bowl with a plastic spatula between churnings. Add the cucumbers and coarsely chop with 5 to 6 staccato pulses. Transfer to a small bowl and reserve.

4. Cover a counter with several thicknesses of paper toweling, and when the beets have cooled, open one foil packet. Using a sharp paring knife and working on the foil, remove the beet top and root, slip off the skin, and quarter the beet. Drop the beet directly into the processor (no need to wash or rinse the work bowl or blade). Crumple the trimmings inside the foil, and discard. Repeat until all beets are in the processor.

5. Add half of the broth and churn for 10 seconds. Scrape the work bowl and stir, pushing larger pieces to the bottom.

6. Add the reserved cucumber mixture, the lime juice, vinegar, and remaining broth, and pulse quickly to combine. The mixture should be quite lumpy.

7. Ladle into soup bowls. To garnish, float 1 tablespoon sour cream in each bowl and sprig with dill.

Potage Crécy (French Carrot Soup)

I'd never tasted carrot soup until I lived in France and I have to say I think it's one of the best soups ever. Before the food processor came into my life, I didn't make it often.

SERVES 6

3 tablespoons unsalted butter

6 medium carrots, trimmed, peeled, and cut into chunks to fit the food processor feed tube

3 medium leeks, trimmed, washed well, and cut into chunks to fit the food processor feed tube

Two 14½- or 15½-ounce cans chicken broth or 4 cups rich homemade chicken stock (page 43)

1 teaspoon salt

¼ teaspoon freshly ground black or white pepper (the French prefer white pepper)

1 cup heavy cream

3 large egg yolks

1. Melt the butter in a large heavy saucepan over low heat.

2. Meanwhile, equip a food processor with the slicing disk and thin-slice the carrots by pushing them down the feed tube, pulsing all the while. Add to the saucepan.

3. Thin-slice the leeks the same way and add to the pan. Raise the heat to moderate and sauté the carrots and leeks, stirring now and then, until limp, about 10 minutes.

4. Add the chicken broth, salt, and pepper, and bring to a boil. Adjust the heat so that the mixture bubbles gently, cover, and simmer until the carrots are very soft, about 30 minutes. Pour the soup into a large heatproof bowl, cover, and cool.

5. Remove the slicing disk from the processor and slip the metal chopping blade into place (no need to wash the work bowl). Purée the soup mixture in two to three batches by churning for 30 seconds. As each batch is puréed, return it to the saucepan.

6. Add the cream and egg yolks to the processor and pulse 2 to 3 times until smooth (again no need to wash the work bowl). Stir into the puréed soup. Set over low heat and cook, stirring constantly, until lightly thickened, about 3 minutes. Do not let the soup boil or it may curdle. Taste for salt and pepper and adjust as needed.

7. Ladle into heated soup bowls and serve. Or, if you prefer, chill well and serve cold (not the French way but delicious nonetheless).

Note: A little chopped parsley or freshly snipped chives makes a colorful garnish, but it's not necessary and a good country French cook would probably do without.

Cream of Cauliflower Soup

Subtly flavored and as smooth as silk, this soup is equally good hot or cold.

SERVES 6

1 medium head of cauliflower (about 2½ pounds), trimmed and divided into florets

4 cups water

2 teaspoons salt

2 tablespoons unsalted butter

¼ teaspoon freshly grated nutmeg

¼ teaspoon freshly ground black pepper

One 14½- or 15½-ounce can chicken broth or 2 cups rich homemade chicken stock (page 43)

1 pint half-and-half cream

1. Place the cauliflower in a large heavy saucepan, add the water and salt, and bring to a boil over moderate heat. Cover and cook until the cauliflower is very tender, about 30 minutes. Drain the cauliflower well, return to the pan, and shake over moderate heat for 1 to 2 minutes to drive off excess moisture.

2. Add half the cauliflower, 1 tablespoon of the butter, the nutmeg, and pepper to a food processor fitted with the metal chopping blade, and purée by churning for 20 seconds. Return to the saucepan.

3. Purée the remaining cauliflower with the remaining butter the same way and add to the pan along with the chicken broth and half-and-half. Set uncovered over moderate heat and bring to serving temperature, 3 to 5 minutes. Do not allow the soup to boil or it may curdle. Taste for salt and pepper and adjust as needed.

4. Ladle into heated soup bowls and serve, or if you prefer, chill for several hours and serve cold.

Curried Cauliflower Soup

Cook and drain the cauliflower as directed. Before returning it to the pan to drive off the excess moisture, melt the 2 tablespoons butter in the pan over moderate heat, add 1 tablespoon curry powder along with the nutmeg and pepper, and cook and stir just until no raw curry taste remains, about 2 minutes. Return the cauliflower to the pan, toss until evenly coated with the curry mixture, then shake 1 to 2 minutes over the heat to evaporate excess moisture. Purée the cauliflower in two batches, return to the pan, and proceed as directed in Steps 3 and 4.

Chestnut Soup

Without dried, peeled Italian chestnuts, I'd never bother to make this soup. Fortunately, most boutique groceries stock them as do nearly all Italian and Middle Eastern food shops. As easy to reconstitute as dried beans, dried chestnuts can be substituted for the fresh in almost any recipe. Stored in plastic zipper bags in the freezer, they keep practically forever.

SERVES 6 TO 8

2 cups dried, shelled and blanched chestnuts, washed and sorted

4 cups cold water

2 medium yellow onions, peeled and cut into slim wedges

2 medium ribs celery, trimmed and cut into 1-inch chunks

3 tablespoons unsalted butter

Two 14½- or 15½-ounce cans chicken broth or 4 cups rich homemade chicken stock (page 43)

½ teaspoon salt

¼ teaspoon freshly ground black pepper

1 cup heavy cream

1 cup half-and-half cream

3 tablespoons freshly snipped chives

1. Bring the chestnuts and water to a boil in a large heavy saucepan over moderate heat, turn off the heat, cover, and let stand for 4 hours. Drain the chestnuts, then sort carefully, removing stubborn bits of skin—it helps to break the nuts in half. Set the chestnuts aside.

2. Place the onions and celery in a food processor fitted with the metal chopping blade and pulse briskly 8 to 10 times until finely chopped.

3. Melt the butter over moderate heat in the pan in which you soaked the chestnuts (no need to wash it). Add the onions and celery and cook, stirring now and then, until limp and lightly golden, about 10 minutes. Do not brown.

4. Add the chestnuts, chicken broth, salt, and pepper, adjust the heat so that the mixture bubbles gently, cover, and simmer until the chestnuts are very soft, about 1 hour. Set off the heat and cool 15 minutes.

5. Purée the saucepan mixture in three or four batches in the food processor, still fitted with the metal chopping blade, churning each 25 to 30 seconds until absolutely smooth. As each batch is puréed, return to the pan.

6. Set the pan of purée over moderate heat, blend in the two creams, and heat just to serving temperature, 3 to 5 minutes. Do not allow the soup to boil or it may curdle. Taste for salt and pepper and adjust as needed.

7. Ladle into heated soup bowls, scatter the snipped chives over each portion, and serve. Or if you prefer, chill several hours and serve cold.

Madeira Onion Soup

Two kinds of onions go into this unusual Portuguese soup, which to my mind, is much nicer than the better known French onion soup. There's no cheese to "string" under the broiler, no soggy slice of bread, only intense onion flavor made all the better with a dash of Verdelho (medium-dry Madeira wine). I can make a meal of this soup.

SERVES 6

2 tablespoons olive oil

2 tablespoons unsalted butter

1 large Spanish, Bermuda or other sweet onion, peeled and cut into wedges slim enough to fit the processor feed tube

4 large yellow onions, peeled and quartered

¼ teaspoon freshly grated nutmeg

Pinch ground cinnamon

Three 14½- or 15½-ounce cans beef broth or 6 cups rich homemade beef stock (page 44)

½ teaspoon salt

¼ teaspoon freshly ground black pepper

2 tablespoons Verdelho wine or medium-dry Port

3 large egg yolks, lightly beaten

1. Place the olive oil and butter in a very large heavy saucepan and set over lowest heat.

2. Equip the food processor with the medium slicing disk, then stand in the feed tube as many Spanish onion wedges as will fit snugly, and guide through the slicing disk with the pusher, pulsing all the while. Add to the saucepan, stirring to glaze with olive oil and butter.

3. Slice the yellow onions the same way and add to the pan. Raise the heat to moderate, and sauté the onions, stirring occasionally, until limp and lightly browned, about 15 minutes.

Note: This browning is important for flavor, so don't rush things. Blend in the nutmeg and cinnamon and mellow for 2 to 3 minutes.

4. Add the broth, salt, and pepper, adjust the heat so the mixture bubbles gently, and simmer uncovered until the onions are very soft, 40 to 45 minutes. Stir in the wine and simmer uncovered 5 minutes more.

5. Quickly whisk a little of the hot soup into the egg yolks, stir back into the pan, and cook, stirring constantly, until lightly thickened, 2 to 3 minutes. Do not allow the soup to boil or it may curdle. Taste for salt and pepper and adjust as needed.

6. Ladle into heated soup plates and serve with crusty chunks of bread. I'd put out a basket of Pão, or Portuguese Farm Bread (page 213). It's the perfect partner for this soup.

Fennel Soup with Pancetta and Parmigiano-Reggiano

Now that fresh fennel (finocchio) is in nearly every supermarket, there's no reason not to make this unusual soup. And if you have a food processor to do the chopping and puréeing, you have no excuse.

Note: I always keep plenty of freshly grated Parmigiano-Reggiano in a one-quart preserving jar in the refrigerator and it goes without saying that I grate my own (see page 13). It is the only Parmesan to use in this soup. Some groceries now carry pancetta, a tightly rolled Italian bacon that is cured with salt and spices but not smoked. If you're unable to find it, substitute bacon. It will add smokiness to the soup and I happen to like this.

Tip: The easiest way to julienne bacon is to stack the slices and cut crosswise at ½-inch intervals with kitchen shears.

SERVES 6

1½ pounds fennel (about 2 medium bulbs)

2 ounces pancetta, diced, or 2 slices smoked bacon, julienned (see tip)

2 tablespoons olive oil

2 large yellow onions, peeled and cut into slim wedges

1 medium baking potato, peeled and cut into 1-inch chunks

1 teaspoon fennel seeds

¼ teaspoon anise seeds

2 medium whole bay leaves

Two 14½-or 15½-ounce cans chicken broth or 4 cups rich homemade chicken stock (page 43)

½ teaspoon salt

¼ teaspoon freshly ground black pepper

¾ cup heavy or light cream or half-and-half

⅓ cup freshly grated Parmigiano-Reggiano, plus 6 tablespoons

6 tablespoons freshly grated Parmigiano-Reggiano, optional

6 small feathery fennel sprigs, optional

1. Slice the feathery tops off the fennel and lightly pack ½ cup of them in a dry measure. Tip into a fine sieve, rinse under cold running water, then roll up and wring as dry as possible in paper toweling.

2. Add the fennel tops to a food processor fitted with the metal chopping blade and pulse briskly 3 to 5 times. Scrape the work bowl, then pulse 3 to 5 times more until moderately finely chopped. Tip onto paper toweling and reserve.

3. Sauté the pancetta in a large heavy saucepan over moderately low heat until all the drippings cook out leaving crisp brown bits, about 10 minutes. Using a slotted spoon, lift the browned bits to paper toweling to drain; reserve. Add the olive oil to the pan.

4. Remove the coarse outer layers from each fennel bulb, then cut the bulbs into 1-inch chunks. Drop into the food processor and coarsely chop with one 5-second churning. Add to the pan.

5. Now coarsely chop the onions and potato together with one to two 5-second churnings, and add to the pan along with the fennel seeds, anise seeds, and bay leaves. Raise the heat to moderate and cook and stir the vegetables until nicely glazed, 2 to 3 minutes. Reduce the heat to its lowest point, cover, and steam the vegetables for 15 minutes.

6. Add the broth, salt, and pepper, adjust the heat so the mixture bubbles gently, cover, and cook until the vegetables are mushy, about 1 hour. Remove from the heat and cool 15 minutes. Discard the bay leaves.

7. Purée the saucepan mixture in 3 to 4 batches, churning each for 30 seconds and scraping the work bowl at half time. As each batch is puréed, return it to the saucepan.

8. Set the pan of puréed soup over moderate heat, smooth in the cream, and bring to serving temperature, about 5 minutes. Stir in the ⅓ cup Parmigiano-Reggiano, reserved pancetta, and chopped fennel. Taste for salt and pepper, and adjust as needed.

9. As soon as the cheese melts—do not allow the soup to boil—ladle into heated soup plates, and garnish, if you like, by scattering 1 tablespoon grated Parmigiano-Reggiano over each portion and sprigging with fennel.

Minestrone

What I like about this husky Italian vegetable soup is that I can set a big heavy kettle on the stove, then dice or chop or mince the various ingredients in the order listed, transferring them directly from processor to kettle. Timing isn't important, so you can work at your own pace. Once the basics are in the pot, turn the heat to its lowest point, clap the lid on, and go about your business. The soup can simmer the better part of the day—in fact, it's better if it does. Just make sure that the burner heat is as low as it can go; the soup should never boil. This recipe makes a lot, it's true, but like most soups, this one profits from a stay in the fridge (it keeps well for about a week).

Note: I prep the salt pork by hand because I don't find the food processor very adept at cutting meat. Besides, an amount this small can be diced in no time.

SERVES 6 TO 8

4 ounces salt pork, diced (see note)

2 large whole cloves garlic, peeled

2 large yellow onions, peeled and cut into 1-inch chunks

2 large ribs celery, trimmed and cut into 1-inch chunks

3 large leeks, trimmed, washed well, and cut into 1-inch chunks

2 large carrots, trimmed, peeled, and cut into 1-inch chunks

1 large all-purpose potato, peeled and cut into 1-inch chunks

4 large ripe tomatoes, cored and cut into 1-inch chunks but not peeled

Two 14½- or 15½-ounce cans beef broth or 4 cups rich homemade beef stock (page 44)

2 large whole bay leaves

Two 3-inch sprigs fresh thyme or ½ teaspoon dried leaf thyme, crumbled

½ teaspoon dried leaf basil, crumbled

½ teaspoon dried leaf marjoram, crumbled

2 tablespoons sugar

½ teaspoon salt

½ teaspooon freshly ground black pepper

2 young zucchini, trimmed and quartered lengthwise

¼ small cabbage, cored and cut in columns to fit the food processor feed tube (see page 11)

4 ounces young green beans, tipped and cut into 1-inch lengths (this you must do by hand)

1. Sauté the salt pork in a large heavy kettle over moderate heat until crisp and brown, 12 to 15 minutes.

2. Meanwhile, drop the garlic into a food processor fitted with the metal chopping blade and churn for 5 seconds. Scrape the work bowl, add the onions, and mince fairly fine by pulsing briskly 5 to 6 times.

3. As soon as all fat has rendered out of the salt pork leaving only crisp browned bits, scoop these up with a slotted spoon, drain on paper toweling, and reserve. Add the garlic and onions to the kettle, stir to coat with drippings, then allow to cook while you get on with the chopping.

4. Add the celery and leeks to the processor and coarsely chop using 5 to 6 quick pulses; add to the kettle.

5. Now coarsely chop the carrots in the processor by churning 8 to 10 seconds; add to the kettle and give the vegetables a good stir.

6. Pulse the potato in the processor 3 to 5 times until very coarsely chopped—no matter if the pieces are irregular—and add to the kettle. Stir all well, then before chopping any more vegetables, allow those in the kettle to sauté lazily until limp but not brown, about 20 minutes.

7. Add a third of the chunked tomatoes to the processor and rough-purée by letting the machine run 8 to 10 seconds. Add to the kettle, then rough-purée the remaining tomatoes the same way in two batches. Add to the kettle along with the beef broth, bay leaves, thyme, basil, marjoram, sugar, salt, and pepper.

8. Bring to a gentle simmer, cover, and cook very slowly for 5 to 6 hours. Meanwhile, wash and dry the processor work bowl and insert the medium slicing disk.

9. About 2 hours before you're ready to serve, slice the zucchini one at a time by reassembling the quarters and pulsing through the small inner feed tube. Fit the cabbage into the broad feed tube and gently guide through the slicing disk with the pusher, pulsing all the while. Add the zucchini and cabbage to the kettle along with the green beans.

10. Cover the soup and simmer slowly until the zucchini, cabbage, and beans are tender, 1½ to 2 hours. This may seem as if you're cooking the vegetables to death, but trust me, the soup is wonderful. Fish out the bay leaves and thyme sprigs and discard. Taste for salt and pepper and adjust as needed.

11. Ladle the minestrone into heated soup plates, scatter the crisp bits of salt pork over each portion, and serve with a good crusty Italian bread.

Mixed Mushroom Soup

Almost any combination of mushrooms will do, but I like equal parts creminis, shiitakes, and chanterelles or white supermarket mushrooms. If I can find morels, I'll add them to the mix, using four equal parts of the four different mushrooms. Or maybe I'll substitute them for chanterelles. Although mushrooms don't win points for nutritional value, they do contain phytochemicals (or nutriceuticals as they're also called) that are believed to help fight a number of diseases. One recent report from Berkeley suggests that shiitakes may—underscore may—possess anti-tumor substances. I certainly don't prescribe this soup as medication, only as something to enjoy on a cool day.

SERVES 6

1 pound mushrooms (see headnote), wiped clean and stemmed (reserve stems)

2 tablespoons olive oil

2 tablespoons unsalted butter

1 large yellow onion, peeled and cut into slim wedges

Two 3-inch sprigs fresh lemon thyme or ½ teaspoon dried leaf thyme, crumbled, plus 6 small sprigs

¼ teaspoon freshly grated nutmeg

3 cups beef broth or homemade beef stock (page 44)

½ teaspoon salt

¼ teaspoon freshly ground black pepper

1½ cups half-and-half cream

3 large egg yolks

1. Equip a food processor with the medium slicing disk, then stand as many mushroom caps on their sides as will fit snugly in the feed tube, and guide through the slicing disk with the pusher, pulsing all the while. Repeat until all mushrooms are sliced.

2. Heat the olive oil and butter in a large heavy saucepan over moderate heat for 2 minutes, add the mushrooms, stir well, and cook while you chop the mushroom stems and onion.

3. Remove the slicing disk from the food processor and insert the metal chopping blade. Add the mushroom stems and chop fairly coarsely with 3 to 5 brisk pulses. Add to the sliced mushrooms in the pan.

4. Coarsely chop the onion the same way and add to the pan along with the thyme and nutmeg. Cook, stirring now and then, until the vegetables are lightly browned and the mushroom juices have evaporated, 10 to 12 minutes.

5. Add the beef broth, salt, and pepper, adjust the heat so the mixture bubbles gently, cover, and simmer until the mushrooms are very soft, about 15 minutes. Pour all into a large fine sieve set over a large heatproof bowl.

6. Place the sieved solids in the processor (no need wash to the chopping blade or bowl) and purée by churning 15 seconds. Using a plastic spatula, scrape the work bowl and stir, pushing any large pieces of mushroom to the bottom. Churn 5 seconds more and if not absolutely smooth, pulse out any lumps. Scoop the purée into the saucepan, add the strained liquid, and set over moderate heat.

7. Quickly whisk the cream with the egg yolks, blend in a little of the hot soup, stir back into the pan, and cook, stirring constantly, until lightly thickened, 2 to 3 minutes. Do not allow the soup to boil or it may curdle. Taste for salt and pepper and adjust as needed.

8. Ladle into heated soup bowls, sprig with thyme, and serve. Or, if you prefer, chill the soup several hours and serve cold.

A Good, Quick Gazpacho

If you insist upon precisely diced vegetables for this cold Andalusian tomato soup, you'll have to cut them by hand. I personally don't mind rough-cut pieces and prefer to let the food processor do the work. Here's one trick I've learned: you can approximate dice—or at least get cleaner cuts—if you feed the cucumber down the small inner feed tube instead of having it slither around the large one.

Note: For gazpacho, you must choose a dense bread that won't go soggy when mixed with chopped tomatoes, onions, and cucumbers (see Pão, or Portuguese Farm Bread, page 213).

SERVES 6

4 ounces stale, firm Italian, Portuguese, or French bread (see note)

¼ cup red wine vinegar

1 large whole clove garlic, peeled

½ teaspoon salt

¼ teaspoon freshly ground black pepper

2 pounds firm, sun-ripened Roma (Italian plum) tomatoes, halved, seeded, and each half halved crosswise

1 large sun-ripened beefsteak tomato (about 1 pound), peeled, cored, and cut into slim wedges

2 medium Kirby (pickling) cucumbers, peeled, one cut into 1-inch chunks, the other quartered lengthwise and each quarter cut in lengths to fit the processor's small inner feed tube

1 medium green bell pepper, cored, seeded, and cut into 1-inch chunks

1 small yellow onion, peeled and cut into slim wedges

6 large scallions, trimmed and cut into 1-inch lengths (include some green tops)

¼ cup olive oil (the fruitiest you can find)

1¾ to 2 cups cold tomato juice

1. Tear the bread into large (approximately 1½-inch) chunks, letting them drop into a food processor fitted with the metal chopping blade. With 8 to 10 staccato pulses, process until the texture of prepared stuffing mix. Empty into a large nonreactive bowl. Sprinkle the vinegar evenly over the bread and toss well.

2. Mince the garlic with the salt and pepper by churning 10 seconds nonstop. Scrape the work bowl well, then pulse quickly 3 to 4 times.

3. Add the Roma tomatoes (in two batches if your work bowl is small), and chop fairly fine with two to three 3-second churnings. Scrape the work bowl between churnings with a plastic spatula, minding the blade, and stir, pushing larger pieces of tomato to the bottom. Scoop all on top of the bread but do not toss.

4. Now rough-chop the beefsteak tomato by pulsing 4 to 5 times. Add to the bread mixture.

5. Add the chunked cucumber to the processor along with half of the bell pepper and all of the yellow onion, and purée by letting the motor run 8 to 10 seconds nonstop. Add to the bowl of tomatoes and bread; again, do not toss.

6. Add the remaining bell pepper and the scallions to the processor and coarsely chop with 3 to 4 fast pulses. Scoop onto a large plate and reserve.

7. Remove the chopping blade from the work bowl and insert the medium slicing disk. Stand the cucumber quarters in the small inner feed tube so they fit together and guide through the slicing disk with the pusher, pulsing all the while. Add to the plate.

8. Drizzle the olive oil over the tomato mixture and toss well. Add 1¾ cups of the tomato juice and stir gently. If the gazpacho seems dry, mix in the remaining ¼ cup tomato juice. Taste for salt and pepper and adjust as needed.

9. Finally, stir in the sliced cucumber, chopped bell pepper, and scallions. Cover and refrigerate for several hours.

10. Ladle the gazpacho into chilled soup plates and serve.

Roasted Garlic and Red Pepper Soup with Tomatoes

Except in the all-too-brief July-August fresh tomato season, I prefer canned tomatoes and use them here so that I can enjoy this pleasantly peppery soup year round. It's good hot or cold. I especially like "fired roasted" diced tomatoes, a new entry in a popular line of organic canned goods. Most of the time I serve the soup "nude"—*sans* garnish. But if company's coming, I spoon a little sour cream into each bowl and add a scattering of freshly snipped chives.

Tip: The most efficient way to deal with bell peppers is to slice off the stem ends, stand the peppers upside-down, then cut straight down, following the natural convolutions and skirting the cores.

SERVES 4 TO 6

4 large red bell peppers (about 2 pounds), cored, seeded, and cut into eighths

4 tablespoons olive oil

1 medium whole head garlic

2 medium leeks, trimmed, washed well, and cut in 1-inch chunks

1 large rib celery, trimmed and cut in 1-inch chunks

2 medium jalapeño peppers, stemmed, cored, seeded, and cut in slim wedges

2 teaspoons dried leaf basil, crumbled

1 teaspoon dried leaf oregano, crumbled

½ teaspoon salt

¼ teaspoon freshly ground black pepper

Two 14½- or 15½-ounce cans chicken broth or 4 cups rich homemade chicken stock (page 43)

One 14½-ounce can fired-roasted diced tomatoes, drained (see headnote)

4 to 6 tablespoons sour cream or plain yogurt, optional

4 to 6 teaspoons finely snipped fresh chives, optional

1. Preheat the oven to 400°F. Place the bell peppers on a 15½ × 10½ × 1-inch jelly roll pan, drizzle with 2 tablespoons of the olive oil, toss well, and spread evenly.

2. Slice ½ inch off the top of the garlic exposing the individual cloves. Double-wrap the garlic in aluminum foil and place in the middle of the pan of peppers. Set the uncovered pan in the oven and roast until the peppers brown and shrivel slightly, 40 to 45 minutes. Remove from the oven and cool until easy to handle.

3. Meanwhile, finely chop the leeks, celery, and jalapeños with the basil, oregano, salt, and pepper in a food processor fitted with the metal chopping blade with two 3-second churnings. Scrape the work bowl between churnings using a plastic spatula, and stir the mixture, pushing any large pieces of leek or celery to the bottom.

4. Heat the remaining 2 tablespoons olive oil in a large, heavy nonreactive pan over moderately high heat for 2 minutes. Add the leek mixture, reduce the heat to moderate, and cook, stirring often, until limp, about 5 minutes.

5. Add the chicken broth and tomatoes, bring to a boil, adjust the heat so the mixture bubbles gently, and simmer uncovered for 15 minutes.

6. Meanwhile, peel the bell peppers (the skins should slip right off). Add to the soup, then squeeze in the roasted garlic. Mix well and simmer, uncovered, for 30 minutes.

7. Cool the soup for 30 minutes, then purée in three batches in the food processor (no need to wash the work bowl or blade) by churning each batch 30 to 40 seconds.

8. Return the soup to the pan, set over moderate heat, and bring to serving temperature, stirring occasionally. Taste for salt and pepper and adjust as needed.

9. Ladle into heated soup plates and serve. Or chill the soup well and serve cold. To garnish, spoon 1 tablespoon sour cream into each bowl and scatter with 1 teaspoon snipped chives.

Golden Bell Pepper Soup with Fresh Rosemary and Marjoram

For 24-karat color, I use a half-and-half mix of orange and yellow bell peppers.

SERVES 6

3 large yellow bell peppers (about 1½ pounds), cored, seeded, and quartered

3 large orange bell peppers (about 1½ pounds), cored, seeded, and quartered

3 tablespoons olive oil

6 medium leeks, trimmed, washed well, and cut in lengths to fit the small inner feed tube

3 large whole cloves garlic, peeled

Two 3-inch sprigs fresh rosemary

Two 3-inch sprigs fresh marjoram or oregano

½ teaspoon salt

¼ teaspoon freshly ground black pepper

2½ cups rich beef stock (page 44) or canned beef broth

1 tablespoon fresh lemon or lime juice

⅓ cup crème fraîche or sour cream

6 tablespoons crème fraîche or sour cream, optional

6 small sprigs fresh rosemary or marjoram, optional

1. Equip the food processor with the medium-slicing disk. Stand as many bell pepper quarters as will fit snugly in the food processor feed tube, then pulse through the slicing disk. Repeat until all the peppers are sliced.

2. Heat the olive oil in a large heavy saucepan over moderate heat 2 minutes, add the peppers, toss well, and cook uncovered until beginning to soften, 3 to 4 minutes.

3. Meanwhile, slice the leeks one by one by pulsing down the processor's small inner feed tube. Slice the garlic the same way. Remove the slicing disk and insert the chopping blade.

4. Add the leeks, garlic, rosemary, marjoram, salt, and black pepper to the pan and toss well. Reduce the heat to its lowest point, cover, and cook, stirring now and then, until the vegetables are very soft, about 1 hour. Check the pan from time to time and if it threatens to cook dry, add a little of the beef stock.

5. Discard the rosemary and marjoram sprigs. Scoop the saucepan mixture into the processor and churn for 30 seconds. Scrape the work bowl, then churn 30 seconds longer. If any lumps remain, quickly pulse them out.

6. Sieve the purée directly back into the saucepan, add the beef stock and lemon juice, set over moderate heat, and bring just to serving temperature. This will take only 2 to 3 minutes. Smooth in the ⅓ cup crème fraîche, then taste for salt and pepper, and adjust.

7. Ladle into heated soup plates, float 1 tablespoon crème fraîche in each portion, if you like, sprig with rosemary, and serve. Or if you prefer, chill the soup well and serve cold.

Sopa de Palmito (Brazilian Hearts-of-Palm Soup)

I'm mad for this soup and have been ever since I tasted it many years ago in Rio. Its flavor is subtle but tart, and it's good hot or cold.

Note: Hearts of palm are the tender young shoots of the palmetto, the state tree of South Carolina. And though palmettos grow across much of the Southeast, the canned hearts of palm sold in supermarkets usually come from Brazil.

SERVES 6

Two 14-ounce cans hearts of palm

2 tablespoons unsalted butter

1 tablespoon finely grated yellow onion

⅛ teaspoon freshly grated nutmeg

¾ cup hearts-of-palm liquid (from the cans above) plus enough chicken broth to total 4 cups

½ teaspoon salt

¼ teaspoon freshly ground white or black pepper (Brazilians would use white)

Pinch ground hot red pepper (cayenne)

2 teaspoons fresh lemon juice

1 cup heavy cream

3 large egg yolks

1. Drain the hearts of palm, reserving ¾ cup of the liquid. Equip the food processor with the slicing disk (the thin-slicing disk if you have one). One by one, push the hearts of palm down the small inner feed tube with the plunger, pulsing all the while. Reserve ½ cup of the sliced hearts of palm to use as a garnish. Remove the slicing disk from the food processor and insert the metal chopping blade. No need to wash the work bowl.

2. Melt the butter in a large, heavy nonreactive saucepan over moderate heat, add the remaining sliced hearts of palm along with the onion and nutmeg and sauté, stirring often, for 5 minutes.

3. Add the hearts-of-palm liquid/chicken broth mixture, the salt, white pepper, and cayenne and simmer uncovered for 20 minutes.

4. Set a large fine sieve over a large heatproof bowl and pour in the saucepan mixture. Add the sieved solids to the food processor along with 1 cup of the strained liquid (reserve the remaining liquid). Purée until uniformly smooth by churning for 30 seconds.

5. Scrape the purée into the saucepan, add the lemon juice and remaining liquid and bring to a simmer over low heat.

6. Quickly whisk the cream with the egg yolks, blend in a little of the hot soup, stir back into the pan, and cook, stirring constantly, until lightly thickened, 2 to 3 minutes. Do not allow the soup to boil or it may curdle. Taste for salt and pepper and adjust as needed.

7. Ladle into heated soup bowls and top each portion with some of the reserved sliced hearts of palm. Or, if you prefer, chill the soup several hours and serve cold.

Green Pea–Scallion Soup with Buttermilk and Fresh Mint

Such an easy soup and one with fresh, tart flavor. I do take a few shortcuts here—like using frozen green peas instead of fresh. Quite frankly, they have better flavor than fresh peas unless you grow your own or gather them at the nearest farm and rush them into the soup kettle. I also use scallions instead of shallots or yellow onions because they're quicker to prep (no peeling needed) and because their flavor is more intense. I slice them by hand instead of by processor because it's easier. Once I've washed and trimmed the scallions, I rebunch them and slice en masse. With a sharp chef's knife, the job's done in seconds, and there's only the knife to wash. One final point. If the flavor of the soup is to be properly rich, it's important that you brown the scallions in the butter before you add the peas.

Note: Only fresh mint will do for this recipe. And chop the mint garnish at the very last minute, otherwise it will turn black.

SERVES 4

2 tablespoons unsalted butter

6 large scallions, trimmed and thinly sliced (see headnote)

One 10-ounce package frozen tiny green peas (no need to thaw)

One 6-inch sprig fresh mint

One 14½-ounce can chicken broth or 2 cups rich homemade chicken stock (page 43)

½ teaspoon salt

¼ teaspoon freshly ground black pepper

6 fresh small mint leaves

1½ cups buttermilk

2 tablespoons coarsely chopped fresh mint

1. Melt the butter in a large heavy saucepan over moderately high heat and as soon as the foam subsides, add the scallions and allow to brown, 4 to 5 minutes.

2. Add the solidly frozen peas, breaking up the block, drop in the mint sprig, and cook and stir until the peas have thawed, 2 to 3 minutes.

3. Add the chicken broth, salt, and pepper, adjust the heat so the liquid bubbles gently, cover, and cook until the peas are very soft, 20 to 25 minutes. Cool the soup to room temperature, then discard the mint sprig.

4. Purée the cooled soup with the mint leaves by churning 30 seconds in a food processor fitted with the metal chopping blade. Scrape down the work bowl sides and churn 30 seconds longer.

5. Pour the puréed soup into a medium-size bowl, stir in the buttermilk, then cover, and refrigerate several hours until cold.

6. Ladle into soup bowls, scatter the chopped mint on top of each portion, and serve.

Cold Cress, Pear, and Potato Soup

Many years ago when I was on assignment in Wales for *Bon Appétit* magazine, I enjoyed this unusual soup at Bodysgallen Hall, a stately country house hotel high above the Irish Sea. The hotel recipe required endless hand-chopping of pears, leeks, onion, potato, celery, and watercress, but the processor makes short shrift of all that. The only tedious part of my streamlined version is sieving the soup after it's puréed (a chinois or conical sieve with a wooden pusher makes things go twice as fast). You can, of course, skip the sieving but your soup will be more rustic than refined.

Note: The pears I like best for this recipe are the buttery Boscs. As with all processor recipes, sequence is everything here. And that means washing the watercress at the outset and rolling it in paper toweling so it's good and dry come chopping time.

SERVES 8

4 cups watercress leaves (do not pack), about 1 large bunch

Two 14½- or 15½-ounce cans chicken broth or 4 cups rich homemade chicken stock (page 43)

1½ teaspoons salt

6 black peppercorns

2 allspice berries

2½ pounds (about 5 medium) Bosc pears, quartered lengthwise, peeled, cored, and cut into 1-inch chunks

3 large leeks, trimmed, washed well, and cut into 1-inch chunks

1 medium yellow onion, peeled and quartered

1 large baking potato, peeled, quartered lengthwise, and cut into 1-inch chunks

1 large rib celery, trimmed and cut into 1-inch chunks

1 cup heavy cream (about)

1. Wash the watercress by lifting gently up and down in a sink full of cool water. Repeat until no grit or sand accumulates at the bottom of the sink. Transfer the watercress to a salad spinner, spin as dry as possible, then spread on several thicknesses of paper toweling, top with more paper toweling, roll up, and refrigerate.

2. Place the chicken broth in a large heavy kettle and add the salt, peppercorns, and allspice.

3. Coarsely chop the pears in a food processor fitted with the metal chopping blade by pulsing 6 to 8 times. Add to the kettle, pushing underneath the chicken broth.

4. Coarsely chop the leeks, onion, potato, and celery together by churning 5 seconds. Add to the kettle.

5. Set over moderately high heat and when the mixture boils, adjust the heat so that it barely bubbles. Cover and simmer, stirring now and then, until the vegetables are mushy, about 1 hour. Set off the heat and cool, still covered, for

30 minutes. Fish out and discard the allspice berries and 3 of the peppercorns.

6. Ladle one-third of the mixture into a food processor fitted with the metal chopping blade and pulse once or twice, then purée by churning 30 seconds nonstop. Pour into a large fine sieve set over a large bowl. Repeat twice until all of the soup has been puréed.

7. Now force as much soup through the sieve as possible—in the end, you should have no more than ¾ cup of solids. Periodically transfer the sieved soup in the bowl to a half-gallon measuring cup so that it never touches the bottom of the sieve.

8. When all soup has been sieved and added to the half-gallon measure, pour in just enough heavy cream to bring the level up to 8 cups. Stir the soup gently, cover with plastic wrap, and refrigerate for at least 2 hours.

9. When ready to serve, coarsely chop the reserved watercress by pulsing briskly 5 to 6 times in a clean dry food processor fitted with the metal chopping blade. Add to the soup and stir gently but thoroughly to mix.

10. Ladle into chilled soup plates and serve. You can, if you like, garnish each portion with a sprig of watercress, but I don't find this necessary.

Vichyssoise

I'm so fond of this cool leek and potato soup that I don't wait for company to make it. With a processor to do all the chopping and puréeing, it couldn't be easier. Vichyssoise keeps well in the refrigerator for several days, and with a tartly dressed green salad, it's all I need for a summer lunch.

Note: If your food processor work bowl holds 12 cups or more, you can chop all of the leeks, onion, and potatoes together. If not, you'll have to do two or three batches.

SERVES 8

4 medium leeks, trimmed, washed well, and cut into 1-inch chunks

1 large yellow onion, peeled and quartered

2 large baking potatoes (about 1½ pounds), quartered lengthwise, peeled, and cut into 1-inch chunks

4 tablespoons (½ stick) unsalted butter

Two 14½- or 15½-ounce cans chicken broth or 4 cups rich homemade chicken stock (page 00)

1½ teaspoons salt

¼ teaspoon freshly ground white pepper

2 cups half-and-half cream

¼ cup freshly snipped chives

1. Coarsely chop the leeks, onion, and potatoes together by churning 3 to 4 seconds in a food processor fitted with the metal chopping blade. A rough chop is what you want.

2. Melt the butter in a very large heavy saucepan over moderate heat. Add the chopped mixture and stir round to coat with butter. Reduce the heat to its lowest point, cover, and "sweat" the vegetables in their own juices for 15 minutes, stirring once or twice.

3. Add the chicken broth, salt, and pepper and bring to a boil. Adjust the heat so that the mixture bubbles very gently, cover, and cook until the vegetables are mushy, about 1 hour. Set off the heat and cool, still covered, for 30 minutes.

4. Purée the soup mixture in two or three batches: first pulse each a couple of times in the food processor, still fitted with the metal chopping blade, then churn for 60 seconds. As each batch is puréed, pour into a large fine sieve set over a large bowl.

5. Now force as much puréed soup through the sieve as possible—in the end, you should have no more than ½ cup of a gluey mixture.

Tip: The best implement for this job is the bowl of a ladle—I just move it round and round pushing the purée through the sieve. Every now and then, I transfer the sieved soup to a second large bowl.

6. Blend the cream into the sieved soup, taste for salt and pepper, and adjust as needed.

7. Cover the Vichyssoise and chill several hours before serving.

8. To serve, ladle the Vichyssoise into chilled soup plates and scatter snipped chives over each portion.

Hot Leek and Potato Soup

Prepare Vichyssoise as directed, but instead of chilling it after the cream has been added, heat just to serving temperature.

Sweet Potato Soup with Coconut Milk, Lemongrass, and Cilantro

One reason I love my job is the chance to travel and eat my way around the world. A restaurant that's a particular favorite is Judy Wicks's White Dog Cafe in Philadelphia. She and Chef Kevin von Klause are an inspired team and this recipe is my processor version of one of their signature soups. Like most soups, this one is better if made one day and served the next.

SERVES 6 TO 8

½ cup lightly packed fresh cilantro leaves

6 large scallions, trimmed and cut into 1-inch chunks (include some green tops)

2 large whole cloves garlic, peeled

One 1-inch cube fresh ginger, peeled

1 small jalapeño pepper, cored, seeded, and cut into 1-inch chunks

3 tablespoons peanut or vegetable oil

2 large sweet potatoes (about 2 pounds), peeled and cubed

Two 5- to 6-inch stalks lemongrass, coarse outer layers discarded and stalks smashed with a cutlet bat or rolling pin (this releases the flavor)

Two 14½- or 15½-ounce cans chicken broth or 4 cups rich homemade chicken stock (page 43)

1 cup water

1 teaspoon salt

¼ teaspoon freshly ground black pepper

One 14-ounce can coconut milk (use light, if you like)

2 tablespoons fresh lime juice

1 tablespoon Thai peanut sauce

1. Coarsely chop the cilantro in a food processor fitted with the metal chopping blade using 4 to 5 fairly long pulses. Tip into a small fine sieve and rinse under cold running water for a few seconds. Drain the cilantro on several thicknesses of paper toweling, roll up, and wring as dry as possible. Set aside.

2. Add the scallions, garlic, ginger, and jalapeño pepper to the processor and churn 4 to 5 seconds until fairly coarsely chopped.

3. Heat the peanut oil in a large heavy saucepan over moderate heat 2 minutes, add the chopped scallion mixture, reduce the heat to moderately low, and cook, stirring occasionally, until limp, about 5 minutes.

4. Add the sweet potatoes, lemongrass, chicken broth, water, salt, and black pepper, cover, and simmer until the potatoes are mushy, about 30 minutes. Cool in the covered pan for 30 minutes. Discard the lemongrass.

5. Purée the saucepan mixture in two to three batches by churning each for 30 seconds.

6. Return to the saucepan, add the coconut milk, lime juice, and peanut sauce and bring just to serving temperature. Taste for salt and pepper and adjust as needed.

7. Stir in the reserved chopped cilantro, ladle into soup bowls, and serve. Or chill well and serve cold.

Fresh Sorrel Soup

Potage Germiny, as this soup is known in France, demonstrates one of the unusual faculties of the food processor: the power to alter flavor. It intensifies the taste of garlic, for example, but strangely, weakens that of fresh sorrel. To learn how to preserve the lemony sourness so essential to a good sorrel soup, I tried several ways of processor-chopping. Mincing the leaves raw produces a flat, grassy taste. Steaming the sorrel before it goes into the food processor leaches out considerable flavor. But warming it briefly in a nubbin of butter preserves most of the original tartness.

SERVES 6

Two 14½- or 15½-ounce cans chicken broth or 4 cups rich homemade chicken stock (page 43)

1 medium yellow onion, peeled and cut into slim wedges

3 tablespoons unsalted butter

1 cup heavy cream

3 large egg yolks

½ teaspoon salt

¼ teaspoon ground hot red pepper (cayenne)

⅛ teaspoon freshly ground black or white pepper

1 pound fresh sorrel, trimmed of coarse stems and wilted leaves, washed well in cool water, and patted as dry as possible between layers of paper toweling

1 to 2 tablespoons fresh lemon juice

1. Pour the broth into a medium-size nonreactive saucepan and bring to a boil over moderate heat. Adjust the heat so the broth bubbles lazily, and boil uncovered until reduced by about one-fourth, about ½ hour.

2. Meanwhile, coarsely chop the onion in a food processor fitted with the metal chopping blade using 3 to 5 quick pulses.

3. Melt the butter in a large, heavy nonreactive skillet over moderate heat, add the chopped onion, and sauté, stirring now and then, until limp and golden, about 5 minutes. Turn the heat under the skillet to its lowest point and allow the onion to mellow while you proceed.

4. Quickly whisk the cream with the egg yolks, salt, cayenne, and black pepper, blend in a little of the hot broth, and stir back into the pan. Cook over low heat, stirring constantly, until lightly thickened, 2 to 3 minutes. Do not boil or the mixture may curdle. Set off the heat and let stand uncovered while you proceed.

5. Pile the sorrel into the skillet with the onion, cover, and warm for 30 seconds. Stir well, re-cover, and warm 30 seconds longer. Scoop all into the food processor and coarsely chop—2 to 3 staccato pulses is all it takes.

6. Stir the sorrel mixture into the soup, set over low heat, and bring to serving temperature, stirring often. Again, don't allow to boil.

7. Stir in 1 to 2 tablespoons lemon juice until as tart as you like. Also taste for salt and pepper and adjust as needed.

8. Ladle into heated soup bowls and serve. Or, if you prefer, chill well and serve cold.

New England Fish Chowder

Such an easy soup, and one of my all-time cold-weather favorites.

SERVES 4 TO 6

¼ cup lightly packed curly parsley

2 ounces salt pork, diced, or 2 slices bacon, stacked and snipped crosswise at ½-inch intervals

1 large yellow onion, peeled and quartered

2 medium all-purpose potatoes, peeled and halved

1¼ cups cold water

1½ teaspoons salt

¼ teaspoon freshly ground black pepper

1 pound cod, scrod, haddock, or flounder fillets

1½ cups milk

½ cup heavy cream

1 tablespoon unsalted butter

1. Coarsely chop the parsley in a food processor fitted with the metal chopping blade using one to two 5-second pulses. Scrape into a large fine sieve and rinse under cool running water. Also rinse the work bowl and blade, letting stray bits of parsley fall into the sieve. Tap the parsley onto several thicknesses of paper toweling, wring dry, and reserve. Return the work bowl to the power base and insert the medium slicing disk.

2. Sauté the salt pork in a large heavy saucepan over moderately low heat until all the drippings cook out leaving crisp brown bits, about 10 minutes. Using a slotted spoon, lift the browned bits to paper toweling and reserve.

3. Slice the onion, then the potatoes, by guiding down the feed tube with the pusher, pulsing all the while.

4. Add to the drippings in the saucepan, and cook over moderate heat, stirring now and then, until the onion is limp and golden, about 10 minutes.

5. Add the water, salt, and pepper, adjust the heat so the mixture bubbles gently, cover, and simmer until the potatoes are nearly tender, 10 to 15 minutes. Lay the fish fillets on top—in a single layer, if possible. Re-cover and simmer just until the fish almost flakes at the touch of a fork, 8 to 10 minutes.

6. Gently fork the fish into chunks, add the milk, cream, butter, and reserved salt pork, and heat just until steaming, 3 to 5 minutes. Do not boil or the mixture may curdle. Taste for salt and pepper and adjust as needed.

7. Ladle the chowder into heated soup plates, top each portion with a sprinkling of chopped parsley, and serve with pilot or common crackers.

Main Dishes

Meats and Meatless, Fish and Fowl

FROM THE VERY beginning, food processors simplified the preparation of main dishes because they chopped, puréed, sliced, and shredded with stunning speed.

What they didn't do well then and—let me be up front about this—don't do particularly well now despite many improvements is slice, mince, or grind raw meat, give or take a couple of exceptions (chicken cutlets, to name one). Most user's manuals will tell you otherwise. But if I must trim all connective tissue from a piece of meat, then chunk the meat, and partially freeze it before it's machine-ready, I'd rather just slice or dice or julienne by hand. Five to ten minutes is all it takes. The new food processors, praised be, are more adept at dealing with cooked meats, fish, and fowl.

Even more important, they prep to perfection nearly everything else needed for main dishes both simple and sophisticated. Let them mince garlic, fresh herbs, and ginger; let them chop onions and bell peppers; let them cut carrots into rounds and celery into crescents. Let them crumb bread for crunchy oven-fried chicken or grate Parmigiano-Reggiano for a quick pasta. Let them purée sauces and gravies.

What you'll find in the pages that follow are main dishes that let the food processor excel.

Mushroom-and-Onion-Smothered Swiss Steak Braised in Beer

Every now and then when I crave comfort food, I'll make Swiss steak. Not the tomatoey recipe but this one reminiscent of Beef Carbonnade, that heavenly Belgian beef stew made with beer.

Note: If you line the roasting pan with aluminum foil, allowing plenty of overhang, you won't have to scrub the pan. The overhang, moreover, can be rolled down to seal in the steak and vegetables.

SERVES 6

2 tablespoons unsalted butter

One 2-inch-thick blade or arm (chuck) steak (about 3 pounds), trimmed of excess fat

1 large yellow onion, peeled and halved lengthwise

1 pound cremini or white mushrooms, stemmed and wiped clean

6 tablespoons all-purpose flour

¼ teaspoon freshly grated nutmeg

¾ teaspoon salt

¼ teaspoon freshly ground black pepper

1 cup beef broth

1 cup stale beer

1. Preheat the oven to 350°F. Line a shallow roasting pan only slightly larger than the steak with heavy-duty aluminum foil, running one strip the length of the pan, a second at right angles to it, and allowing about 6 inches of overhang all around. Set the pan aside.

2. Melt the butter in a large heavy skillet over moderately high heat and when the foam subsides, add the steak, and brown well, allowing about 5 minutes per side. Center the steak in the foil-lined pan and set the skillet off the heat.

3. Equip the food processor with the medium slicing disk, fit the onion halves snugly in the feed tube, then pulse through the slicing disk. Slice the cremini the same way, standing the caps on end in the feed tube, concave sides all facing the same way.

Note: If your work bowl is not big enough to accommodate both the onion and mushrooms, tip the onion into the skillet before slicing the mushrooms.

4. Empty the onion and mushrooms into the skillet and cook over moderate heat, stirring occasionally, until lightly browned, 10 to 12 minutes.

5. Blend in the flour, nutmeg, salt, and pepper, and cook and stir 1 to 2 minutes. Add the broth and beer and cook, stirring constantly, until thickened, 3 to 5 minutes.

6. Pour the skillet mixture over the steak, then roll the foil down enclosing everything in a snug package.

7. Place on the middle oven rack and bake until the steak is fork-tender, about 1½ hours. Test by thrusting a sharp knife through the foil into the steak—it should offer little resistance.

8. To serve, cut the steak across the grain into slices about ½ inch thick, and ladle plenty of mushrooms and gravy over each portion. Accompany with fluffy boiled rice or tiny redskin potatoes cooked in their jackets.

Ossobuco

Ossobuco, veal shanks braised the Italian way until falling-off-the-bone tender, is a terrific make-ahead. It's my favorite main dish for a small dinner party. If you're making the ossobuco a day or two ahead, cool to room temperature, cover, and refrigerate until about an hour before serving. Let stand at room temperature 30 to 40 minutes, then set the covered kettle over moderately low heat, and bring to serving temperature. This will take about 20 minutes.

Note: If you have a mini food processor, you can use it to prepare the gremolata (a mix of minced garlic, parsley, and lemon zest added shortly before serving). To provide the abrasiveness needed to speed the mincing, I've added a little salt. If you hand-mince the gremolata, increase the salt in the ossobuco by one-half teaspoon.

SERVES 6

⅓ cup lightly packed Italian parsley leaves

½ cup lightly packed fresh basil leaves

1 tablespoon fresh marjoram leaves or 1 teaspoon dried leaf marjoram, crumbled

1 teaspoon fresh rosemary leaves or ½ teaspoon dried leaf rosemary, crumbled

Six 2½-inch-thick veal shanks measuring about 4 inches in diameter

¾ cup unsifted all-purpose flour

3 tablespoons unsalted butter

2 tablespoons olive oil

1 to 1½ teaspoons salt (see note)

½ teaspoon freshly ground black pepper

1 large whole clove garlic, peeled and halved

1 large Spanish onion, peeled and cut into 1½-inch chunks

1 medium rib celery, trimmed and cut into 1-inch lengths

2 medium carrots, peeled and cut into 1-inch lengths

Two 3-inch strips lemon zest, removed with a vegetable peeler

2 medium ripe tomatoes, cored and cut into slim wedges (no need to peel)

2 cups dry white wine such as Pinot Grigio

GREMOLATA (SEE NOTE)
2 medium whole cloves garlic, halved

Five 3-inch strips lemon zest, removed with a vegetable peeler

½ teaspoon salt

¼ cup lightly packed Italian parsley leaves, rinsed in cool water and wrung as dry as possible in paper toweling

1. Churn the parsley, basil, and fresh marjoram and rosemary, if using, in a food processor fitted with the metal chopping blade 5 seconds. Scrape the work bowl and churn 2 to 3 seconds more until moderately fine. Tip into a large fine sieve, then rinse the work bowl and blade directly over the sieve so that all stray bits of herbs fall into it. Rinse the herbs well under cool running water, transfer to paper toweling, roll up, and wring dry. Set aside.

2. Dredge the veal shanks well on all sides in the flour, shaking off the excess. Heat the butter and 1 tablespoon of the olive oil in a large, heavy nonreactive kettle over fairly high heat for 2 minutes.

3. Add half the shanks, brown well on all sides, and lift to paper toweling to drain. Add the remaining tablespoon olive oil to the kettle, heat 1 minute, then add the remaining shanks, and brown the same way. Transfer to paper toweling to drain and slide the kettle off the heat. Sprinkle the shanks well on both sides with the salt and pepper.

4. Add the garlic to the processor and mince fine by churning 4 to 5 seconds. Scrape the work bowl well, add half the onion, the dried marjoram and rosemary, if using, and pulse 5 to 6 times until moderately coarsely chopped; add to the drippings in the kettle. Coarsely chop the remaining onion with the celery the same way and add to the kettle.

5. Add the carrots to the processor and churn 10 to 15 seconds until fairly finely chopped. Add to the kettle along with the lemon zest and reserved chopped parsley and herbs. Stir well to mix.

6. Set the kettle over low heat and sauté, stirring occasionally, until the vegetables are very soft but not brown.

7. Meanwhile, add the tomatoes to the processor (no need to wash the bowl or blade), and reduce to juice by churning 30 seconds.

8. Add the tomatoes to the kettle together with the wine and stir well to mix. Return the veal shanks to the kettle, pushing down under the liquid. Bring to a boil over moderately high heat, then adjust the heat so the mixture bubbles gently, cover, and simmer very slowly until the meat almost falls from the bones, 3½ to 4 hours. Remove the strips of lemon zest and discard. Taste for salt and pepper and adjust as needed—but remember, if you machine-prep the gremolata, it will contain salt.

9. For the gremolata: Coarsely chop the garlic and lemon zest with the salt in a mini food processor using two 5-second churnings, scraping the work bowl and lid in between. Use the "grind" mode if your mini offers that option. Add the parsley and coarsely chop with three 2-second churnings, again scraping the work bowl and lid between each.

Note: If your mini has a "chop" mode, use it for the parsley.

10. Scatter the gremolata evenly over the veal shanks, cover, and simmer 5 minutes more.

11. Serve the ossobuco with boiled rice—either bedded on or beside it.

Vitello Tonnato (Cold Poached Veal with Tuna Sauce)

If you want a party dish to wow guests, try this Italian classic, which can be made a day ahead. Pre-processor, it was the very devil to make—but not so today.

Note: Have your butcher roll the veal tight and tie it at frequent intervals—important if the slices are to hold together.

SERVES 8

VEAL

3 tablespoons olive oil

One 4-pound boned and rolled veal rump roast (see note)

2 medium yellow onions, peeled and cut into slim wedges

2 medium ribs celery, trimmed and cut into 1-inch chunks

2 medium carrots, peeled and cut into 1-inch chunks

2 large branches Italian parsley

2 large whole cloves garlic, peeled

5 anchovy fillets, rinsed and patted dry on paper toweling

One 6- to 7-ounce can chunk white tuna, drained well (use water-packed, if you like)

1 cup dry white wine (an Italian Soave, for example)

2 tablespoons fresh lemon juice

Two 3-inch sprigs fresh lemon thyme or ½ teaspoon dried leaf thyme

1 large whole bay leaf, preferably fresh

½ teaspoon freshly ground black pepper

TUNA SAUCE

The kettle mixture in which the veal cooked

1½ cups mayonnaise (use light, if you like)

2 tablespoons fresh lemon juice

¼ cup well-drained small capers

¼ cup finely chopped Italian parsley (I chop this small amount by hand)

OPTIONAL GARNISHES

1 tablespoon well-drained small capers

1 lemon, cut into slim wedges

1. For the veal: Heat the olive oil in a large heavy kettle over high heat 1 minute, add the veal, and brown lightly on all sides. Reduce the heat to low.

2. Mince the onions fairly fine in a food processor fitted with the metal chopping blade by pulsing briskly 3 to 5 times. Scrape into the kettle. Chop the celery the same way and add to the kettle.

3. Add the carrots to the processor and churn for 10 seconds. Add to the kettle along with the parsley and cook uncovered over moderate heat, stirring now and then, until the vegetables are limp but not brown, about 10 minutes. Reduce the heat to low.

4. Add the garlic and anchovies to the processor and mince fine by churning for 5 seconds. Scrape the work bowl well, add the tuna, breaking it into large chunks, then flake moderately fine by pulsing 2 to 4 times. Scoop the tuna mixture into the kettle, add the wine, lemon juice, thyme, bay leaf, and pepper, and stir well.

5. Bring the kettle liquid to a boil, adjust the heat so that it barely trembles, cover, and cook until the veal is fork-tender, 2 to 2½ hours. Meanwhile, wash and dry the processor work bowl and blade and reassemble.

6. When the veal is tender, cool 30 minutes in the kettle mixture. Discard the parsley and bay leaf and lift the veal to a large nonreactive bowl.

7. Purée the kettle mixture in three batches by churning each for about 1 minute. As each batch is puréed, pour over the veal. Cover the bowl with plastic wrap and refrigerate for 24 hours, turning the veal in the purée once or twice.

8. Remove the veal from the refrigerator, lift from the purée, and set on a cutting board. Scrape as much of the purée from the veal as possible and place in a clean food processor fitted with the metal chopping blade.

9. For the sauce: Add one-third of the remaining purée together with ½ cup of the mayonnaise and all of the lemon juice. Whiz for 30 seconds and scrape into a medium-size bowl.

Churn the remaining purée in two batches the same way, each time adding another ½ cup of the mayonnaise, then combining with the purée in the bowl. Mix in the capers and parsley.

10. Remove the strings from the veal, then slice ¼ inch thick, keeping the slices in order. Overlap the slices on a large platter, spooning a little of the tuna sauce over each. When all slices are in place, spoon a little more sauce on top. Cover loosely with plastic wrap and refrigerate for several hours. Also cover and refrigerate the remaining sauce.

11. Before serving, let the vitello tonnato stand at room temperature, still covered, for half an hour. Uncover and garnish, if you like, by scattering capers on top and tucking lemon wedges in here and there. Pour the remaining sauce into a sauceboat and pass separately.

Turkey Tonnato

The only difference here is that you substitute turkey breast for veal—and, I might add, save a significant amount of money. Have your butcher cut and roll it as needed so that it's the size and shape of the rolled veal rump. The finished turkey roll should weigh 4 pounds. Otherwise, follow the veal recipe exactly.

Rôti de Porc à la Boulangère
(Pork Roasted in the Manner of the Baker's Wife)

A perfect party dish but imagine hand-slicing a dozen potatoes and a dozen onions! Before the food processor came into my life, I did it because this classic French dish—roast loin of pork bedded on thinly sliced potatoes and onions—never failed to impress. It gets its name from the fact that the baker's wife would roast the pork on residual brick-oven heat after her husband's loaves of bread were done.

Note: I usually processor-mince parsley before I wash it because it stays fluffier. Here it doesn't matter. Besides, by washing the parsley first, I don't have to rinse and dry the work bowl and blade and can move right along.

SERVES 8 TO 10

1 cup lightly packed curly parsley leaves, washed and wrung dry

2 large whole cloves garlic, peeled

2 tablespoons fresh sage leaves or 2 teaspoons rubbed sage

1 tablespoon fresh thyme leaves or 1 teaspoon dried leaf thyme, crumbled

2 teaspoons salt

¾ teaspoon freshly ground black pepper

One 8-pound, bone-in pork loin (have the butcher crack the backbone along the ribs to simplify carving)

12 large baking potatoes, peeled and halved lengthwise

12 medium yellow onions, peeled and halved lengthwise

½ cup (1 stick) unsalted butter, melted

1. Preheat the oven to 450°F.

2. Mince the parsley fairly fine in a food processor fitted with the metal chopping blade using 6 to 8 staccato pulses. Tap onto paper toweling and reserve.

3. Add the garlic, sage, thyme, 1 teaspoon of the salt, and ½ teaspoon of the pepper to the processor and churn to paste—this will take 8 to 10 seconds.

4. Rub the pork loin well all over with the garlic paste, then place in a large open roasting pan so that the pork rests on its rib ends. Let stand at room temperature for half an hour, then set uncovered on the middle oven rack and roast for 30 minutes. Reduce the heat to 350°F and roast 1 hour longer. Lift the pork to a large wire rack and allow to rest while you slice the potatoes and onions. Also drain all drippings from the pan.

5. Remove the chopping blade from the processor and insert the slicing disk, the thin slicing disk if you have one (no need to wash the bowl or blade). Stand as many potato halves in the feed tube as will fit snugly, then exerting steady pressure on the pusher, guide the potatoes through the slicing disk. Continue slicing until potatoes fill the work bowl, then tip these into the roasting pan. Repeat until all of the potatoes have been sliced. Add to the roasting pan along with the reserved parsley.

6. Thin-slice the onions the same way and add to the pan along with the remaining 1 teaspoon salt and ¼ teaspoon pepper. Drizzle the melted butter evenly over all, toss well, and spread the vegetables to the edges of the pan.

7. Center the pork on the vegetables, raise the oven temperature to 400°F and roast uncov-
ered until the potatoes are tender and a meat thermometer inserted into the center of the pork, not touching bone, registers at least 150°F, 1 to 1½ hours. You'll have to stir the vegetables occasionally to keep those on top from drying and those underneath from over-cooking.

8. To serve, carve the roast into chops and accompany with hefty portions of vegetables.

Ham and Sausage Loaf with Capers and Lemon

When I began developing this processor ham loaf, I wanted something different, not the usual spicy brown-sugar-glazed loaf (for those who insist upon it, I offer a variation that comes close). What I discovered while working up this recipe is that you can grate the lemon zest while you crumb the bread because it offers just enough abrasiveness to speed things along. Years ago I'd learned that I could grate citrus zest with granulated or confectioners' sugar—a huge time-saver for all manner of sweets. But until this recipe I'd never tried processor-grating zest with something savory.

Note: There's no salt in this recipe because the ham, sausage, and capers are plenty salty. For the same reason, I've made the bacon topping optional.

Tip: You can mix in some of the ground ham by processor but no more than half of it because the loaf will be too dense. Break the ham into chunks and add at the end along with the eggs.

SERVES 10 TO 12

1½ pounds ground smoked ham

1 pound ground pork shoulder

5 slices firm-textured white bread

4 strips lemon zest about 3 inches long and ½ inch wide, cut crosswise at ½-inch intervals

1 cup lightly packed curly parsley sprigs

2 tablespoons fresh marjoram leaves or 2 teaspoons dried leaf marjoram, crumbled

1 teaspoon fresh lemon thyme leaves or ½ teaspoon dried leaf thyme, crumbled

1 medium yellow onion, cut into slim wedges

½ teaspoon dry mustard

¼ teaspoon freshly ground black pepper

1 cup evaporated milk (use fat-free, if you like)

½ pound bulk sausage meat (not too sagey and not too peppery)

¼ cup ketchup

2 tablespoons well-drained small capers

2 large eggs

4 thick slices smoked bacon (about ¼ pound), halved crosswise, optional

1. Preheat the oven to 350°F. Coat a 10 × 5 × 4-inch loaf pan well with nonstick cooking spray and set aside.

2. Place the ground ham and pork in a large mixing bowl. Tear 1 slice of bread into large pieces, letting drop into a food processor fitted with the metal chopping blade. Scatter the lemon zest on top, then churn for 2 minutes, giving the machine several quick pulses every 30 seconds. Tear the remaining 4 slices of bread into the work bowl and buzz to coarse crumbs, about 5 seconds. Tip the crumb mixture into the bowl of pork and ham.

3. Add the parsley, fresh marjoram and thyme leaves, if using, to the work bowl and coarsely chop with three 5-second pulses. Transfer to a large fine sieve and set under cool running water for several seconds. Also rinse the bowl and blade under the cold tap, letting stray bits of herb fall into the sieve. Tap the parsley mixture onto several thicknesses of paper toweling, roll up, wring dry, and add to the crumbs and meat.

4. Drop the onion wedges into the processor, add the mustard, pepper, and dried marjoram and thyme, if using, and pulse 2 to 3 times until very coarsely chopped.

5. Add the evaporated milk, then break the sausage meat into 2-inch chunks, letting fall directly into the work bowl. Add the ketchup, capers, and eggs and pulse quickly 3 to 4 times.

6. Transfer to the mixing bowl and mix thoroughly with your hands, scooping down to the bottom of the bowl often. Pat the ham mixture firmly into the prepared pan and, if you like, lay the bacon strips across the top, overlapping them slightly.

7. Bake uncovered until an instant-read thermometer, inserted in the center of the loaf, registers 170°F, about 1¾ hours.

8. Cool the ham loaf to room temperature in the upright pan on a wire rack Drain off all drippings, then slice the loaf about ¾ inch thick and serve. Better yet, wrap the loaf in aluminum foil and refrigerate overnight. The perfect accompaniment? Sour Cream Mustard-Dill Sauce (page 50).

Spicy Ham Loaf with Orange

Prepare as directed but substitute orange zest for lemon zest and fresh orange juice for evaporated milk. Also, omit the dry mustard and use dried marjoram and thyme instead of fresh, incorporating in Step 4 along with ¼ teaspoon each ground ginger, cinnamon, and allspice.

Note: You can use fresh ginger instead of ground: add a 1-inch peeled cube at the beginning of Step 4 before adding the onion, and churn about 1 minute until finely minced. Proceed as Step 4 directs. In Step 5, add 2 tablespoons honey-mustard along with the orange juice, sausage, ketchup, capers, and eggs. Proceed as directed but omit the optional bacon topping. About 25 minutes before the loaf is done, spread with 2 to 3 tablespoons orange or ginger marmalade.

Note: Both of these ham loaves freeze well. When cool, wrap snugly in aluminum foil and pop into a plastic zipper bag, pressing out all air. Label, date, and store in a 0°F freezer. Use within 3 months and bring to room temperature before serving.

Beef and Vegetable Loaf

I bake this meatloaf in a 13 × 9 × 2-inch pan for three reasons: it cooks a little faster than it would in a standard loaf pan, it's easier to serve, and there's more "crust"—my favorite part.

SERVES 10 TO 12

2 pounds lean ground beef chuck

½ cup lightly packed Italian parsley leaves, washed and wrung dry in paper toweling

6 slices stale firm-textured white bread, torn

2 tablespoons sweet paprika

2 teaspoons dried leaf marjoram, crumbled

1 teaspoon dried leaf thyme, crumbled

1 teaspoon salt

½ teaspoon freshly ground black pepper

½ cup freshly grated Parmesan cheese

2 large whole cloves garlic, peeled

2 medium carrots, trimmed, peeled, and cut into 1-inch chunks

1 medium red or yellow onion, peeled and cut into 1-inch chunks

1 medium red bell pepper, cored, seeded, and cut into 1-inch pieces

One 8-ounce can tomato sauce

⅓ cup ketchup

⅓ cup mustard relish

2 large eggs

1 tablespoon Worcestershire sauce

1. Preheat the oven to 350°F. Coat a 13 × 9 × 2-inch baking pan well with nonstick cooking spray and set aside. Place about two-thirds of the ground chuck in a large mixing bowl.

2. Churn the parsley, 2 slices of the bread, the paprika, marjoram, thyme, salt, and black pep- per together in a food processor fitted with the metal chopping blade for 5 seconds.

3. Add the remaining bread and the Parmesan and pulse quickly 3 times. Scrape the work bowl and push larger pieces of bread to the bot- tom. Pulse 2 to 3 times—you want a few large (about ¼-inch) crumbs. Add to the meat.

4. With two 5-second churnings, chop the garlic and carrots very fine, scraping the work bowl at halftime.

5. Add the onion and red bell pepper and pulse until coarsely chopped.

6. Add all remaining ingredients and whiz for 2 seconds. Crumble in the reserved ground chuck and churn 2 seconds.

7. Pour into the mixing bowl and with your hands, mix thoroughly.

8. Pack the mixture into the prepared pan, mounding slightly in the middle and making a trough all around the edge to catch juices.

9. Bake uncovered on the middle oven rack until richly browned and no longer soft to the touch, about 1 hour and 20 minutes.

10. Cool the meatloaf in the upright pan on a wire rack for at least 30 minutes, pouring off the drippings as they accumulate. Cut into large squares and serve.

Crispy Parmesan-Crumbed Chicken

Many years ago when I was a junior food editor at *The Ladies' Home Journal* in New York, we developed the recipe from which this one evolved. This was pre-food processor and I remember how tedious it was to grate the bread by hand. I continued to serve the recipe after I left the *Journal* and continued to change it, too. Some years later when my friend Sara Moulton was chef tournant at La Tulipe, an acclaimed Greenwich Village restaurant, she asked me to suggest something for the chef's table. I handed her the Parmesan-Crumbed Chicken recipe, she made it for the troops, and it was a huge hit. Fast-forward to the late '90s and Sara's Food Network show *Cooking Live*. She demonstrated the recipe one night and it's now one of her most requested recipes.

Note: The best chicken to use is a broiler-fryer weighing about three and a half pounds. Have it disjointed and if the breasts are outsize, halve them crosswise.

SERVES 4

¾ cup (1½ sticks) unsalted butter

½ cup lightly packed curly parsley sprigs

1 large clove garlic, peeled and halved

6 slices day-old firm-textured white bread

1 teaspoon salt

½ teaspoon dried leaf thyme

½ teaspoon freshly ground black pepper

½ cup freshly grated Parmesan cheese

One 3½-pound chicken, cut up for frying

1. Preheat the oven to 350°F. Melt the butter in a medium-size saucepan over low heat.

2. Churn the parsley in a food processor fitted with the metal chopping blade 5 seconds. Scrape the work bowl and churn 5 seconds more. Tip into a large fine sieve, rinse the work bowl and blade over the sieve so that all stray bits of parsley fall into it. Roll the parsley up in paper toweling, wring absolutely dry, and set aside.

3. Dry the processor work bowl and blade and reassemble. Snap the motor on, drop the garlic down the feed tube and churn 5 seconds. Scrape the work bowl and pulse the garlic 4 to 5 times until finely chopped; add to the butter.

4. Working directly over the processor, tear the bread into small chunks and drop into the work bowl. Add the salt, thyme, and pepper, churn 3 seconds, then pulse 5 to 6 times until the crumbs are moderately coarse. Add the Parmesan and reserved parsley and pulse 6 to 8 times. Transfer to a pie pan.

5. Dip the pieces of chicken into the melted garlic butter, then roll in the crumb mixture, coating well on all sides. Arrange the chicken on an ungreased 15½ × 10½ × 1-inch jelly roll pan and drizzle the remaining butter evenly over all.

6. Bake uncovered on the middle oven shelf until the chicken is crusty-brown, 45 to 50 minutes.

7. Serve hot, or cool to room temperature and serve. This is great picnic fare. If you double the recipe, you won't need twice the amount of butter, so multiply it by 1½.

Flavors-of-Asia Shiitake-Crusted Chicken

Fresh shiitakes can be oven-dried, buzzed to crumbs and used to "bread" chicken cutlets. I cook these just as I do Wiener Schnitzel—in a skillet that's hot, hot, hot.

Note: Do not attempt this recipe in rainy or humid weather because the shiitakes will absorb atmospheric moisture as soon as they come from the oven and be impossible to "crumb."

SERVES 4

½ pound shiitake mushrooms, stemmed, wiped clean, and quartered

4 slices firm-textured white bread

½ teaspoon salt

½ teaspoon freshly ground black pepper

1 medium whole clove garlic, peeled and halved

One 1-inch cube fresh ginger, peeled and halved

½ cup vegetable oil (about)

¼ cup chicken broth

2 tablespoons Japanese soy sauce

2 tablespoons Asian roasted sesame oil

2 tablespoons sherry or port (not too dry)

4 chicken cutlets of equal size, about 1 pound

1. Preheat the oven to 350°F. Spread the mushrooms on an ungreased 15½ × 10½ × 1-inch jelly roll pan, set uncovered on the middle oven rack, and roast, stirring occasionally, until crisp and dry, 35 to 40 minutes. The mushrooms will stick a bit but that's okay.

2. Cool the mushrooms 5 minutes, scrape into a food processor fitted with the metal chopping blade, and chop until uniformly fine, four 10-second churnings. Scrape work bowl between churnings, and stir mushrooms, pushing large pieces to the bottom. Transfer chopped mushrooms to a pie pan.

3. Tear the bread into the work bowl, add salt and pepper and pulse to coarse crumbs. Toss with the mushrooms.

4. Add the garlic, ginger, ¼ cup of the vegetable oil, the chicken broth, soy sauce, sesame oil, and sherry to the processor and churn for 10 seconds. Scrape the work bowl and lid and churn 10 seconds longer. Pour into a second pie pan.

5. Dip the chicken cutlets first into the liquid mixture, then into the shiitake crumbs, patting until both sides are thickly coated. Arrange the breaded cutlets, not touching, on a wire rack set over a wax-paper-covered counter and air-dry 30 minutes. This makes the breading stick.

6. Heat the remaining ¼ cup vegetable oil in a large heavy skillet over moderately high heat for 2 minutes, arrange the cutlets in the pan so they do not touch, and brown for 3 minutes. Do not poke the cutlets as they brown and do not turn them. They will stick to the skillet.

7. Using a nonstick pancake turner, very carefully turn the cutlets, and if the skillet has cooked dry, add another 1 to 2 tablespoons vegetable oil. Brown the flip sides 3 minutes, then lift the cutlets to paper toweling to drain.

8. Serve at once with roasted asparagus, steamed broccoli, snow peas, or sugar snaps.

Stir-Fry of Chicken, Red Onion, and Bell Peppers

I must confess that I am not convinced that slicing meat in the food processor is faster or easier than doing it by hand because you must first cut it into pieces that fit the food processor feed tube, then partially freeze them so that they offer some resistance to the slicing disk. Even then, I find that in the stir-frying, little bits come off so the meat loses its clean-cut look. If you want to processor-slice the chicken for this recipe (and the beef for the variation that follows), by all means do so. After cutting the meat to fit the feed tube, wrap each piece individually in plastic food wrap, lay directly on the freezing surface of a 0°F freezer, and freeze until almost firm, 35 to 45 minutes should do it if you turn the slices over at halftime. To slice, equip the processor with the medium slicing disk (standard equipment for most machines), remove the plastic and stack as many slices on end in the feed tube as you can for a snug fit, then with staccato pulses, ease the meat through the slicing disk with the pusher.

Note: I've sequenced the ingredients in this recipe so that there's no need to wash, rinse, or even wipe the food processor parts between steps.

SERVES 4 TO 6

1 large red onion, peeled and halved from stem end to root end

1 medium-large green bell pepper, cored, seeded, and quartered

1 medium-large red bell pepper, cored, seeded, and quartered

4 chicken cutlets of equal size (thin slices of boned and skinned chicken breast), about 1 pound, cut crosswise into strips about ⅜ inch wide (see headnote)

3 tablespoons peanut or vegetable oil

MARINADE
One 1-inch cube fresh ginger, peeled and halved

1 large whole clove garlic, peeled and halved

2 tablespoons soy sauce

2 tablespoons Thai peanut sauce

2 tablespoons Asian roasted sesame oil

2 tablespoons sherry (not too dry)

1 tablespoon cornstarch

CORNSTARCH MIXTURE
¾ cup chicken broth

2 tablespoons cornstarch

1 tablespoon soy sauce

1 teaspoon light brown sugar

1. Equip the food processor with the medium slicing disk, arrange the onion halves in the feed tube so that the half-circle layers face down, then push through the slicing disk, pulsing briskly all the while. Transfer to a pie pan and reserve.

2. Slice the green and red bell peppers the same way in two batches and add to the onion.

If you want to processor-slice the chicken, now is the time to do so (see headnote).

3. Place the chicken strips in a large shallow bowl. Remove the slicing disk from the food processor and insert the metal chopping blade.

4. For the marinade: Churn all ingredients 10 seconds, and with a plastic spatula, scrape both the work bowl and lid. Repeat twice until the ginger and garlic are finely chopped. Pour over the chicken, toss well, and let stand at room temperature 20 minutes, tossing once or twice as the chicken marinates.

5. Meanwhile, prepare the cornstarch mixture. Whiz all ingredients in the food processor 3 to 5 seconds to combine. Leave in the work bowl until needed—this way you can pulse the mixture just before you add it to the stir-fry.

6. Heat 2 tablespoons of the peanut oil in a large heavy skillet over moderately high heat 2 minutes. Add the onion, green and red bell peppers and cook, stirring and tossing frequently, just until they begin to lose their crunch, about 5 minutes. With a slotted spoon, scoop the vegetables to a large plate and reserve.

7. Add the remaining 1 tablespoon peanut oil to the skillet, heat 1 minute over moderately high heat, then add the marinated chicken strips. Stir-fry just until nearly all the strips turn white, about 3 minutes.

8. Quickly pulse the cornstarch mixture in the food processor, pour into the skillet, and cook, stirring constantly, until it begins to thicken, about 2 minutes.

9. Return the onion and bell peppers to the skillet and cook, tossing and stirring, 1 to 2 minutes longer until the juices thicken and clear.

10. Serve at once over fluffy boiled rice.

Stir-Fry of Beef, Red Onion, and Bell Peppers
Prepare as directed but substitute 1 pound thin strips of eye round for the chicken.

Caldeirada (Portuguese Fishermen's Stew)

Once while exploring Portugal (my favorite thing to do), I fetched up on a beach south of Lisbon just as the fishermen were making Caldeirada. They used an oil drum and tossed a variety of fresh-caught fish into it (even an octopus) along with plenty of onions, tomatoes, and garlic. My reward for waiting until the stew was done was a bowl filled to the brim plus big chunks of Pão (see page 213). I've updated that wonderful fish muddle for the food processor and impressively shortcut prep time—if not cooking time.

Note: For a proper Portuguese Caldeirada, you must use a combination of fish, half lean (cod, flounder, haddock, etc.) and half oily (mackerel, tuna, bluefish, etc.). If you want no bones in your Caldeirada, use fillets, but the Portuguese never do.

SERVES 6

½ cup lightly packed Italian parsley leaves

3 large whole cloves garlic, halved

2 large yellow onions, peeled and cut into 1½-inch chunks

5 tablespoons olive oil (the Portuguese would use a gutsy one)

2 large whole bay leaves, preferably fresh

2 pounds red-ripe tomatoes, peeled, cored, and cut into slim wedges

2½ pounds mixed lean and oily fish, cleaned and cut into 2-inch chunks (see note)

1 cup fish stock or bottled clam juice

½ cup dry white wine

2 teaspoons salt

½ teaspoon freshly ground black pepper

⅛ to ¼ teaspoon ground hot red pepper (cayenne)

1. Churn the parsley in a food processor fitted with the metal chopping blade 5 seconds. Scrape the work bowl and pulse 2 to 3 times more until moderately coarsely chopped. Tip the chopped parsley into a large fine sieve, then rinse the work bowl and blade directly over the sieve so that all stray bits of parsley fall into it. Rinse the parsley well under cool running water, transfer to paper toweling, roll up, and wring dry. Set aside.

2. Dry the processor work bowl and blade and reassemble. Snap the motor on, drop the garlic down the feed tube into the spinning blade, and churn for 5 seconds. Scrape the work bowl and pulse the garlic 2 to 3 times until finely chopped. Add the onions and pulse 3 to 5 times until moderately coarsely chopped.

3. Heat the oil in a large, heavy nonreactive kettle over moderate heat 2 minutes, add the garlic, onions, parsley, and bay leaves, and cook, stirring occasionally, until the onions are limp, about 5 minutes. Reduce the heat to its lowest point, cover, and allow the mixture to "sweat" for 10 minutes. Check the kettle occasionally and if the mixture threatens to cook dry, set off the heat for the balance of the cooking time. This is a Portuguese technique called *refogado* and its purpose is to "sweeten" the onions and garlic.

4. Rough-chop the tomatoes in two batches in the food processor (no need to wash the work bowl or blade) using 8 to 10 staccato pulses. As each batch is chopped, add to the kettle.

5. Simmer uncovered over moderate heat just until the flavors mellow and the mixture is the consistency of marinara sauce, about 20 minutes.

6. Push the fish down into the sauce, then add the stock, wine, salt, black pepper, and cayenne (the Portuguese fishermen used explosive little *piri-piri* or malaguete chiles half the size of my little finger).

7. Bring to a boil, adjust the heat so the mixture bubbles gently, cover, and simmer until the flavors meld, about 30 minutes. If the mixture seems too soupy (it should be the consistency of Manhattan clam chowder), boil uncovered for a few minutes. Remove and discard the bay leaves. Taste for salt and pepper and adjust as needed.

8. Ladle into heated soup plates and serve with chunks of good, chewy country bread.

Salmon Loaf with Fresh Dill and Sweet Red Pepper

For coarse cracker crumbs, you must do three batches. Buzzing one big batch of crackers will reduce most of them to dust and that will mean a gluey salmon loaf.

Note: This recipe calls for finely grated lemon zest but because the cracker crumbs must be coarse and there is no other abrasive ingredient here with which to machine-grate it, I use a rasp or microplane, that new miracle gadget that grates zest quickly, completely, and cleanly. For an intensely salmony loaf, use the can liquid, for a more delicate one, chicken broth. The amount of bone in cans of salmon varies wildly. When developing this recipe, one can was bone-free, the second chock-full. Salmon bones are edible and—no surprise here—rich in calcium. Because of the saltiness of the salmon, crackers, and capers, this recipe calls for no salt.

SERVES 8

Sixty 2-inch-square soda crackers (slightly less than ½ pound)

Two 14¾-ounce cans pink salmon, drained, flaked, and dark skin removed (reserve can liquid)

¼ cup lightly packed Italian parsley leaves

¼ cup lightly packed sprigs fresh dill

6 medium scallions, trimmed and cut into 1-inch chunks (include some green tops)

1 medium rib celery, trimmed and cut into 1-inch chunks

1 small red bell pepper, cored, seeded, and cut into 1-inch pieces

½ teaspoon freshly ground black pepper

Salmon can liquid plus enough evaporated milk (use fat-free, if you like) to total 2 cups or 1½ cups chicken broth plus ½ cup evaporated milk (see note)

1 tablespoon finely grated lemon zest (see note)

2 tablespoons fresh lemon or lime juice

¼ cup well-drained small capers

3 large eggs

1. Preheat the oven to 325°F. Coat a 9 × 5 × 3-inch loaf pan well with nonstick cooking spray and set aside.

2. Equip the food processor with the metal chopping blade, then working with 20 crackers at a time, pulse briskly 6 to 8 times until you have coarse crumbs. As each batch is done, tip the crumbs into a large mixing bowl. Add the salmon to the crumbs but do not mix.

3. Add the parsley and dill to the processor and chop fairly fine using three 5-second churnings. Using a plastic spatula and skirting the blade, scrape the work bowl between churnings and stir the herbs. Transfer to a large fine sieve and set under cool running water for several seconds. Also rinse the bowl and blade under the cold water tap, letting stray bits of parsley and dill fall into the sieve. Tap the parsley mixture onto several thicknesses of paper toweling, roll up, wring dry, and add to the crumbs and salmon.

4. Add the scallions, celery, bell pepper, and black pepper to the processor and coarsely chop using four to five 1-second churnings. Stir and scrape about half way along.

5. Add the salmon liquid-milk mixture, the lemon zest and juice, the capers, and eggs and pulse briskly 4 to 5 times to combine.

6. Pour into the mixing bowl and with your hands, mix all ingredients well, scooping again and again to the bottom of the bowl.

7. Pack the salmon mixture into the prepared pan, set on the middle oven rack, and bake uncovered until the loaf is lightly browned, feels set, and begins to pull from the sides of the pan, 1 to 1¼ hours.

8. Remove the salmon loaf from the oven and cool in the upright pan on a wire rack to room temperature.

9. Without removing the loaf from the pan, cut into slices about ¾ inch thick and serve with either Cucumber Sour Cream Sauce (page 51) or Lemon Sauce (page 47).

Shrimp de Jonghe

This old Chicago recipe was the specialty of the de Jonghes, a Dutch family of hoteliers who had settled in the Windy City. Their hotel is no more but their shrimp dish lives on as an American classic. With a food processor to crumb the bread and mince the herbs, it's easy. And if you can coax your fishmonger into shelling and deveining the raw shrimp, it's easier still.

SERVES 6

1½ pounds shelled and deveined raw medium shrimp

2 quarts boiling water

1 small yellow onion, peeled and quartered

1 small rib celery, halved (include leaves)

8 peppercorns

1 large bay leaf, preferably fresh

1 teaspoon salt

½ cup (1 stick) unsalted butter, melted

3 tablespoons dry sherry or port

1 large whole clove garlic, peeled and halved

¼ cup lightly packed curly parsley sprigs, washed and wrung dry in paper toweling

2 tablespoons fresh tarragon leaves, washed and wrung dry in paper toweling or 1 teaspoon dried leaf tarragon

4 slices firm-textured white bread, torn into small pieces

1 teaspoon sweet paprika

⅛ teaspoon ground hot red pepper (cayenne)

1. Preheat the oven to 375°F. Lightly coat a shallow 6-cup casserole or au gratin dish with nonstick cooking spray and set aside.

2. Place the shrimp in a large heavy saucepan, add the boiling water, onion, celery, peppercorns, bay leaf, and salt. Set over moderate heat and as soon as the water returns to a boil, adjust the heat so that it bubbles gently. Cook the shrimp uncovered just until they turn pink, about 2 minutes. Drain at once, transfer the shrimp (and only the shrimp) to a large bowl, add ¼ cup of the melted butter and the sherry, and toss well.

3. Equip a food processor with the metal chopping blade, snap the motor on, and drop the garlic down the feed tube into the spinning blade. Scrape the work bowl, then pulse the garlic 2 to 3 times until finely minced.

4. Add the parsley and tarragon and pulse quickly 3 to 4 times until fairly finely chopped. Add the bread, paprika, and cayenne, and with two 5-second churnings, reduce to moderately fine crumbs. Drizzle the remaining ¼ cup butter on top and pulse quickly to combine.

5. Arrange half the shrimp in the prepared casserole, scatter half the crumb mixture evenly on top, then repeat with the remaining shrimp and crumb mixture.

6. Bake uncovered on the middle oven shelf until bubbly and tipped with brown, about 30 minutes. Serve at once.

Eastern Shore Crab Imperial

On Maryland's Eastern Shore, watermen make a living pulling the "beautiful swimmers" (blue crabs) out of Chesapeake Bay. This recipe was given to me many years ago by a waterman's wife—pre-food-processor.

Note: This one's for the mini food processor because amounts are small.

SERVES 6

1 pound lump crabmeat, bits of shell and cartilage removed

2 slices firm-textured white bread

2 tablespoons unsalted butter, melted

2 tablespoons curly parsley leaves, rinsed and wrung dry in paper toweling

½ teaspoon salt

⅛ teaspoon freshly ground black pepper

Pinch ground hot red pepper (cayenne)

⅔ cup mayonnaise (use light, if you like)

½ teaspoon dry mustard

1. Preheat the oven to 400°F. Lightly coat 6 large scallop shells with nonstick cooking spray or, if you prefer, lightly coat a 6-cup au gratin pan or shallow casserole; set aside. Place the crab in a medium-size mixing bowl and set aside also.

2. Tear the bread into small chunks, letting them drop into a mini food processor fitted with the metal chopping blade. Using 3 to 4 brisk pulses, reduce to moderately coarse crumbs. Drizzle the melted butter over all and pulse 2 to 3 times to incorporate. The crumbs should now be moderately fine. Tip onto a piece of wax paper and reserve.

3. Add the parsley, salt, black pepper, and cayenne to the processor (no need to wash the bowl or blade), and pulse briskly 3 to 5 times until the parsley is coarsely chopped.

4. Add the mayonnaise and mustard and churn until smooth, about 5 seconds. Scoop on top of the crab and toss lightly to mix.

5. Mound the crab mixture in the scallop shells or spread evenly in the au gratin dish, and scatter the buttered crumbs on top.

6. Bake uncovered on the middle oven rack until bubbling and touched with brown, 12 to 15 minutes.

7. Serve at once, accompanying with a tartly dressed salad of greens. Roasted asparagus spears also make a delicious accompaniment.

Crab Louis

Although the original Crab Louis is a West Coast classic made with Dungeness, "the only crab," say those living within the sound of the Pacific, I use the more widely available East Coast blue crabs. The traditional way to serve Crab Louis is on a bed of shredded lettuce with quartered tomatoes and hard-cooked eggs to garnish. I like to mound it in avocado or papaya halves and skip the garnishes. I also add capers to the dressing, an unauthentic but welcome edge.

SERVES 4

DRESSING

Four 1-inch squares green bell pepper

2 large scallions, trimmed and cut into 1-inch chunks (include some green tops)

1 cup mayonnaise (use light, if you like)

3 tablespoons chili sauce or ketchup

2 tablespoons well-drained small capers

1 tablespoon fresh lemon juice

1 teaspoon Worcestershire sauce

¼ teaspoon hot red pepper sauce

CRAB

1 pound lump crabmeat, picked over for bits of shell and cartilage

2 large avocados or 2 small papayas, halved and pitted or seeded but not peeled

1. For the dressing: Coarsely chop the green pepper and scallions by pulsing briskly 4 to 5 times in a food processor fitted with the metal chopping blade. Scrape the work bowl. Add the remaining dressing ingredients and churn 5 seconds to combine. Set aside.

2. For the crab: Place the crab in a large mixing bowl, add half the dressing, and toss lightly but thoroughly.

Note: You can prepare the recipe up to this point a day ahead of time. Cover the crab and refrigerate until ready to serve. Also cover and refrigerate the remaining dressing.

3. To serve, mound the crab in the avocado halves and spoon the remaining dressing on top, dividing the total amount evenly.

Tuna Salad with Lime and Fresh Herbs

This is a recipe I've evolved over time specifically for the food processor. I like it best with fresh dill, fresh lemon thyme and marjoram, and in most high-end supermarkets, these are now available year round. If you can't find them, substitute dried herbs. But do try this recipe again when the fresh are available—there's a world of difference in flavor.

Note: Because of the saltiness of the tuna and capers, this recipe probably won't need any salt. But taste before serving and adjust as needed.

Tip: The fastest way to remove leaves from a sprig of thyme or marjoram is to run your fingers along the stem against the grain—from top to bottom. The leaves will pop right off.

SERVES 4 TO 6

1 medium yellow onion, cut into slim wedges

3 tablespoons well-drained small capers

3 tablespoons coarsely snipped fresh dill or 1 teaspoon dill weed

2 tablespoons fresh marjoram leaves or 1½ teaspoons dried leaf marjoram, crumbled

1 tablespoon fresh lemon thyme leaves or ½ teaspoon dried leaf thyme, crumbled

¼ teaspoon freshly ground black pepper

2 tablespoons fresh lime juice

¾ cup light or low-fat mayonnaise

Two 12-ounce cans water-packed solid white tuna, drained well

½ cup finely diced celery (about 1 small rib), optional

1 to 2 tablespoons milk, if needed to moisten the tuna salad

1. Pulse the onion, 1 tablespoon of the capers, the dill, marjoram, thyme, and black pepper 6 to 7 times in a food processor fitted with the metal chopping blade until coarsely chopped.

2. Add the lime juice and mayonnaise and pulse 4 to 5 times to combine.

3. While the tuna is still in the cans, flake by slashing down through it with a sharp knife in a deep criss-cross pattern. Empty the tuna directly into the food processor, add the remaining capers and pulse 3 to 4 times, just enough to combine. Quickly pulse in the celery, if desired. And if the mixture seems dry, pulse in the milk. Easy does it. If you prefer coarser textured tuna salad, pulse in one can of tuna only, then mix the second can in by hand after all the other ingredients have been incorporated. You can do this right in the work bowl if you first remove the chopping blade.

4. Transfer the tuna salad to a serving dish, cover with plastic food wrap, and refrigerate several hours before serving. This give the flavors a chance to mellow.

Four Onion Tart with Smoky Bacon

I find this tart the perfect centerpiece for a light luncheon, but I also serve it as the first course of a dinner party.

Note: Caramelizing the onions is what gives this tart its lovely sweetness, and for that reason I omit all of the sugar in the pastry. The easiest way to julienne bacon is to stack the slices, then snip crosswise at one-fourth-inch intervals with sharp kitchen scissors.

SERVES 6 TO 8

1 recipe Processor Pastry for Tarts and Pies (page 72), prepared as directed but omit the sugar

1 egg white, whisked until frothy

4 thick slices lean smoky bacon, julienned (see note)

1 large red onion, peeled and quartered

1 medium yellow onion, peeled and quartered

4 medium leeks (about 1½ pounds untrimmed), trimmed, washed, and cut in lengths to fit the small inner food processor feed tube

6 large whole shallots, peeled

1½ teaspoons caraway seeds

¼ teaspoon freshly grated nutmeg

½ cup heavy cream

½ cup half-and-half cream

3 large eggs

¾ teaspoon salt

½ teaspoon freshly ground black pepper

1. Preheat the oven to 350°F.

2. Roll the pastry on a well-floured pastry cloth with a stockinette-covered rolling pin into a circle 13 inches across. Lop the pastry over the rolling pin and ease into a 10½-inch tart tin with a removable bottom. Press the pastry against the bottom of the tin and up the sides, then roll the rolling pin across the rim, cutting off the overhang. Place the tart tin on a heavy baking sheet and brush the bottom and sides of the pastry shell with the beaten egg white. Allow to air-dry while you prepare the filling.

3. Brown the bacon in a large heavy skillet over moderate heat until all the drippings cook out and only crisp brown bits remain—this will take 8 to 10 minutes. Using a slotted spoon, lift the bacon bits to paper toweling to drain. Pour all the drippings from the skillet, then spoon 2 tablespoons of them back into the skillet. Set off the heat.

4. Equip the food processor with the medium slicing disk. Arrange as many red onion quarters in the feed tube as you can for a snug fit, then push through the slicing disk, pulsing all the while. Repeat with the yellow onion quarters. Now slice the leeks, by pushing one by one through the small inner feed tube, again pulsing all the while. Finally, arrange as many shallots as you can in the inner feed tube, and slice by pulsing the same way. Most processor work bowls are now big enough to hold all the onions, so you don't have to stop midway and empty it.

5. Heat the drippings in the skillet 2 minutes over moderately high heat, add all the onions, the caraway seeds, and nutmeg and cook, stirring often, until the onions are limp, about 10 minutes. Reduce the heat to low and continue cooking, stirring occasionally, until the onions caramelize lightly, 20 to 25 minutes. Remove from the heat and cool for 15 minutes.

6. Meanwhile, remove the slicing disk from the food processor and insert the metal chopping blade. There's no need to wash, rinse, or even wipe the processor work bowl. Add the two creams, the eggs, salt, and pepper and pulse quickly 3 to 5 times to combine.

7. Fill the tart shell (still on the baking sheet) with the onion mixture, smoothing to the edge, scatter the reserved bacon on top, and pour the cream mixture evenly over all.

8. Bake uncovered on the middle oven rack until the filling puffs and sets like custard, about 40 minutes.

9. Remove the tart from the oven and the baking sheet, set on a wire rack, and cool 30 to 40 minutes.

10. Using your sharpest knife, cut into wedges and serve.

Provençal Spinach and Basil Omelet

I not only shortcut this recipe by processor-chopping the garlic, onion, and herbs but also by using frozen chopped spinach, one of the few frozen vegetables I like. Fresh spinach, even the "triple-washed," is too labor-intensive for a recipe in which it will be cooked dry.

Note: I've altered my usual method of mincing herbs here—washing them first, so that I can add the eggs, Parmesan, and seasonings without having to wash the processor work bowl and blade.

For this omelet, you'll need a well seasoned flameproof 10- to 12-inch omelet pan or skillet with sides that slope up gently from the bottom. I've never mastered the art of flipping large omelets, I'm afraid, so I take the coward's way out and finish this one in the broiler.

SERVES 6

2 thick slices lean smoky bacon, stacked and snipped crosswise at ½-inch intervals

3 tablespoons olive oil (the fruitiest you can find)

1 large whole clove garlic, peeled

1 medium red onion, peeled and cut into slim wedges

Two 10-ounce packages frozen chopped spinach, thawed and drained

½ cup lightly packed fresh basil leaves, rinsed and wrung dry in paper toweling

½ cup lightly packed fresh Italian parsley leaves, rinsed and wrung dry in paper toweling

5 large eggs

½ cup freshly grated Parmesan cheese

¼ teaspoon freshly grated nutmeg

¾ teaspoon salt

¼ teaspoon freshly ground black pepper

1. Brown the bacon in 1 tablespoon of the olive oil in a large heavy skillet over moderate heat until all the drippings cook out and only crisp brown bits remain, 8 to 10 minutes.

2. Meanwhile, coarsely chop the garlic and onion in a food processor fitted with the metal chopping blade by churning 4 to 5 seconds.

3. Add to the skillet and cook until limp, about 5 minutes. Do not brown.

4. Add the spinach and cook, stirring often, until dry, 10 to 12 minutes; cool 10 minutes.

5. Preheat the broiler. Add the basil and parsley to the processor and coarsely chop using 4 to 5 fairly long pulses.

6. Add the eggs, Parmesan, nutmeg, salt, and pepper and pulse quickly. Add the cooled spinach mixture and pulse until well blended.

7. Heat the remaining 2 tablespoons olive oil in a well-seasoned flameproof 10- to 12-inch omelet pan over moderate heat 1 minute, swirling to coat the pan sides. Add the spinach and egg mixture and cook without stirring until crusty-brown on the bottom (the top will be quite moist), about 5 minutes.

8. Transfer the omelet to the broiler, setting about 6 inches from the heat, and cook until browned and set in the middle, 3 to 5 minutes.

9. Carefully loosen the omelet around the edge, then slide a pancake turner underneath, shaking the pan gently if it seems to stick.

10. Cut into wedges and serve.

Falafel

Many years ago during a prolonged visit to Lebanon, I tasted falafel for the first time and couldn't get enough of these chickpea "burgers." I liked them best in pita pockets with crunchy shreds of lettuce, slices of cucumber and tomato, and a hefty ladling of tahini sauce (see the note with the Hummus recipe on page 94). My Beirut guide gave me this recipe, an old one from her family, which uses ground raw potato to help bind everything together. With a food processor to do all the chopping and grinding, this falafel is so easy there's no excuse to use a mix. The classic way to cook falafel is in deep fat (365°F is just right). But I've also fried them in a skillet containing no more than ¼ inch of oil and they are just as good.

SERVES 6

¼ cup firmly packed Italian parsley leaves

¼ cup firmly packed fresh cilantro leaves

One 1 pound, 3-ounce can chickpeas, drained well and patted dry on paper toweling

1 small yellow onion, peeled and quartered

1 very small all-purpose potato (about 2 ounces), peeled and quartered

1 medium whole clove garlic, peeled

2 tablespoons chickpea flour, all-purpose flour, or fine dry bread crumbs (about)

1 teaspoon ground coriander

¾ teaspoon salt

¼ teaspoon freshly ground black pepper

⅛ teaspoon ground hot red pepper (cayenne)

Pinch baking soda

6 cups vegetable oil for deep-fat frying (see headnote)

1. Coarsely chop the parsley and cilantro together in a food processor fitted with the metal chopping blade using 8 to 10 fairly long pulses.

2. Empty the chopped herbs into a large fine sieve and set under cold running water for a few seconds. Also rinse the bowl and blade under the cold tap, letting any stray bits of herb fall into the sieve. Drain the herb mixture on several thicknesses of paper toweling, roll up, and wring as dry as possible. Set aside. Wipe the processor bowl and blade dry and reassemble.

3. Add the chickpeas, onion, potato, garlic, chickpea flour, coriander, salt, black and red peppers, and baking soda to the processor and churn for 15 seconds. Scrape down the sides of the work bowl, add the reserved chopped herbs, and churn 15 seconds longer. Again scrape the work bowl sides, then pulse quickly 2 to 3 times until fairly smooth. If the mixture seems too soft to shape, pulse in a little additional all-purpose flour or crumbs.

4. Shape the mixture into 18 little "burgers," each one measuring about 1¾ inches across and ½ inch thick. Arrange, not touching, on a small baking sheet lined with wax paper and set in the freezer while you heat the oil.

5. Pour the oil into a 12-inch skillet at least 2 inches deep, set over moderate heat, and when the oil registers 365°F on a deep-fat thermometer, it's time to cook the falafel.

6. Ease 6 of the falafel into the hot oil, spacing as evenly as possible (they will sputter, so stand back). Fry until richly browned on both sides, about 3 minutes in all, raising and lowering the burner heat as needed to maintain the 365°F temperature of the oil.

7. With a slotted spoon, lift the falafel to paper toweling to drain. Skim any burned bits from the hot oil, then cook and drain the remaining falafel the same way, 6 at a time.

8. Serve as is or top with cucumber-mint-yogurt (to each 1 cup of plain yogurt, add ¼ cup diced cucumber and 1 tablespoon coarsely chopped fresh mint).

Falafel Sandwich

Scoop about ⅓ cup thinly sliced iceberg lettuce into a pita pocket, add 3 crisply fried falafel, a generous ladling of tahini sauce (see headnote), and tuck in a few thin slices of cucumber and cherry or plum tomato.

Fusilli with Mushrooms and Parsley and Thyme

The combination of mushrooms and thyme (especially lemon thyme) is one of those made-in-heaven marriages. But only fresh thyme will do. Use any combination of mushrooms you fancy.

SERVES 4

⅓ cup lightly packed Italian parsley leaves

1 tablespoon fresh lemon thyme leaves

1 large whole clove garlic, peeled

1 small red onion, peeled and cut into slim wedges

4 tablespoons olive oil

½ pound porcini mushrooms, stemmed, the caps wiped clean and cut to fit the food processor feed tube

½ pound cremini or white mushrooms, stemmed and wiped clean

¼ teaspoon freshly ground black pepper

¾ cup chicken broth blended with 1 tablespoon all-purpose flour

¼ teaspoon salt

1 pound fusilli, cooked and drained by package directions (reserve a little cooking water)

1 tablespoon unsalted butter

¼ cup freshly grated Parmesan cheese

1. Coarsely chop the parsley and thyme together in a food processor fitted with the metal chopping blade using 5 to 6 fairly long pulses. Tip into a small fine sieve and rinse under cold running water for a few seconds. Also rinse the bowl and blade under the cold tap, flushing any stray bits of herb into the sieve. Drain the herbs on several thicknesses of paper toweling, roll up, and wring dry.

2. Coarsely chop the garlic and onion by churning 4 to 5 seconds.

3. Heat 2 tablespoons of the olive oil in a very large heavy skillet over moderate heat 2 minutes, add the garlic and onion and cook until golden, about 5 minutes. Do not brown.

4. Remove the chopping blade from the work bowl and insert the medium slicing disk. Stand as many pieces of porcini in the feed tube as will fit snugly, then ease through the slicing disk with the pusher, pulsing quickly. Repeat until all porcini are sliced. Slice the cremini the same way, standing the caps on end.

5. Add the remaining 2 tablespoons olive oil to the skillet, warm a minute or two, then add the mushrooms and the pepper, and cook, stirring occasionally, until the mushrooms are limp and most of their juices have evaporated, 12 to 15 minutes.

6. Add the broth mixture and the salt and cook, stirring constantly, until the mixture thickens, about 5 minutes.

7. Mix in the reserved chopped parsley and thyme, then add the hot drained fusilli, the butter, and Parmesan, and toss well, adding a little of the pasta cooking water if needed for creamy consistency.

8. Taste for salt and pepper, adjust, and serve.

Penne with Midsummer Tomato Sauce

Wait till home-grown tomatoes come to the farmer's market before making this sauce. Any variety will do as long as the tomatoes are plump and full of flavor.

Note: I usually chop fresh herbs before I rinse them under cool running water. But basil, first cousin to mint, darkens when wet or bruised. To minimize the problem, I rinse the basil as I do spinach, gently lifting it up and down in a sink full of cool water. I get most of the water out in a salad spinner and blot up the rest on paper toweling. Finally, I chop the basil in the processor at the last minute.

SERVES 4

1 large whole clove garlic, peeled

1 medium yellow onion, peeled and cut into slim wedges

¼ teaspoon freshly ground black pepper

3 tablespoons olive oil (the fruitiest you can find)

2 pounds red-ripe tomatoes, peeled, cored, and cut into slim wedges (see headnote)

½ teaspoon salt

1 cup lightly packed fresh basil leaves, rinsed and patted dry on paper toweling (see note)

1 pound penne, cooked and drained by package directions (reserve a little cooking water)

1 tablespoon unsalted butter

1. Coarsely chop the garlic and onion wedges with the pepper in a food processor fitted with the metal chopping blade by churning 4 to 5 seconds.

2. Heat the oil in a very large, heavy nonreactive skillet over moderate heat 2 minutes, add the garlic and onion, and cook, stirring now and then, until limp and golden, about 5 minutes. Do not brown.

3. Meanwhile, rough-chop the tomatoes in two batches in the food processor using 8 to 10 staccato pulses.

4. Add to the skillet along with the salt, bring to a boil over moderate heat, then adjust the heat so that the mixture bubbles easily. Cover and simmer until the flavors mellow, about 20 minutes. Uncover, raise the heat to moderate, and boil, stirring occasionally, until the sauce thickens slightly, about 5 minutes.

5. Meanwhile, rinse the processor chopping blade and work bowl, dry, and reassemble. Add the basil to the processor and coarsely chop using 3 to 4 fairly long pulses.

6. Add the hot drained penne to the skillet along with the butter and chopped basil. Toss well, adding a little of the pasta cooking water if needed for creamy consistency.

7. Taste for salt and pepper, adjust as needed, and serve.

Sides and Salads

FROM THE OUTSET, food processors were speed demons when it came to slicing, shredding, and chopping vegetables. Still, these miracle workers weren't perfect.

Motors often lacked the prowess to tackle tough jobs. And certain feed tubes were wrongly shaped or oversized, meaning that vegetables, no matter how carefully cut to fit them, slithered about producing ragged slices and shreds. Some work bowls, moreover, were too big to mince or chop small amounts effectively—a couple of cloves of garlic, for example, half a cup of fresh parsley leaves.

Early models also lacked pulse buttons. Some had no on-off switches and the only way to start or stop the motor was to swivel the lid. Pair that with sluggish braking action and it's easy to understand why onions, bell peppers, tomatoes, and oh so many other fruits and vegetables were more often reduced to mush than minced.

Now comes a whole new generation of food processors. There are minis as well as mini bowl-and-blade inserts for full-size models—just right for mincing herbs, a lone clove of garlic, or a cube of fresh ginger. Redesigned work bowls include such welcome new features as small inner feed tubes that make it possible—at long last—to slice and shred carrots, cucumbers, and other long skinny vegetables with near surgical precision.

The vegetable and salad recipes that follow are designed to teach you how to use the new food processors properly, thereby solving, indeed eliminating, nearly all the old problems.

Stuffed Artichokes

I've been fond of artichokes ever since I was a little girl, but I'd never had them stuffed until I spent some time in Italy.

Tip: The fastest way to prepare artichokes for stuffing is to slice off the stems so they will stand without wobbling. Next, lay the artichokes on their sides and cut off about three-fourths inch of the tops, exposing the lavender chokes deep inside. Spread the leaves and with a melon baller, scoop out all the prickly, fuzzy chokes leaving the meaty bottoms and roomy hollows for the stuffing. Pluck out and discard all coarse leaves around the base of each artichoke, usually 15 to 20 leaves. Finally, snip off the prickly leaf tips. When it comes to tearing the bread into small chunks, I do so right over the processor work bowl.

SERVES 4

4 quarts cold water

Juice of 1 large lemon

1 tray ice cubes

4 large globe artichokes (about 2½ pounds), prepared for stuffing (see tip)

STUFFING
1 medium whole clove garlic, peeled

½ teaspoon salt

¼ teaspoon freshly ground black pepper

⅓ cup lightly packed Italian parsley leaves, washed and wrung dry in paper toweling

6 slices stale firm-textured white bread, torn into small chunks

⅓ cup freshly grated Parmesan cheese

¼ cup olive oil

FOR COOKING THE ARTICHOKES
6 cups cold water

1 cup dry white wine such as a Pinot Grigio

1. Place the water, lemon juice, and ice in a large nonreactive bowl, add the artichokes, then weight with a plate so that they're submerged. Let stand for 1 hour.

2. Meanwhile, prepare the stuffing: Place the garlic, salt, and pepper in a food processor fitted with the metal chopping blade and with two 5-second churnings, whiz until uniformly fine. Scrape the work bowl with a plastic spatula and stir.

3. Add the parsley and churn 5 seconds. Again scrape the work bowl and stir. Add the bread and the Parmesan and pulse briskly 3 times. Scrape the bowl and stir the mixture. Drizzle the olive oil evenly over all and pulse 3 to 4 times, just enough to combine. Lift the chopping blade from the work bowl and set it aside.

4. Drain the artichokes well by standing upside-down on several thicknesses of paper toweling.

5. To stuff, stand the artichokes right-side-up on wax paper (to catch spills). Using a teaspoon and scooping the stuffing directly from the work bowl, fill the hollows of each artichoke, mounding it up slightly in the center. Now working from the bottom row of leaves and moving upward, bend the leaves outward and spoon in a little stuffing (use whatever spills onto the wax paper, too). Repeat until all artichokes have been stuffed.

6. To cook, stand the artichokes in a large nonreactive kettle, add the water and wine, and bring to a boil over moderately high heat. Adjust the heat so the liquid bubbles gently, cover, and cook the artichokes until you can remove a leaf easily, 35 to 40 minutes.

7. With tongs or a skimmer, lift the artichokes to a baking sheet lined with paper toweling and cool to room temperature.

8. Meanwhile, boil the kettle liquid uncovered over high heat until reduced to about 1 cup—this will take nearly an hour, so keep your eye on the pot.

9. Spoon a little of the reduced kettle liquid over each artichoke, cool 10 minutes, and serve.

Viennese Beets with Horseradish and Sour Cream

I first tasted these beets many years ago in Vienna paired with a gorgeous joint of roebuck. They've been a favorite of mine ever since and are particularly good, I think, as an accompaniment to roast veal, pork, chicken, or turkey. You may wonder why I use such small beets here—they should be no bigger than cherry tomatoes. There's good reason for this: once the beets are cooked, all I have to do is peel them and feed them through the processor shredding disk. Large beets must be chunked and for me, that usually means wearing a lot of beet juice.

Tip: To minimize the spatter when dealing with larger beets, I foil-wrap them and roast them (see Cool Summer Soup of Roasted Beets and Cucumbers, page 107).

SERVES 4

20 small beets (about 2½ pounds), scrubbed but not peeled, the root ends and 2 inches of the tops left intact (see headnote)

2 tablespoons unsalted butter

2 tablespoons prepared horseradish

1 teaspoon salt

¼ teaspoon freshly ground black pepper

½ cup sour cream, at room temperature (use light, if you like)

1. Place the beets in a large heavy saucepan, add enough cold water to cover, and bring to a boil over moderate heat. Adjust the heat so the water bubbles steadily, cover, and cook the beets until firm-tender, about 30 minutes.

2. Drain the beets, cool until easy to handle, then working over several thicknesses of paper toweling, remove the tops and root ends, and slip off the skins.

3. Equip the food processor with the medium shredding disk, then fit as many beets in the feed tube as you can. Exerting light pressure on the pusher, pulse the beets through the shredding disk. Repeat until all beets are shredded.

4. Scoop the beets into a medium-size saucepan, add the butter, horseradish, salt, and pepper, and warm over moderate heat for 5 minutes, stirring now and then.

5. Smooth in the sour cream and warm 2 to 3 minutes longer—don't allow to boil or the sour cream will curdle.

6. Taste for salt and pepper, adjust as needed, then dish up and serve.

Broccoli and Parmesan Pudding

This custard-smooth pudding is best with something simple—grilled chicken, lamb chops, or shrimp, for example. Or lightly browned turkey or veal scaloppine.

SERVES 6

4 cups broccoli florets (1¾ to 2 pounds broccoli)

1 cup cold water

1 medium yellow onion, peeled and cut into slim wedges

5 tablespoons unsalted butter

¼ teaspoon freshly grated nutmeg

¼ teaspoon freshly ground black pepper

6 tablespoons all-purpose flour

2 cups milk

1⅔ cups light cream or half-and-half cream

1½ teaspoons salt

4 large eggs, lightly beaten

½ cup freshly grated Parmesan cheese

1. Preheat the oven to 350°F. Butter a 2-quart soufflé dish and set aside.

2. Cook the broccoli in the water in a covered large saucepan over moderate heat until tender, 12 to 15 minutes. Drain well, then purée in a food processor fitted with the metal chopping blade by churning 10 seconds. Scrape into a large mixing bowl and set aside.

3. Drop the onion wedges into the processor (no need to wash the bowl or blade) and mince fairly fine by pulsing briskly 6 to 8 times.

4. Melt the butter in the saucepan over moderate heat, add the minced onion, nutmeg, and pepper, and sauté, stirring now and then, until the onion is lightly browned, 8 to 10 minutes.

5. Blend in the flour, then the milk, cream, and salt, and cook and stir until thickened and no raw starch taste remains, about 5 minutes.

6. Blend a little of the hot sauce into the beaten eggs, stir back into the pan, add the Parmesan, and cook and stir over low heat for 1 minute—no longer or the eggs may curdle.

7. Pour the sauce over the broccoli and using a gentle over-and-over motion, fold the two together until no streaks of green or white remain. Pour into the prepared soufflé dish.

8. Set a large shallow baking pan on the middle oven rack, pour hot water into the pan to a depth of 1½ inches, then center the soufflé dish in the water bath.

9. Bake uncovered until the pudding barely quivers when you nudge the dish, 1 to 1¼ hours.

10. Remove the pudding from the water bath and cool 30 minutes before serving. Don't worry, it will still be plenty warm. The point of the cooling is to allow the custard to firm up slightly. Its texture will be about halfway between a custard and a soufflé.

Red Cabbage Braised the Bavarian Way

It was Hedy Würz, my co-author on *The New German Cookbook*, who introduced me to this delicious sweet-sour cabbage. We included her recipe—but not this faster processor version—in that book and it never fails to impress. I especially like this red cabbage with roast pork, chicken, and turkey. As a matter of fact, I've served it with the Thanksgiving bird. If this recipe seems overly large, let me just add that the leftovers are wonderful—reheated, of course. But I can eat them straight out of the refrigerator.

SERVES 6 TO 8

1 large yellow onion, peeled and cut into 1-inch cubes

2 large Granny Smith apples, peeled, cored, and cut into slim wedges

2 tablespoons unsalted butter

1 tablespoon sugar

1 medium-large red cabbage (about 2 pounds), trimmed of coarse outer leaves, quartered, cored, and cut into columns to fit the food processor feed tube

¼ cup red wine vinegar

1 cup beef broth

½ teaspoon salt

¼ teaspoon freshly ground black pepper

2 large whole bay leaves

3 tablespoons all-purpose flour

1 cup dry red wine

2 tablespoons red currant jelly

1. Coarsely chop the onion and apples together in a food processor fitted with the metal chopping blade by pulsing briskly 10 to 12 times.

2. Melt the butter in a very large, heavy nonreactive skillet over moderately high heat, sprinkle in the sugar, and stir until dissolved, 2 to 3 minutes.

3. Add the onion-apple mixture and cook, stirring often, until golden, about 5 minutes. Meanwhile, remove the processor chopping blade and insert the medium slicing disk.

4. Fit as many columns of cabbage in the feed tube as you can, arranging so that the blade cuts across the layers, then guide through the slicing disk with the pusher, pulsing all the while. Repeat until all the cabbage is sliced.

5. Add the cabbage to the skillet and cook, stirring, until nicely glazed, about 5 minutes.

6. Add the vinegar, ½ cup of the beef broth, the salt, pepper, and bay leaves, pushing these down into the cabbage. Adjust the heat so the mixture bubbles gently, cover, and cook until the cabbage is crisp-tender, 20 to 25 minutes.

7. Sprinkle the flour evenly over the cabbage and toss well. Add the wine and remaining ½ cup beef broth and cook uncovered, stirring gently, until lightly thickened and no raw starch taste remains, about 5 minutes.

8. Discard the bay leaves, add the jelly, and toss gently. Simmer uncovered 5 minutes more, dish up, and serve.

Cabbage as Curried in Madras

Cabbage, like broccoli and cauliflower, is one of those healthful cruciferous vegetables we're supposed to eat as often as possible ("cruciferous" refers to their cross-shaped flowers). Unless shredded into slaw, however, cabbage isn't likely to top anyone's favorite-vegetable list because it's been cooked to death for years. Well, this quick curried cabbage made a convert of me. It was served with roast lamb at the government inn in Mahabalipuram where I stayed while touring the Indian temple towns south of Madras. Sarala, the college student who was my guide, was amused by my enthusiasm for curried cabbage—to her it was routine. But when we returned to Madras, she gave me her grandmother's recipe for curried cabbage, neatly typed out. I make it often, using the food processor to mince the ginger, chop the onion, and slice the cabbage.

Note: Curry leaf, integral to Sarala's grandmother's recipe, is at long last sold at many specialty grocers. If you can't find it, substitute minced green bell pepper, which approximates the flavor. Ghee (clarified butter) is what most good Indian cooks use as a sautéing medium. You can buy little jars of it in Indian groceries, but what you make yourself will be fresher and sweeter. Here's how: Melt ½ cup (1 stick) unsalted butter very, very slowly in a small heavy saucepan over lowest heat—the butter should never brown. Set off the heat and let stand until the milk solids settle to the bottom and the froth solidifies on top. Carefully skim off the froth, then slowly pour the liquid butter into a small jar taking care not to disturb the white milk solids. The advantage of ghee, apart from its pure-sunshine flavor, is that it can be brought to higher temperatures without browning than unclarified butter (it's the milk solids that burn). Stored tightly capped in the refrigerator, ghee will keep for several weeks.

SERVES 4

One 1-inch cube fresh ginger, peeled

1 small yellow onion, peeled and cut into slim wedges

3 tablespoons ghee (see note) or unsalted butter

2 teaspoons mustard seeds

2 curry leaves or 2 tablespoons finely minced green bell pepper (see note)

One 2-pound cabbage, quartered, cored, and cut in columns to fit the food processor feed tube

2 teaspoons curry powder

Pinch ground cinnamon

½ teaspoon salt

¼ teaspoon freshly ground black pepper

1. Equip the food processor with the metal chopping blade, snap the motor on, and drop the ginger down the feed tube into the spinning blade. Scrape the work bowl, add the onion wedges, and pulse 2 to 3 times until coarsely chopped.

2. Heat the ghee in a large heavy skillet over moderately high heat for 1 minute, add the mustard seeds, and heat, stirring often, until the seeds sputter and pop, about 2 minutes.

3. Reduce the heat to moderate, add the curry leaves and onion-ginger mixture, stir well, and sauté until limp and golden, 3 to 5 minutes.

4. Meanwhile, remove the chopping blade from the food processor and insert the medium slicing disk. Stand as many columns of cabbage in the feed tube as will fit snugly, arranging so that the blade will cut across the layers, then exerting light pressure on the pusher, pulse the cabbage through the slicing disk. Repeat until all the cabbage is sliced.

5. Blend the curry powder and cinnamon into the skillet mixture and mellow a minute or two over moderate heat.

6. Add the sliced cabbage, salt, and pepper, and stir-fry over moderate heat until the cabbage is nicely glazed, about 5 minutes. Reduce the heat to low, and cook uncovered, stirring often, until the cabbage is as crisp-tender as you like it, 5 to 10 minutes. Remove and discard the curry leaves.

7. Taste for salt and pepper, adjust as needed, and serve with grilled chicken or lamb chops. It's good, too, with roast pork or baked ham.

Carottes Râpées (Shredded Carrots)

For me there is no better way to prepare carrots than this sunny South-of-France sauté. It calls for a pound of shredded carrots and for a cleaner cut, I use the small inner feed tube because the carrots don't slip around as they often do in the wide feed tube. For optimum flavor, I use fresh young carrots with crinkly tops, not the topless golden agers bagged in plastic.

SERVES 4

¼ cup lightly packed fresh chervil or tarragon leaves

1 large whole clove garlic, peeled

1 medium yellow onion, peeled and cut into slim wedges

¼ cup olive oil (the fruitiest you can find)

1 pound tender young carrots, trimmed of green tops, peeled, and cut in lengths to fit the small inner processor feed tube

¼ teaspoon salt

¼ teaspoon freshly ground black pepper

3 to 4 tablespoons fresh lemon juice

1. Coarsely chop the chervil by pulsing 4 to 5 times in a food processor fitted with the metal chopping blade. Tip into a large fine sieve, then rinse the work bowl and blade directly over the sieve so that all stray bits of chervil fall into it. Rinse the chervil well under cool running water, transfer to paper toweling, roll up, and wring dry. Set aside.

2. Dry the processor work bowl and blade and reassemble. Snap the motor on, and drop the garlic down the feed tube into the spinning blade. Scrape the work bowl, add the onion wedges, and chop moderately fine by pulsing 4 to 6 times.

3. Heat the olive oil in a large heavy skillet over moderately high heat for 1 minute, add the chopped garlic and onion, stir well, reduce the heat to low, and allow to sauté slowly.

4. Remove the chopping blade from the food processor and insert the medium shredding disk. Pulse the pieces of carrot down the small inner feed tube one by one.

5. Add the shredded carrots to the skillet along with the salt and pepper, raise the heat to moderate, and sauté, stirring frequently, just until the carrots are crisp-tender, 8 to 10 minutes, depending upon how young the carrots are.

6. Mix in the lemon juice and reserved chervil, taste for salt and pepper, and adjust as needed.

7. Serve hot or at room temperature with grilled meats, fish (especially salmon or tuna), or chicken. I even like these carrots refrigerator-cold.

Skillet Carrots with Lime and Lemon Thyme

As with Carottes Râpées, which precedes, the best option is to pulse the carrots down the small inner feed tube one by one even though you are slicing them here instead of shredding. If you have no fresh lemon thyme, substitute fresh rosemary.

SERVES 4

1 pound medium carrots, trimmed of green tops, peeled, and cut in lengths to fit the small inner processor feed tube

2 tablespoons olive oil (the fruitiest you can find)

¼ cup rich chicken or vegetable broth

4 small sprigs fresh lemon thyme or rosemary

½ teaspoon salt

¼ teaspoon freshly ground black pepper

1 tablespoon fresh lime juice

1. Equip the food processor with the thin or medium slicing disk, then feed the pieces of carrot down the small inner feed tube one by one, pulsing all the while.

2. Heat the olive oil in a large heavy skillet over moderate heat for 2 minutes, add the carrots, and toss until lightly glazed with oil. Mix in the broth, thyme, salt, and pepper.

3. Adjust the heat so the mixture bubbles gently, cover, and cook, stirring once or twice, until the carrots are tender, 10 to 15 minutes. Taste for salt and pepper and adjust.

4. Remove the sprigs of thyme, add the lime juice, toss well, and serve with roast veal, lamb, turkey, or chicken.

Old-Timey Corn Custard

Because sweet corn season is so short and because what most groceries sell is too long off the stalk, I use frozen whole-kernel corn for this recipe. My preference: "butter and sugar corn," the one with white and yellow kernels on the same cob (a one-pound bag gives me the four cups I need).

Note: If you want to use fresh sweet corn for this recipe, you'll need eight to ten medium ears. The easiest way to cut the kernels from the cob is to stand the cob in a shallow pan, then using a sharp knife, to slice straight down from top to bottom, freeing several rows of kernels at a time. You needn't alter this recipe if you substitute fresh corn for frozen except that in Step 5, one ten-second churning should be sufficient.

SERVES 6

6 medium scallions, trimmed and cut into 1-inch chunks (include some green tops)

2 tablespoons bacon drippings or unsalted butter

4 cups solidly frozen whole-kernel corn (see headnote)

2 tablespoons sugar

2 tablespoons all-purpose flour

1 teaspoon salt

½ teaspoon freshly ground black pepper

One 12-ounce can fat-free evaporated milk

¼ cup half-and-half or heavy cream

4 large eggs

1. Preheat the oven to 325°F. Coat a 2½-quart casserole with nonstick cooking spray and set aside.

2. Churn the scallions 2 to 3 seconds in a food processor fitted with the metal chopping blade until coarsely chopped.

3. Heat the bacon drippings in a small heavy skillet over moderate heat for 1 minute, add the chopped scallions, and cook, stirring often, until limp and golden, 3 to 5 minutes.

4. Meanwhile, add the frozen corn, sugar, flour, salt, and pepper to the food processor and churn 10 seconds.

5. Scrape the work bowl, add the hot scallions and bacon drippings, and churn 10 seconds more. Scrape the bowl well and churn for another 10 seconds. You're performing two operations in one here: converting whole-kernel corn to cream-style and blending in the seasonings.

6. Add the evaporated milk, half-and-half, and eggs and pulse quickly 4 to 5 times to combine.

7. Pour into the prepared casserole, set in a shallow roasting pan, and add enough hot water to come halfway up the sides of the casserole.

8. Bake uncovered on the middle oven rack until the custard is golden brown, set, and a cake tester inserted in the middle comes out clean, about 1½ hours.

9. Serve straight from the oven. Corn custard is especially good with roast chicken or turkey, fried chicken, roast pork, or baked ham.

Mushrooms Paprika with Parsley and Dill

I used to make this recipe with ordinary white mushrooms, but now that so many different species are available, I like to mix them up. I usually go for cremimis ("baby bellas") and chanterelles or shiitakes, most often equal parts of each. If I can get fresh morels, I'll use them to the exclusion of all others. And if white mushrooms are all that's available, I'll settle for them. This recipe is completely flexible, so choose the mushrooms you like best. When do you serve this? Anytime you've got a big roast—beef, veal, pork, turkey, or chicken.

Note: I usually mince fresh herbs in the processor before I wash them, then I rinse and wring them dry in paper toweling. Chopped dill is so small, however, that no sieve is fine enough to contain it when set under the cold tap. So I wash the parsley and dill, then wring them dry before committing them to the chopping blade.

SERVES 4 TO 6

½ cup lightly packed fresh dill sprigs, rinsed and wrung dry in paper toweling

⅓ cup lightly packed Italian parsley leaves, rinsed and wrung dry in paper toweling

2 pounds mixed, medium mushrooms, stemmed and wiped clean (see headnote)

¼ cup (½ stick) unsalted butter

1 large yellow onion, peeled and halved lengthwise

1½ tablespoons sweet paprika, preferably Hungarian sweet rose paprika

¾ teaspoon salt

¼ teaspoon freshly ground black pepper

¼ teaspoon freshly grated nutmeg

1 cup chicken broth

1 cup sour cream, at room temperature

4 to 6 slices firm-textured white bread, halved diagonally, lightly toasted, and buttered

1. Coarsely chop the dill and parsley together in a food processor fitted with the metal chopping blade using 6 to 8 fairly long pulses. Tip onto paper toweling and reserve. Remove the chopping blade and insert the medium slicing disk.

2. Stand as many mushroom caps on end in the feed tube as will fit, concave sides all facing the same way, then exerting gentle pressure on the pusher, quickly pulse through the slicing disk. Repeat until all mushrooms are sliced.

3. Melt the butter in a large heavy skillet over moderate heat, add the mushrooms, and toss until nicely coated.

4. Now stand the two onion halves on end in the processor feed tube and pulse through the slicing disk just as you did the mushrooms.

5. Mix into the skillet and sauté along with the mushrooms, stirring now and then, until limp and most of the juices have evaporated, about 10 minutes.

6. Blend in the paprika, salt, pepper, and nutmeg and mellow over moderate heat 1 to 2 minutes. Add the broth and cook uncovered until reduced by half—this will take about 15 minutes, perhaps slightly longer.

7. Smooth in the sour cream, dill, and parsley and heat just until steaming, 3 to 5 minutes. Do not boil or the sour cream will curdle.

Taste for salt and pepper and adjust as needed.

8. Ladle over the lightly buttered toast, allowing two triangles per person, and serve as an accompaniment to the main dish.

Note: A friend to whom I gave this recipe says she likes to toss these mushrooms with hot, well-drained fusilli or bowties and call it a meal. Sounds good to me.

Gratin of Prosciutto and Two Mushrooms

Although I group this dish with the vegetables, it's hearty enough to serve as the main course of a light lunch or supper. Because the gratin is brown, accompany it with something colorful—stir-fried broccoli florets, roasted asparagus, or a tartly dressed salad of radicchio and arugula.

SERVES 4 TO 6

⅓ cup lightly packed Italian parsley leaves

2 tablespoons lightly packed fresh tarragon leaves

4 large shallots, peeled and quartered

3 tablespoons unsalted butter

½ pound portabella mushrooms, stems removed and the caps wiped clean and quartered

½ pound medium white mushrooms, stems removed and the caps wiped clean

½ cup half-and-half cream

½ cup heavy cream

3 large egg yolks

½ teaspoon salt

¼ teaspoon freshly ground black pepper

2 ounces thinly sliced prosciutto ham, the slices stacked, halved lengthwise, then restacked and sliced crosswise at ⅛-inch intervals

¼ cup freshly grated Parmesan cheese

1. Preheat the oven to 350°F. Lightly coat a flameproof 6-cup au gratin dish or a 9-inch flameproof glass pie plate with nonstick cooking spray and set aside.

2. Coarsely chop the parsley and tarragon by pulsing 6 to 8 times in a food processor fitted with the metal chopping blade. Tip the chopped herbs into a large fine sieve, then rinse the work bowl and blade directly over the sieve so that all stray bits fall into it. Rinse the herbs well under cool running water, transfer to paper toweling, roll up, and wring dry. Set aside.

3. Dry the processor work bowl and blade and reassemble. Add the shallots and chop fairly fine using two 3-second churnings. If any large pieces remain, pulse them out.

4. Melt 2 tablespoons of the butter in a large heavy skillet over moderate heat, add the shallots, and cook, stirring now and then, until limp and lightly browned, 5 to 6 minutes.

5. Meanwhile, remove the processor chopping blade and insert the medium slicing disk. Stand as many portabella quarters in the wide feed tube as will fit snugly, then ease through the slicing disk with the pusher, pulsing all the while. Repeat with the remaining portabellas, then slice the white mushrooms the same way.

6. When the shallots are lightly browned, drop the remaining 1 tablespoon butter into the skillet and when it melts, add the mushrooms, and cook, stirring often, until very tender, 15 to 20 minutes.

7. Meanwhile, lightly whisk together the two creams, egg yolks, salt, and pepper in a spouted 2-cup measure and set aside.

8. As soon as the mushrooms are tender, add the prosciutto, the reserved herbs, and the cream mixture and cook, stirring often, just until bubbly, 2 to 3 minutes.

9. Transfer to the prepared au gratin dish and scatter the Parmesan evenly on top.

10. Set on the middle oven rack and bake uncovered until bubbly and set like custard, about 25 minutes. If your broiler is separate from the oven, preheat it toward the end of baking.

11. Transfer the gratin to the broiler, setting about 4 inches from the heat, and broil 2 to 3 minutes until tipped with brown.

12. Serve at once as an accompaniment to roast beef, veal, lamb, pork, turkey, or chicken.

Yankee Hashed Onions

The best possible onions to use here are big sweet ones—Spanish onions, for example, Bermudas, Vidalias, Walla Wallas. Before being fed into the food processor, they're simmered gently in a mixture of milk and water, which makes them sweeter still. These onions are good with almost any meat, but I personally like them best with roast pork, turkey, or chicken.

SERVES 6

⅓ cup lightly packed curly parsley leaves

4 large Spanish or other sweet onions, peeled and halved crosswise (see headnote)

¾ cup cold milk

2 cups cold water

1 teaspoon salt

2 tablespoons unsalted butter

¼ teaspoon freshly ground black pepper

¼ teaspoon freshly grated nutmeg

¼ cup half-and-half cream

¼ cup heavy cream

1. Coarsely chop the parsley by pulsing 6 to 8 times in a food processor fitted with the metal chopping blade. Tip into a large fine sieve, then rinse the work bowl and blade directly over the sieve so that all stray bits of parsley fall into it. Rinse the parsley well under cool running water, transfer to paper toweling, roll up, and wring dry. Set aside. Dry the processor work bowl and blade and reassemble.

2. Place the onions, milk, water, and salt in a large heavy saucepan, bring to a simmer over moderate heat, adjust the heat so the mixture barely trembles, cover, and cook until the onions are crisp-tender, about 15 minutes. Drain well.

3. Meanwhile, melt the butter in a large heavy skillet over low heat, then set off the heat.

4. When the onions are crisp-tender, quarter each, then very coarsely chop them one by one in the food processor—two staccato pulses is about all it takes. As you chop each onion, add it to the skillet. If you try to chop all the onions at once, or even half of them, there will be mush at the bottom of the work bowl and big pieces on top. Properly chopped, the onions will be uniformly coarse, about the texture of hash. And the only way to achieve this is to chop them one at a time.

5. Set the skillet of onions over moderate heat, mix in the pepper and nutmeg, and allow to mellow for a minute or two. Add the half-and-half and heavy cream, bring to a gentle simmer, adjust the heat so the mixture bubbles gently, and cook uncovered, stirring occasionally, until the onions are tender and the flavors marry, 10 to 12 minutes. Never let the mixture boil or the cream may curdle. Taste for salt and pepper and adjust as needed.

6. Stir in the reserved chopped parsley, warm a minute or two longer, and serve.

Purée of Potato, Carrots, and Leek

One valuable lesson I've learned while working with the food processor is that you can indeed use it to mash Irish potatoes if—and this is a big if—you mix them fifty-fifty with another vegetable. Carrots, for example. Or celery root. The best potatoes to use for this recipe are Russets or "bakers" because they are less waxy than all-purpose potatoes and make a lovely purée. Have the cream at room temperature so it doesn't cool the hot purée as it's beaten in.

SERVES 4

6 cups water

2 teaspoons salt

1 large baking potato (about ¾ pound), peeled and cut into 2-inch chunks

6 medium carrots (about ¾ pound), trimmed, peeled, and sliced about ½ inch thick

1 medium leek, trimmed, washed well, and sliced about ½ inch thick

¼ teaspoon freshly ground black pepper

4 to 6 tablespoons heavy cream, at room temperature

1. Bring the water and salt to a boil over moderate heat in a large heavy saucepan. Add the potato, carrots, and leek, adjust the heat so the water bubbles gently, cover, and cook until the vegetables are very tender, 18 to 20 minutes.

2. Drain the vegetables well, return the pan to the stove, and shake over moderate heat to drive off excess moisture. This is important if the purée is to be light and fluffy.

3. Transfer the vegetables to a food processor fitted with the metal chopping blade, add the pepper and 4 tablespoons of the cream, and whiz for 5 seconds. Using a plastic spatula, scrape the work bowl, and minding the blade, stir the purée well. Churn for another 5 seconds and again scrape the bowl and stir.

4. If the purée seems thick, add the remaining 2 tablespoons cream, and churn for 5 seconds more. Taste for salt and pepper and adjust as needed.

5. Transfer to a heated vegetable dish and serve with any roast of meat or fowl. This purée is equally delicious with baked ham or fish.

Potato and Celery Root Purée

For me, this is the best of all vegetable purées. Better than mashed potatoes. I had never tasted celery root until I was in my late twenties and living on a shoestring in Paris. My neighborhood bistro prided itself on its potato-celery root purée and I like to think that this one is just as good. Certainly the food processor eliminates the elbow grease that French chef used.

Note: Before making this recipe, read what I have to say about celery root in the note for Celery Rémoulade (page 186). A good way to trim the calories in this recipe is to use evaporated milk, preferably fat-free, in place of heavy cream. Its delicately caramel flavor is the perfect complement for potatoes and celery root.

Tip: Don't throw away the cooking liquid. Freeze it and add it to your next soup.

SERVES 4 TO 6

4 cups water

One 14½- or 15½-ounce can chicken broth or 2 cups rich homemade chicken stock (page 43)

2 teaspoons salt

2 pounds celery root, trimmed, peeled, and cut into 1½-inch cubes (see note)

2 medium-large baking potatoes (about 1¼ pounds), peeled and cut into 1½-inch cubes

½ cup heavy cream or evaporated milk (use fat-free, if you like), at room temperature

1 tablespoon unsalted butter, at room temperature

¼ teaspoon freshly ground black pepper

1. Bring the water, chicken broth, and salt to a boil in a large heavy saucepan over moderate heat. Add the celery root and potatoes, adjust the heat so the water bubbles gently, cover, and cook until the vegetables are very tender, 18 to 20 minutes.

2. Drain the vegetables well, return them in the pan to the stove, and shake over moderate heat to drive off excess moisture. This is important if the purée is to be light and fluffy.

3. Transfer the vegetables to a food processor fitted with the metal chopping blade, add the cream, butter, and pepper and churn for 3 seconds. Using a plastic spatula, scrape the work bowl and minding the blade, stir the purée well, pushing any large chunks of potato to the bottom. Churn for another 3 seconds and again scrape the bowl and stir. Now with two or three 5-second churnings, process until smooth and silky. Taste for salt and pepper and adjust as needed.

4. Transfer to a heated vegetable dish and serve with roast beef, veal, lamb, pork, chicken, or turkey.

Potatoes Dauphinoise

For this recipe, the potatoes should be sliced about ⅛ inch thick, a job the thin-slicing disk does to perfection, but not every processor has one. The regular slicing disk, standard equipment for most machines, cuts them about ¼ inch thick, and that means that this casserole of scalloped potatoes will take longer to bake. It also means that the cream in which they bake is more likely to curdle. To minimize the risk, I've blended in a little flour. I use Idaho or Russet potatoes in my Dauphinoise for two reasons: These "bakers" have nuttier flavor than all-purpose potatoes and their elongated shape makes them better candidates for the processor feed tube. A true French Dauphinoise will specify white pepper, but I frankly prefer the taste of black.

SERVES 6

2 medium whole cloves garlic, peeled

1 teaspoon salt

½ teaspoon freshly ground black pepper

2 cups half-and-half cream or milk

2 tablespoons all-purpose flour

3 large baking potatoes (about 2½ pounds), peeled and cut in long chunks about the height of the food processor feed tube

2 tablespoons unsalted butter, cut into small pieces

3 tablespoons freshly grated Parmesan cheese, optional

1. Preheat the oven to 425°F. Lightly butter a shallow (2-inch-deep), 2-quart casserole or coat with nonstick cooking spray and set aside.

2. Churn the garlic, salt, and pepper 3 to 5 seconds in a food processor fitted with the metal chopping blade. Scrape down the work bowl sides, add the cream and flour, and pulse several times until smooth.

3. Transfer to a small heavy saucepan, set over moderately low heat, and bring to a boil, stirring now and then.

4. Meanwhile, remove the chopping blade from the processor and insert the slicing disk (preferably the thin-slicing disk). There's no need to wash the work bowl. Arrange as many chunks of potato in the feed tube as will fit, and pulse them through the slicing disk. Repeat until all potatoes have been sliced.

5. Spread half the sliced potatoes over the bottom of the prepared casserole, pour half the boiling cream mixture on top, then repeat with the remaining potatoes and cream mixture. Dot evenly with the butter.

6. Bake uncovered on the middle oven rack for 35 to 40 minutes or until the potatoes are nicely crusted with brown and tender—fork one up and taste it. If you want to add the Parmesan, do so 10 minutes before the potatoes are done, making sure to sprinkle it evenly over them.

7. Serve at once with roast beef, veal, pork, or lamb, with roast chicken or turkey, or with baked ham. I sometimes make a meal of these potatoes, accompanying with nothing more than a tartly dressed salad of bitter greens.

Jansson's Temptation

What I've done here is turn my favorite potato recipe upside down so that it can be made almost entirely by food processor. It's a Swedish classic, named some say, for Erik Jansson, a religious zealot who led his disciples to Bishop Hill, Illinois. Homesick and hungering for this crusty casserole of potatoes, onions, and anchovies, Jansson succumbed to temptation, and dove in. The true Swedish recipe calls for dotting layers of potatoes and onions with minced anchovies and bits of butter, then topping them off with milk and cream. I've simplified things by substituting anchovy paste for anchovy fillets, softening the butter, and whizzing them up with the milk and cream in the food processor. It goes without saying that I slice the potatoes and onions in the processor. Swedes don't stint on anchovies when making Jansson's Temptation—two ounces of anchovy paste seems just right to me, but if you want more delicate flavor, use only half the amount called for below. Because of the saltiness of the anchovy paste, this recipe needs no salt.

SERVES 6 TO 8

8 medium all-purpose potatoes (about 3¾ pounds), peeled and halved lengthwise

2 large yellow onions, peeled and halved lengthwise

One 2-ounce tube anchovy paste (see headnote)

3 tablespoons unsalted butter, at room temperature

1 tablespoon all-purpose flour

¼ teaspoon freshly ground black pepper

1 cup heavy cream, at room temperature

1½ cups milk, at room temperature

1. Preheat the oven to 425°F. Lightly coat a shallow 3-quart baking dish with nonstick cooking spray and set aside.

2. Equip the food processor with the slicing disk (the thin slicing disk, if you have one). Stand as many pieces of potato in the feed tube as will fit, then pulse the potatoes through the slicing disk. Repeat until all the potatoes have been sliced. As the work bowl fills, scoop the potatoes onto a large piece of wax paper.

Scoop the last batch onto the wax paper, too, and reserve.

3. Slice the onions just as you did the potatoes, transfer to a second sheet of wax paper, and reserve. Remove the slicing disk from the processor and insert the metal chopping blade.

4. Add the anchovy paste, butter, flour, pepper, and half the cream to the processor and churn 3 to 5 seconds until smooth. Add the remaining cream and the milk and pulse 4 to 5 times to incorporate.

5. Layer one-third of the potatoes in the prepared casserole, spreading evenly, top with one-third of the onions and one-third of the anchovy mixture. Repeat twice. The anchovy mixture should just be visible in the casserole; it should not cover the onions and potatoes.

6. Bake uncovered on the middle oven rack until nicely browned, about 1 hour.

7. Remove from the oven and let stand 10 minutes before serving.

Two Potato Gratin with Bacon and Leeks

I love sweet potatoes but I do not love them sugared. In this savory gratin, they pair superbly with baking potatoes, bacon, and leeks. This gratin is particularly good with roast pork, chicken, or turkey.

SERVES 6

4 thick slices lean, deeply smoky bacon, snipped crosswise at ½-inch intervals

5 small leeks (1¾ to 2 pounds untrimmed), trimmed, washed well, and cut into 1-inch lengths

2 medium whole cloves garlic, peeled

1 tablespoon fresh lemon thyme leaves or 1 teaspoon dried leaf thyme, crumbled

1 teaspoon salt

½ teaspoon freshly grated nutmeg

¼ teaspoon freshly ground black pepper

2 large baking potatoes (about 1½ pounds), peeled and cut in chunks to fit the food processor feed tube

1 large sweet potato (about ½ pound), peeled and cut in chunks to fit the food processor feed tube

2 tablespoons all-purpose flour

One 14½- or 15½-ounce can chicken broth

¼ cup freshly grated Parmesan cheese

1. Preheat the oven to 425°F. Lightly coat a shallow, 2-quart casserole or au gratin dish with nonstick cooking spray and set aside.

2. Cook the bacon in a medium-size heavy skillet over moderately low heat until the drippings render out and only crisp brown bits remain, about 10 minutes. Using a slotted spoon, lift the browned bacon to paper toweling to drain. Pour the drippings from the skillet, then spoon 3 tablespoons of them back in.

3. Churn the leeks, garlic, thyme, salt, nutmeg, and pepper for 3 seconds in a food processor fitted with the metal chopping blade. Scrape down the work bowl, then churn 3 seconds more until finely chopped.

4. Scrape the leek mixture into the skillet, stir well to coat with drippings, then reduce the heat to low, and cook, stirring now and then, until limp and golden, about 10 minutes.

5. Meanwhile, replace the processor chopping blade with the coarse or medium shredding disk (no need to wash the work bowl). Arrange as many chunks of potato in the feed tube as you can for a snug fit (I mix the sweet potatoes and the "bakers'), and pulse through the shredding disk. Repeat until all potatoes have been shredded. Transfer to a large mixing bowl and add the reserved bacon.

6. Blend the flour into the sautéed leek mixture and mellow over moderate heat for 1 minute. Add the chicken broth and cook and stir until the mixture boils, about 3 minutes.

7. Pour over the potato mixture, mix well, then turn into the prepared casserole.

8. Bake uncovered on the middle oven rack for 25 minutes. Scatter the Parmesan evenly on top and bake 10 to 15 minutes longer until bubbly and lightly browned.

9. Let stand 15 minutes before serving—this gives the potatoes time to absorb the juices.

Rösti (Shredded Swiss Potato Pancake)

This giant butter-browned pancake contains three ingredients only—coarsely shredded potatoes, salt, and pepper. In Switzerland, *rösti* is the traditional accompaniment to *émincé de veau* (creamed strips of veal), but I like it just as well with roast beef or veal, grilled steaks or veal chops. It's lovely, too, with roast chicken.

Note: It's important to use waxy potatoes (redskins or California long whites) for *rösti* because they hold together far better than baking or all-purpose potatoes. Also key: using a well-seasoned skillet with sides that slope gently up from the bottom. Even thus, *rösti* can be tricky to turn. To minimize the risk of breakage, carefully loosen the *rösti* around the edges, invert on a dinner plate, then ease back into the skillet, browned-side-up.

SERVES 6

2½ pounds large redskin potatoes, peeled and halved lengthwise (see note)

4 tablespoons (½ stick) unsalted butter

½ teaspoon salt

¼ teaspoon freshly ground black pepper

1. Equip the food processor with the medium shredding disk, stand as many pieces of potato in the feed tube as will fit, then pressing firmly on the pusher, pulse through the shredding disk. Repeat until all the potatoes have been shredded.

2. Melt 3 tablespoons of the butter in a well-seasoned, heavy 10-inch skillet over moderately high heat. When it froths, swirl the skillet gently so that the butter coats the sides.

3. Scoop the shredded potatoes into the skillet, spreading to the edges, then press down hard with a pancake turner to form one giant pancake.

4. Brown for 5 minutes, continuing to press and flatten with the pancake turner. Reduce the heat to moderate, cover the skillet, and cook the *rösti* for 5 minutes. Uncover and cook 5 to 8 minutes more, pressing and flattening, until the surface looks fairly dry.

5. Using a small, thin-blade spatula, carefully loosen the *rösti* all around the edge, slide a pancake turner underneath, then invert on a large flat plate that's been lightly coated with nonstick cooking spray. Easy does it. Scrape up any stuck bits of potato on the skillet bottom and pat onto the pancake.

6. Melt the remaining 1 tablespoon butter in the skillet and when it foams, ease the *rösti* back into the skillet, browned-side-up. Raise the heat to moderately high, sprinkle the *rösti* with the salt and pepper, and cook until the flip side is crusty-brown, about 5 minutes.

7. Slide the *rösti* onto a heated round platter, cut into wedges, and serve.

Garlic Mashed Sweet Potatoes

We all know that the food processor can't mash Irish potatoes—it turns them to glue. On the other hand, it purées sweet potatoes like a dream. That got me to thinking. I dearly adore garlic mashed potatoes and wondered if garlic mashed sweet potatoes wouldn't be just as good. What I discovered while developing this recipe is that baked sweet potatoes and roasted garlic are so rich they don't need gobs of butter. As a result, garlic mashed sweet potatoes are more nutritious and less caloric than garlic mashed Irish potatoes. And I truly think they're wonderful.

SERVES 4 TO 6

3 large sweet potatoes (about 2½ pounds), scrubbed

1 small head garlic (about 2 ounces)

1 tablespoon unsalted butter

1 teaspoon salt

¼ teaspoon freshly ground black pepper

1. Preheat the oven to 400°F.

2. Place the sweet potatoes in an ungreased open roasting pan, prick each with the tines of a kitchen fork, and bake for 30 minutes.

3. Meanwhile, slice the top off the head of garlic, exposing the individual cloves. Double-wrap the garlic in aluminum foil and set aside.

4. When the potatoes have baked 30 minutes, add the foil-wrapped garlic to the pan and continue baking until a fork will pierce the potatoes easily, about 30 minutes more. Remove the pan from the oven, halve the potatoes lengthwise, then turn cut-sides up. Also unwrap the garlic. Allow the potatoes and garlic to cool for 15 minutes.

5. Scoop the sweet potato flesh into a food processor fitted with the metal chopping blade. Holding the head of garlic directly over the work bowl, cut-side-down, squeeze out the roasted garlic, letting it fall on top of the potatoes.

6. Add the butter, salt, and pepper and churn 10 seconds. Scrape the work bowl, then carefully skirting the chopping blade, stir the potato mixture up from the bottom. Repeat the 10-second churning/scraping/stirring sequence twice or until the purée is absolutely smooth.

7. Serve at once as an accompaniment to baked ham, roast beef, lamb, pork, turkey, or chicken.

Crookneck Squash Casserole

Yellow crookneck squash is hands down the best for this old southern classic. It has a nuttier flavor than other summer squash and it's a lot less watery. Track down the freshest, smallest crooknecks you can find for this recipe—baby squash are perfect. And do try to use fresh herbs, too. This casserole takes a while to cook, I'll admit. But only long, slow cooking will caramelize the natural sugars in the squash and this is what gives the dish such heavenly flavor. At least you don't have to baby-sit the recipe—it cooks almost unattended.

SERVES 4 TO 6

1 large yellow onion, peeled and cut into 1-inch cubes

1 tablespoon fresh marjoram leaves or 1 teaspoon dried leaf marjoram, crumbled

2 teaspoons fresh lemon thyme leaves or ½ teaspoon dried leaf thyme, crumbled

¼ cup (½ stick) unsalted butter

2½ pounds baby yellow crookneck squash, scrubbed, trimmed, and cut into 1-inch chunks

1 tablespoon packed light brown sugar

1 teaspoon salt

¼ teaspoon freshly ground black pepper

1. Coarsely chop the onion, marjoram, and thyme in a food processor fitted with the metal chopping blade by pulsing 8 to 10 times.

2. Melt the butter in a large heavy skillet over moderately high heat and when the foam subsides, add the onion mixture and cook, stirring often, until nicely browned, 10 to 12 minutes.

3. Meanwhile, coarsely chop the squash in two to three batches, using 3 to 4 quick pulses for each.

4. When the onion is nicely browned, mix in the squash, brown sugar, salt, and pepper. Reduce the heat to moderately low, cover the squash, and cook until very soft and almost dry, 40 to 45 minutes. As the squash cooks, give it an occasional stir to keep it from sticking to the skillet. If you keep the heat low enough, this shouldn't happen because the squash releases considerable liquid as it cooks. Your aim is to evaporate all liquid.

5. When the squash has cooked 25 to 30 minutes, preheat the oven to 350°F. Also coat a shallow 3-quart casserole with nonstick cooking spray or butter lightly.

6. As soon as the squash is done, turn the skillet mixture into the prepared casserole, set uncovered on the middle oven shelf, and bake until nicely browned on top, 1 to 1¼ hours.

Note: This casserole reheats beautifully, in fact the squash gets even crustier and browner and sweeter. Take the casserole from the refrigerator, set uncovered in a 300°F oven, and bake 25 to 30 minutes.

Celery Rémoulade

With supermarkets now selling pasteurized eggs, it's safe to make this refreshingly tart French recipe—I don't know whether to call it a salad or a vegetable because it can be both. It can also be the first course of an elegant meal. Celery Rémoulade goes particularly well with roast pork, chicken, or turkey, also with grilled or cold poached salmon. The sauce is also superb with boiled or grilled shrimp, grilled tuna or salmon.

Note: Because of its convoluted shape and fibrous skin, there's considerable waste with celery root. For the one pound of peeled and trimmed celery root called for here, you'll need two and a half to three pounds.

Tip: Choose small, firm specimens, not whoppers. The best way to peel celery root is to slice off each end, then stand the root on a cutting board. With a sharp knife, remove the coarse outer layer in strips by cutting from top to bottom, always following the shape of the root. To divide into chunks, halve the celery root lengthwise, place cut-side-down on a chopping board, then cut into chunks about the height and width of the processor feed tube. Easier than it sounds. A mini processor—if its work bowl can hold as much as a quart—is a good choice for the rémoulade because it chops the herbs more evenly and emulsifies the dressing more quickly. The key here is adding the olive oil in the thinnest of streams with the machine running flat-out.

SERVES 6

CELERY ROOT
  1 pound peeled and trimmed celery root, cut in chunks to fit the food processor feed tube (see note and tip)

  2 tablespoons fresh lemon juice

  2 tablespoons tarragon vinegar

  ½ teaspoon salt

RÉMOULADE
  ⅓ cup lightly packed fresh Italian parsley leaves

  ⅓ cup lightly packed fresh tarragon leaves

  ¼ cup Dijon mustard

  3 pasteurized large egg yolks

  ¼ teaspoon freshly ground black pepper

  ⅓ cup boiling water

  3 tablespoons tarragon vinegar

  1 cup olive oil

1. For the celery root: Equip a food processor with the coarse or medium shredding disk. Arrange enough pieces of celery root in the feed tube as needed for a snug fit, then guide down the feed tube with the pusher, pulsing all the while. Repeat until all celery root has been shredded.

2. Transfer to a large nonreactive mixing bowl, add the lemon juice, vinegar, and salt. Toss well, cover, and refrigerate for at least an hour before proceeding.

3. For the rémoulade: Place the parsley and tarragon leaves in a food processor (preferably a mini) fitted with the metal chopping blade, churn for 5 seconds, scrape the work bowl, and pulse once or twice until coarsely chopped.

4. Tip the chopped herbs into a large fine sieve, then rinse the work bowl and blade directly over the sieve so that all stray bits fall into it. Rinse the herbs well under cool running water, transfer to paper toweling, roll up, and wring absolutely dry. Set aside.

5. Dry the processor work bowl and blade and reassemble. Add the mustard, egg yolks, and pepper to the processor and whiz 2 to 3 seconds until smooth.

6. Combine the boiling water and vinegar, then with the motor running, drizzle down the feed tube. The mixture will fluff up like zabaglione. Scrape the work bowl.

7. Again with the motor running, add the olive oil in a stream as fine as thread. If you add it too fast, the rémoulade will not emulsify. You can stop and rest every now and then but keep the machine running. Continue drizzling in the olive oil in the thinnest of streams, and when all of it has been incorporated, churn the sauce for 60 seconds nonstop.

8. Add the reserved chopped parsley and tarragon and pulse quickly to combine.

9. To finish the Celery Rémoulade, pour 2 cups of the sauce over the shredded celery root and toss well. Cover and refrigerate for at least 2 hours. Also cover and refrigerate the remaining sauce (there'll be about ½ cup).

10. Just before serving, toss the celery root well again. If it seems dry, add a little of the remaining sauce and toss once again.

Cucumber Crescents with Yogurt and Mint

There are so many reasons to prepare this cool Middle Eastern salad. I've had it in Istanbul paired with lamb cooked a dozen ways. I've had it in Beirut ladled into pita bread with falafel. And I've had it in Amman in a forty-course mezze. The most suitable cucumbers to use are Kirbys or small pickling cucumbers. They are firmer than everyday cucumbers, they have fewer seeds, they are less likely to have been waxed, and finally, I think they have better flavor. You can also use the long, slender, shrink-wrapped English or hothouse cucumbers. These have even fewer seeds and can be sliced whole, skin and all. I do peel the Kirbys although I sometimes stripe them with a vegetable peeler.

Tip: The fastest way to prep cucumbers is to halve them lengthwise and scoop out the seeds with a teaspoon. For slicing, I use the processor's small inner feed tube, which will exactly accommodate one whole cucumber or two reassembled halves. I also pulse the machine as I push the cucumbers down the feed tube instead of letting it rip because pulsing gives me greater control.

SERVES 4 TO 6

1 cup fresh mint leaves, washed and patted dry on paper toweling

1 cup plain yogurt

1 tablespoon olive oil

½ teaspoon salt

½ teaspoon freshly ground black pepper

6 medium Kirby cucumbers, halved lengthwise, seeded, and cut in lengths to fit the food processor feed tube (see tip)

1. Churn the mint, yogurt, olive oil, salt, and pepper in a food processor fitted with the metal chopping blade for 5 seconds until the mint is fairly finely chopped. Scrape down the work bowl, remove the chopping blade, and insert the thin or medium slicing disk.

2. Place 2 cucumber halves in the small inner feed tube, concave sides facing one another so that you have a "hollow" cucumber. Push the cucumber down the feed tube with the pusher, pulsing all the while and letting the slices fall into the yogurt mixture. Repeat until all cucumbers have been sliced.

3. Transfer to a nonreactive mixing bowl, toss well, cover, and refrigerate for at least 1 hour.

4. Toss well again and serve as an accompaniment to roast lamb, grilled salmon or tuna. Or use in making falafel sandwiches (page 159).

Swedish Cucumbers with Sour Cream and Dill

Prepare as directed but omit the olive oil and substitute sour cream for yogurt. Also substitute ½ cup loosely packed tender young dill sprigs for the 1 cup mint. Delicious with grilled or cold poached salmon.

Down South Marinated Slaw

As long as you're going to make slaw, you might as well make a big batch, especially if it keeps as well as this one. It's sweet-sour (Southerners, believe it or not, would use twice the amount of sugar called for here) and it's the traditional "side" for pork barbecue in North Carolina and elsewhere Down South.

Note: If your processor has a thin-slicing disk, use it to cut the cabbage. When you prep the cabbage for the processor, be sure to remove all of the core so that there are no tough or woody strands in the slaw. Finally, when arranging the columns of slaw in the processor feed tube, lay them flat so that you'll get uniformly thin slices.

SERVES 6 TO 8

DRESSING
1 cup cider vinegar

⅔ cup vegetable oil

½ cup sugar

2 tablespoons spicy brown mustard

1 teaspoon salt

1 teaspoon celery seeds

½ teaspoon freshly ground black pepper

SLAW
1 medium yellow onion, peeled and cut into slim wedges

1 large green bell pepper, cored, seeded, and cut into 1-inch pieces

1 large green cabbage (about 3 pounds), trimmed of coarse outer leaves, quartered, cored, then cut in columns the width of the food processor feed tube

1. For the dressing: Place all ingredients in a food processor fitted with the metal chopping blade and blend by churning 3 to 5 seconds. Empty into a small nonreactive saucepan, set over low heat, and bring slowly to the boil, stirring occasionally.

2. Meanwhile, begin the slaw: Add the onion and green pepper to the processor (no need to wash the bowl or blade) and with three 3-second churnings, chop very fine. Using a plastic spatula and minding the blade, scrape the bowl and stir the mixture between churnings. Empty into a large nonreactive mixing bowl.

3. Remove the chopping blade and insert the slicing disk, preferably the thin-slicing disk. Lay a column of cabbage on its side in the feed tube, top with as many more as will fit, then exerting gentle pressure on the pusher, pulse through the slicing disk. Repeat until all the cabbage has been sliced. Add to the bowl with the onion and green pepper.

4. As soon as the dressing boils, pour over the cabbage mixture and toss well. Cool to room temperature, toss well again, cover, and refrigerate for several hours.

5. Toss the slaw well again just before serving, then dish up with tongs (the cabbage oozes considerable water as it marinates).

Red Slaw with Sauerkraut and Caraway

One summer while spending time on my Aunt Florence's Illinois farm, I went to a community potluck picnic, and among the salads laid out underneath the trees was this unusual coleslaw. The lady who brought it must have had German roots because I've enjoyed similar dishes in Germany. My slaw, reconstructed entirely from memory and updated for the food processor, fills a big bowl—just as well because the longer it sits in the fridge, the better it gets.

Note: When cutting the cabbage to fit the processor feed tube, do so that when the columns are laid in it flat, the slicing disk will cut across the grain producing thin slices. Also use the thin-slicing disk if you have one. Because of the saltiness of the sauerkraut, I've added no salt to my recipe.

SERVES 6 TO 8

1 medium yellow onion, peeled and cut into slim wedges

1 tablespoon vegetable oil

2 cups sauerkraut (preferably fresh), with all liquid

1 tablespoon prepared yellow mustard

1 cup mayonnaise (use light, if you like)

2 tablespoons sugar

2 teaspoons caraway seeds

1 teaspoon celery seeds

½ teaspoon freshly ground black pepper

½ medium red cabbage (about 1½ pounds), trimmed, cored, and cut in columns the width of the food processor feed tube

1 cup sour cream (use light, if you like)

1. Pulse the onion 5 times in a food processor fitted with the metal chopping blade, scrape the work bowl, then pulse 2 to 3 more times until moderately fine chopped.

2. Heat the oil for 1 minute in a large, heavy nonreactive saucepan over moderate heat. Add the onion and sauté, stirring now and then, until limp and golden, 3 to 5 minutes.

3. Add the sauerkraut, mustard, mayonnaise, sugar, caraway and celery seeds, and pepper. Reduce the heat to low and cook, stirring occasionally, just until steam rises from the mixture, 8 to 10 minutes. Do not allow to boil or the mayonnaise may curdle.

4. Meanwhile, remove the chopping blade from the processor and insert the thin or medium slicing disk. Lay a column of red cabbage on its side in the feed tube, top with as many more as will fit, then exerting gentle pressure on the pusher, pulse through the slicing disk. Repeat until all the cabbage is sliced, transferring it to a large nonreactive bowl as the work bowl fills.

5. Blend the sour cream into the sauerkraut mixture, cook and stir 1 to 2 minutes more—again, do not allow to boil—then pour over the sliced cabbage.

6. Mix well and serve with baked ham, grilled or fried chicken. This slaw keeps well in the refrigerator for nearly a week, so it's a great make-ahead.

Sweet and Mild
Red Pepper Salad with Tomatoes

If I had to julienne the bell peppers by hand, I'd make this recipe only once in a blue moon. Fortunately, the food processor trims prep time to nearly nothing. If I find firm-ripe Romas (plum tomatoes) at the farmer's market, I'll substitute them for canned tomatoes in this recipe. I'll use four medium Romas, halve them lengthwise, scoop out the seeds, and halve each half crosswise. Then into the processor they go for a rough chop—a couple of fast pulses is all it takes. Before adding the tomatoes to the salad, I drain them in a large sieve.

SERVES 4

One 14½-ounce can diced tomatoes, drained well

3 tablespoons tomato ketchup

2 tablespoons fresh lemon juice

1 large whole clove garlic, peeled and halved

½ teaspoon salt

½ teaspoon freshly ground black pepper

⅓ cup lightly packed Italian parsley leaves, washed and wrung dry in paper toweling

4 large red bell peppers (about 2 pounds), cored, seeded, and quartered

3 tablespoons olive oil

1. Place the tomatoes, ketchup, and lemon juice in a large nonreactive bowl; set aside.

2. Equip the processor with the metal chopping blade and with the motor running, drop the garlic, salt, and black pepper down the feed tube. Scrape the work bowl, then churn 8 to 10 seconds until the garlic is finely minced.

3. Scrape the work bowl, add the parsley, distributing evenly, and coarsely chop with two 3-second churnings, scraping the work bowl in between. Add to the tomato mixture.

4. Remove the chopping blade and insert the medium slicing disk. Stacking the red pepper pieces on end with convex side against concave side (just as you would stack spoons), fit as many in the feed tube as you can—you need a snug fit. With the quickest of pulses, ease the peppers through the slicing disk. Repeat until all the peppers have been sliced.

5. Heat the olive oil in a large heavy skillet over moderately high heat for 2 minutes, add the sliced peppers, and stir-fry just until crisp-tender, 6 to 8 minutes.

6. Add to the tomato mixture and toss well. Let stand uncovered at room temperature for half an hour. Or, cover with plastic wrap, and refrigerate for several hours. This salad is even better after a stint in the fridge.

7. Serve as an accompaniment to barbecue, roast pork, chicken, or turkey. Good, too, with grilled salmon or tuna steaks.

Sweet and Hot Red Pepper Salad with Tomatoes
Prepare as directed but substitute one well drained 10-ounce can diced tomatoes with green chiles for the 14½-ounce can diced tomatoes.

Panzanella (Italian Bread and Tomato Salad)

This bread and tomato salad, a Tuscan classic, is beloved all over Italy. It's a main dish, a frugal way to recycle stale bread and clean up the garden. For Panzanella, buy a sturdy round loaf of country bread or use Pão (page 213). If the bread is not sufficiently dry, slice it thick, spread the slices on a baking sheet and set in a "keep-warm" oven for about half an hour.

Tip: The easiest way to chiffonade basil is to stack the leaves, roll them into a tight "cigar," and slice at ¼-inch intervals. Or you can simply stack the leaves and snip crosswise with kitchen scissors.

SERVES 6

8 ounces stale, firm Italian, Portuguese, or French bread (see headnote)

3 tablespoons red wine vinegar

3 tablespoons white balsamic vinegar

½ teaspoon salt

¼ teaspoon freshly ground black pepper

2 pounds firm, sun-ripened Roma (Italian plum) tomatoes, halved lengthwise, seeded, and each half halved crosswise

2 Kirby (pickling) cucumbers, peeled, quartered lengthwise, and each quarter trimmed to fit the processor's small inner feed tube

6 large scallions, trimmed and cut in lengths to fit the processor's small inner feed tube (include some green tops)

1 small red onion, peeled and cut in columns to fit the processor's small inner feed tube

⅓ cup olive oil (the fruitiest you can find)

12 large fresh basil leaves, cut into chiffonade (see tip)

1. Tear half the bread into 1½-inch chunks, letting them drop into a food processor fitted with the metal chopping blade. Pulse until the texture of prepared stuffing mix—3 to 4 zaps should do it; the pieces of bread should be fairly large. Empty into a large nonreactive bowl. Repeat with the remaining bread.

2. Drizzle the two vinegars evenly over the bread, sprinkle with salt and pepper, and toss.

3. Place the tomatoes in the processor (in two batches if your work bowl is small), and rough-chop using 8 to 10 staccato pulses. Add to the bread but do not toss.

4. Remove the chopping blade and insert the medium slicing disk. Stand 4 cucumber quarters in the small inner feed tube so they fit together (you're simply reassembling the cucumber), then pulse through the slicing disk. Repeat with the second cucumber.

5. Stand as many pieces of scallion in the inner feed tube as will fit snugly and slice the same way; repeat until all scallions are sliced. Using the same technique, slice the red onion.

6. Add the sliced vegetables to the bread and tomatoes, drizzle the olive oil over all, and toss well. Taste for salt and pepper and adjust.

7. Add the basil, toss once again, and serve on dinner plates. Panzanella keeps well for several hours in the refrigerator—good to know if you want to make it ahead of time.

Quick Breads and Yeast Breads

IT WASN'T UNTIL I'd worked with food processors for some time that I discovered how adept they are at making bread dough.

For most quick breads I use the muffin method of mixing, that is, I combine all the dry ingredients by machine, and as soon as they're emptied into a large shallow mixing bowl, I buzz up the liquids (milk, oil, egg, etc.), and pour them into the well I've made in the dry ingredients.

The final step—combining the dries and wets—I usually do by hand with a big wooden spoon or rubber spatula. But there are exceptions.

With the new generation of food processors, especially top-of-the-line models with hair-trigger pulsing and powerful braking, I find that I can mix scones, biscuits, even muffins entirely by machine. The key is mastering the art of staccato pulses—and remembering that quick-bread batters and doughs should be lumpy. In fact, it's good for a few floury specks to show because they prove you aren't guilty of overmixing, the sure-fire way to toughen any quick bread.

On the whole, yeast breads are even easier to make by food processor, especially if you use a new technique I've developed. It calls for whizzing dry yeast with the other dry ingredients before a drop of liquid is churned in. And it works for a variety of breads.

In one simple yeast bread (Pāo, or Portuguese Farm Bread, page 213), I tried something different. I proofed the yeast in the work bowl. I processor-mixed the dough, processor-kneaded it, even let it rise in the work bowl, then punched it down by pulsing.

In short, I turned the processor into a sort of bread machine, which goes to show that it can trim clean-up as impressively as it does prep time.

PROCESSOR BREAD-MAKING TIPS

Here are the tricks and shortcuts I've learned while developing bread recipes for the food processor. And the problem-solvers that make things go smoothly:

■ To grate citrus zest more quickly and uniformly, process with a little sugar from the recipe—granulated sugar, brown, even confectioners'. The fastest way to remove zest (the colored part of the rind) from a lemon, lime, or orange is to strip it off with a swivel-blade vegetable peeler.

■ To keep nuts from churning to paste when they're to be chopped fine or moderately fine, add a little sugar from the recipe. Even a bit of flour is a good preventive. It usually helps, too, to processor-chop nuts in several small batches instead of in a single big one.

■ For cleanly shredded or sliced cheese, refrigerate several hours before you push it through the shredding or slicing disk. And if the cheese is soft, freeze it.

■ To prevent dried fruits (raisins, currants, blueberries, cranberries, etc.) from gumming up in the processor, freeze them. I never found a successful way to chop dates or candied cherries in the processor. Fortunately, some of these can be bought already diced and ready to use.

■ To keep dry ingredients from spewing out of the processor when you pulse or churn them, lay a piece of plastic food wrap over the top of the bowl before you snap the lid into place. Depending upon your particular brand and model of food processor, you may need to make a slit to expose the locking mechanism.

■ To avoid a stuck processor lid, as often happens when dry ingredients are churned, lightly coat the locking mechanism and work bowl rim with nonstick cooking spray before snapping the lid into place.

■ Use the metal chopping blade for combining dry ingredients, even when making yeast doughs. Longer than the stubby dough blade, the chopping blade mixes dry ingredients more quickly and thoroughly.

■ For most kneading jobs, use the plastic or metal dough blade. It's dull and doesn't slash the strands of gluten that provide the framework of every good loaf.

■ To keep your food processor from "walking" off the counter when you're kneading yeast dough, set it back against the wall and keep an eye on it.

Note: If you're in the market for a new food processor, buy one with a heavily weighted base.

■ If your machine balks while kneading yeast dough, snap it off and let it rest five minutes before proceeding. For big batches or doughs that are unusually heavy, periodically interrupt the kneading and give both the machine and the dough a breather. This way the dough won't overheat and kill the yeast.

■ Always use the freshest yeast you can find, one with an expiration date a year or more down the line. This is especially important for the quick and easy method I've developed for processor yeast breads in which I combine the yeast with the other dry ingredients instead of proofing it in warm water.

Note: Some of my recipes call for yeast by the tablespoon instead of by the envelope and there's good reason for this. Occasionally one envelope of active dry yeast is not enough to leaven a loaf of bread and two envelopes are too much. Yeast is sold by both the jar and the envelope. For the record, one ¼-ounce envelope of active dry yeast equals 2¼ teaspoons.

■ Note that flours vary from one part of the country to another, indeed from season to season, which means that even though you follow a yeast bread recipe to the letter, your dough may be softer or stiffer than that the recipe describes. A good processor yeast dough will be malleable (rather like Play-Doh), not sticky, not crumbly. Watch carefully as you add liquid to the combined dry ingredients. The minute the dough comes together in the ball, the consistency is just right. If the dough seems crumbly after all of the liquid has been incorporated, drizzle a little warm water down the feed tube with the motor running. If, on the other hand, the dough seems sticky, remove the processor lid, sprinkle in about ¼ cup flour, and continue mixing. If the dough still does not form a ball, repeat the process.

■ Be meticulous when measuring salt for yeast breads. In addition to adding flavor, it "brakes" the leavening power of yeast. Too much salt and your loaves won't rise properly. Too little and they will over-rise and coarsen.

■ Always bake yeast loaves until richly—sometimes deeply—brown and hollow-sounding when thumped on the bottom of the loaf. The tendency among inexperienced bakers, I find, is to underbake yeast breads and that means they'll be doughy.

■ Do not slice yeast bread until it has come to room temperature. I'm always tempted to cut the loaf as soon as I pull it from the oven because its yeasty smell is irresistible. But I've learned that hot bread will squish down the minute I slice it. For the same reason, always use a sharp serrated knife and a gentle see-saw motion when slicing fresh-baked yeast bread.

■ For tender quick breads, use refrigerator-cold butter that the processor can chip and distribute evenly throughout the dry ingredients. If a recipe calls for pats, use the wrapper markings as a cutting guide. If the butter is to be diced, here's a quick way to do it: Unwrap the cold stick of butter, halve lengthwise, roll the stick over one-quarter turn, halve lengthwise again, then cut into pats. This, by the way, is the pastry method of mixing, which I find particularly good for biscuits, scones, and certain baking-powder loaves.

■ Always cool quick loaves in their upright pans on a wire rack 10 to 15 minutes before removing from the pan. Turn right-side-up and cool on the wire rack to room temperature before cutting. For neat slices, use a sharp serrated knife and, unless a recipe directs otherwise, space the cuts about ½ inch apart.

■ Choose plain aluminum or other pale metal pans for baking breads, not dark pans, which absorb heat faster, retain it, and thus often overbrown loaves before they are done. This applies to muffin pans and baking sheets, too.

Cheddar Scones

These scones are so quick, and considering the fact that they were mixed by machine, amazingly tender. Choose a well-aged sharp Cheddar to make them, preferably a bright orange one.

MAKES 8 SCONES

6 ounces refrigerator-cold sharp Cheddar cheese, cut in chunks to fit the food processor feed tube

1½ cups sifted all-purpose flour

½ teaspoon baking powder

¼ teaspoon salt

6 tablespoons (¾ stick) refrigerator-cold unsalted butter, cut into pats (use the wrapper markings)

½ cup milk

1. Preheat the oven to 450°F.

2. Equip the food processor with the shredding disk (a coarse shredding disk if your machine has one). Place as many chunks of cheese in the feed tube as will fit, then pulse the machine briskly, pushing the cheese through the shredding disk. Continue until all cheese has been shredded. Remove the shredding disk, tip the cheese onto a piece of wax paper, and reserve.

3. Fit the metal chopping blade in place. Add the flour, baking powder, and salt to the processor and pulse 3 to 4 times to combine.

4. Scatter the butter pats evenly on top and with 8 to 10 fairly long pulses, cut in until the mixture resembles coarse meal. Scrape the work bowl sides well.

5. Scatter the reserved cheese over the dry ingredients and pulse quickly 4 to 5 times to incorporate.

6. Pour the milk evenly over all and pulse briskly 5 to 6 times, just until the dough begins to come together. It will look dry and crumbly.

7. Transfer the dough to a lightly floured surface and knead gently 3 or 4 times, working in all loose bits of dough and cheese. Shape into a ball, then roll into a circle ⅝ inch thick. Using a floured 2¾-inch round cutter (preferably a fluted one), cut into rounds. Reroll the scraps and cut (these scones won't be quite as tender as the "first rolls").

8. Space the scones 1 inch apart on an ungreased baking sheet and bake on the middle oven rack until golden brown and irresistible smelling, about 15 minutes.

9. Serve at once with or without butter. These scones are also good at room temperature and pure heaven when split, lightly buttered, and toasted in a 350°F oven for 6 to 8 minutes—watch closely because these burn easily.

Pumpkin Scones with Toasted Pine Nuts

With pumpkin you expect lots of sugar and spice. Well, these scones are the exception. They contain black pepper only and just two tablespoons of sugar. Overworking this fragile dough will produce tough scones, so the trick is to use frozen butter and pulse it in quickly—the processor reduces the butter to tiny chips, then distributes them evenly in the dry ingredients. The first order of business is to toast the pine nuts. Here's how: Spread the nuts in a 9- or 10-inch pie pan and set uncovered in a preheated 350°F oven for 8 to 10 minutes. Watch closely and stir the nuts well at halftime so they brown evenly—they should be the color of pale caramel.

MAKES 8 SCONES

1 cup lightly toasted pine nuts (see headnote)

2 cups unsifted all-purpose flour

2 tablespoons sugar

1½ teaspoons baking powder

1 teaspoon baking soda

1 teaspoon salt

½ teaspoon freshly ground black pepper

¼ cup (½ stick) frozen unsalted butter, cut into 4 pats and each of these quartered

1 cup packed canned pumpkin (pure unsweetened pumpkin, not pie mix or filling)

¼ cup milk

1 tablespoon heavy cream or half-and-half cream

1. Preheat the oven to 400°F. Lightly coat a baking sheet with nonstick cooking spray and set aside.

2. Coarsely chop the pine nuts with 2 tablespoons of flour by pulsing quickly 4 to 5 times in a food processor fitted with the metal chopping blade.

3. Add the remaining flour, the sugar, baking powder, soda, salt, and pepper and pulse 4 to 5 times to incorporate.

4. Scatter the frozen butter evenly over the flour mixture, then pulse 10 to 12 times until the mixture is the texture of coarse meal.

5. Combine the pumpkin and milk, spoon evenly over the flour mixture, then with a spatula, push down into the flour mixture. Pulse 3 to 4 times—no more or you will toughen the scones.

6. Turn the pumpkin mixture onto a lightly floured surface and with floured hands, knead gently 2 or 3 times to make a soft, sticky dough.

7. Center the dough on the prepared baking sheet and pat into a circle about 9 inches across. Score the top with a sharp knife, marking off 8 wedge-shaped scones of equal size, then glaze by daubing on the cream with a pastry brush.

8. Bake the scones on the middle oven rack for 20 to 25 minutes until lightly browned and hollow-sounding when tapped.

9. Cut at once into wedges and serve hot with plenty of sweet butter.

Angel Biscuits

It took me three tries to come up with a good processor version of the South's favorite biscuit. My biggest challenge was finding a way to machine-mix the dough without destroying the biscuits' tenderness. My solution was to substitute low-gluten cake flour for some of the all-purpose flour. What's unusual about Angel Biscuits—also called Bride's Biscuits or Riz' (as in Risen) Biscuits—is that they contain three different leavenings. Yeast, baking powder, and baking soda make them foolproof enough for brides who don't know their way around a kitchen. But the yeast, I have to say, is more for flavor than for lift. The beauty of this biscuit dough is that it can be refrigerated, scooped out as needed, shaped, and baked.

Note: Because vegetable shortening is so soft, I find that the only way to cut it into the dry ingredients without creaming it is to freeze it. Using the vegetable shortening sold as sticks with handy cutting guides on the wrapper, I slice off ¾ cup, halve the block lengthwise, give it a quarter-turn, halve lengthwise once again, then slice crosswise at half-inch intervals. To keep the cubes of shortening from fusing as they freeze, I spread them on a triple thickness of foil folded to fit my available freezer space, set directly on the freezing surface, and leave for at least three hours.

MAKES ABOUT 3 DOZEN (INCLUDING REROLLS)

1 tablespoon active dry yeast

2 tablespoons plus 1 teaspoon sugar

¼ cup very warm water (110° to 115°F)

4 cups sifted all-purpose flour

1 cup sifted cake flour

1 tablespoon baking powder

1 teaspoon baking soda

2 teaspoons salt

¾ cup vegetable shortening, diced and frozen (see note)

¼ cup (½ stick) refrigerator-cold unsalted butter, diced

1¼ cups cold buttermilk

1. Set the oven rack in the slot just below the middle and preheat the oven to 425°F. Line 3 baking sheets with aluminum foil, placing dull-side up; do not grease the foil.

2. Whisk the yeast with the 1 teaspoon sugar and the water in a spouted 1-cup measure and set in a warm spot until frothy, about 10 minutes.

3. Meanwhile, combine the remaining 2 tablespoons sugar with the two flours, baking powder, soda, and salt by churning 10 seconds in a food processor fitted with the metal chopping blade.

4. Scatter the frozen diced shortening and refrigerator-cold butter evenly on top and with two 5-second churnings, process until the texture of coarse meal. If any large pieces remain, pulse quickly once or twice.

5. Scrape the yeast sponge into the work bowl, pour the buttermilk evenly over all, and churn until a soft dough forms, about 5 seconds.

6. Turn onto a well-floured pastry cloth and with well-floured hands, knead the dough lightly 3 to 5 times. This dough is very soft, very moist, so you'll have to keep flouring the cloth and your hands, adding each time only enough to keep the dough from sticking.

7. With a floured, stockinette-covered rolling pin, roll the dough into a circle ½ inch thick.

8. Using a floured 2¼- to 2½-inch cutter, cut into rounds and space 1 inch apart on the prepared baking sheets (a standard baking sheet will hold 12 biscuits). Gather the scraps, roll, and cut until no dough remains. Cover each pan of biscuits with a clean dry cloth and let stand 15 minutes. Remove the cloths.

9. Bake the biscuits, one sheet at a time, in the lower third of the oven until lightly browned, about 10 minutes.

10. Lift at once to wire racks. I like these biscuits better warm than right out of the oven—warm enough, however, to melt the butter tucked inside when the biscuits are split.

Note: If you do not bake all of the biscuits, shape the remaining dough into a ball, place in a bowl lightly coated with nonstick cooking spray, smooth plastic wrap flat on the surface of the dough, and refrigerate. Stored this way, the dough will keep for as long as five days. A wonderful time-saver because you can scoop up the dough as needed, roll, cut, and bake.

Parmesan Biscuits

Cheddar biscuits are so familiar I thought I'd try something a little different (for those who insist, I include a Cheddar Biscuit variation at the end of this recipe). What I like about Parmesan Biscuits—apart from their delicate cheese flavor—is that the metal chopping blade does it all. No need to use the shredding disk. There's another bonus, too: Parmesan is so finely grated it spreads evenly throughout the dough—no rubbery strands as so often happens with Cheddar biscuits.

MAKES 12 TO 15 (INCLUDING REROLLS)

1½ cups sifted all-purpose flour

¾ cup freshly grated Parmesan cheese (see headnote)

2 teaspoons baking powder

½ teaspoon salt

⅛ teaspoon ground hot red pepper (cayenne)

6 tablespoons (¾ stick) refrigerator-cold unsalted butter, diced

½ cup cold milk

1. Set the oven rack in the slot just below the middle and preheat the oven to 450°F. Line a baking sheet with aluminum foil, placing dull-side up; do not grease the foil.

2. Combine the flour, Parmesan, baking powder, salt, and cayenne by churning 5 seconds in a food processor fitted with the metal chopping blade.

3. Scatter the butter evenly on top and churn 5 seconds. Using a plastic spatula and minding the blade, scrape the work bowl and stir, pushing larger butter lumps to the bottom. Now pulse quickly 2 to 3 times until the texture of coarse meal.

4. Pour the milk evenly over all, and churn just until a stiff dough forms, about 3 seconds.

5. Turn the dough onto a lightly floured pastry cloth and with lightly floured hands, knead quickly 2 to 3 times.

6. With a floured, stockinette-covered rolling pin, roll the dough into a circle ½ inch thick.

7. Using a floured 2¼- to 2½-inch cutter, cut into rounds and space 1 inch apart on the prepared baking sheet. Gather the scraps, roll, and cut until no dough remains.

8. Bake the biscuits in the lower third of the oven until lightly browned, 8 to 10 minutes.

9. Serve hot with plenty of butter.

Cheddar Biscuits

Equip a food processor with the medium shredding disk, then cut 3 ounces sharp Cheddar cheese into columns to fit the processor's small inner feed tube. Using the pusher and pulsing all the while, guide the cheese through the shredding disk. Remove the shredding disk (but not the cheese) and insert the metal chopping blade. Now follow the recipe for Parmesan Biscuits exactly, omitting the Parmesan in Step 2.

Basic Processor Muffins

Muffin has become a euphemism for cupcake; store-bought muffins certainly are as sweet as cake. And they've ballooned out of all proportion. These muffins—together with those that follow—are more like the ones Grandma used to make, that is, they're of normal size and not very sweet. More important, every one of them can be made entirely—or almost entirely—by food processor.

Tip: For muffins of uniform size, drop the batter into the pan with a spring-release ice cream scoop (the No. 24 is perfect for standard muffin pans). Use silver pans, not darkly coated ones, which tend to overbrown muffins.

MAKES 10 TO 12

2 cups sifted all-purpose flour

2 tablespoons sugar

2½ teaspoons baking powder

1 teaspoon salt

1 cup milk

⅓ cup vegetable oil

1 large egg

1. Preheat the oven to 425°F. Lightly coat a 12-muffin pan with nonstick cooking spray and set aside.

2. Combine the flour, sugar, baking powder, and salt by pulsing 3 to 4 times in a food processor fitted with the metal chopping blade.

3. Add the milk, vegetable oil, and egg and pulse very briskly 2 to 3 times. Using a plastic spatula and minding the blade, scrape the work bowl and stir gently. Pulse twice more—just staccato bursts—then lift out the chopping blade, scraping any batter clinging to it back into the work bowl; set the blade aside. Stir once round the work bowl with the spatula.

4. Scoop the batter directly from the work bowl into the prepared muffin pan, filling each cup three-quarters full.

5. Bake on the middle oven rack 18 to 20 minutes until nicely browned.

6. Serve at once with plenty of butter and jam.

Date Muffins

Prepare through Step 2 as directed, empty the combined dry ingredients into a large mixing bowl, add 1 cup diced pitted dates, and toss to dredge. Make a well in the center of the dry ingredients. Combine the milk, oil, and egg by pulsing 3 to 4 times in the processor, pour into the well and stir to form a stiff, lumpy batter—it's okay for a few floury specks to show. Spoon into the muffin pan and bake 18 to 20 minutes. Serve hot. Makes 1 dozen.

Fresh Blueberry Muffins

Prepare Date Muffins as directed but increase the sugar to ¼ cup. Place the combined dry ingredients in the mixing bowl, add 1 cup stemmed, washed, and dried fresh blueberries and toss well to dredge. Combine the milk with ⅓ cup melted unsalted butter and the egg by pulsing 3 to 4 times, pour into the well in the dry ingredients, mix, and bake as directed. Serve hot. Makes 1 dozen.

Orange-Cranberry Muffins

I use dried cranberries in these muffins for two reasons: they're available right around the calendar and they retain their bright ruby color.

Tip: You'll find that dried cranberries chop more cleanly in the food processor if you freeze them (set them in the freezer the night before you plan to make the muffins). Because it's humid where I live, I routinely store dried cranberries in the freezer. This way they stay dry and I can just reach in and scoop out whatever I need.

MAKES 1 DOZEN

¼ cup sugar

½ teaspoon salt

Zest of ½ medium orange, removed in strips with a vegetable peeler

1 cup dried cranberries (see tip)

2 cups sifted all-purpose flour

2½ teaspoons baking powder

½ teaspoon baking soda

½ cup fresh orange juice

½ cup milk

¼ cup vegetable oil

1 large egg

1. Preheat the oven to 425°F. Lightly coat a 12-muffin pan with nonstick cooking spray and set aside.

2. Churn the sugar, salt, and orange zest 15 seconds in a food processor fitted with the metal chopping blade. Using a plastic spatula and taking care to skirt the blade, scrape the work bowl and stir. Churn 15 seconds longer until the zest is finely grated. If large bits remain, quickly pulse them out.

3. Add the dried cranberries and rough-chop using 10 to 12 staccato pulses. There will be a few large pieces and that is perfectly okay.

4. Add the flour, baking powder, and soda and pulse 4 to 5 times to incorporate. Tip into a large mixing bowl and make a well in the center of the dry ingredients.

5. Add the orange juice, milk, oil, and egg to the processor and pulse 3 to 4 times to combine. Pour into the well in the dry ingredients and using a large spoon or rubber spatula, fold in lightly but thoroughly to form a stiff, lumpy batter. There may be a few specks of flour showing but these will vanish as the muffins bake. Resist the temptation to mix them in because you risk toughening the muffins.

6. Scoop the batter into the prepared muffin pan, filling each cup three-quarters full.

7. Bake on the middle oven rack 18 to 20 minutes until the muffins are nicely browned.

8. Serve hot with butter and jam.

Popovers

Popover batter must be vigorously beaten and nothing does this job better than a food processor. Mixing time? Less than 20 seconds. I've learned, however, that popovers will puff more dramatically if you let the batter stand at room temperature for half an hour, then spoon it into a hissing-hot pan (five minutes in the preheating oven will do it).

Note: Next time you make roast beef with Yorkshire Pudding, use this popover batter (see the variation that follows).

MAKES 10 TO 12

2 large eggs

¾ cup milk

¼ cup water

½ teaspoon salt

1 cup sifted all-purpose flour

1. Churn the eggs, milk, water, and salt in a food processor fitted with the metal chopping blade for 3 seconds. Scrape the work bowl.

2. Sprinkle the flour evenly over the egg mixture and churn 10 seconds, scrape the work bowl, and churn 5 seconds longer. Let the batter rest in the covered work bowl ½ hour.

3. Meanwhile, preheat the oven to 450°F Also oil a 12-popover pan or 12-muffin pan well and set aside.

4. Five minutes before you're ready to bake the popovers, set the pan in the 450°F oven. Remove the pan from the oven and ladle in the batter, filling each cup two-thirds full.

5. Set the pan of popovers on the middle oven rack and bake until puffed and richly browned, 25 to 30 minutes.

6. Serve immediately with plenty of "sweet" butter.

Yorkshire Pudding

Prepare the popover batter as directed in Steps 1 and 2. Preheat the oven to 500°F—after you've taken a beef roast (preferably a standing rib) from the oven for its resting period. Spoon ¼ cup of the beef drippings into a 13 × 9 × 2-inch baking pan and set on the middle rack in the 500°F oven for 2 minutes. Churn the batter in the processor just until bubbles appear on the surface, about 5 seconds. Pour into the hot drippings in the pan, return to the oven, and bake uncovered for 10 minutes. Lower the oven temperature to 450°F and continue baking until richly browned and crisp, about 10 minutes more. Cut into large squares and serve with roast beef. Serves 8 to 10.

Buttermilk Corn Bread

I wasn't sure if I could make good corn bread in a food processor, but I thought I'd give it a whirl (no pun intended). What I discovered is that this speed demon whizzes up a corn bread just as good as Mama's. Like hers, this one should be served straight from the oven.

Note: Use this corn bread the next time you want corn bread stuffing for your turkey. If you bake it a day or two ahead of time, it will be plenty dry when you go to crumble it.

SERVES 6 TO 8

1½ cups yellow cornmeal, preferably stone-ground

1 cup sifted all-purpose flour

1 tablespoon sugar

1 tablespoon baking powder

1 teaspoon baking soda

1 teaspoon salt

½ teaspoon freshly ground black pepper

1 cup buttermilk or sour milk

½ cup corn oil

2 large eggs

1. Preheat the oven to 400°F. Lightly coat an 8 × 8 × 2-inch baking pan with nonstick cooking spray and set aside. I use an old-fashioned shiny aluminum pan; dark ones tend to over-brown whatever is baked in them.

2. Combine the cornmeal, flour, sugar, baking powder, soda, salt, and pepper by pulsing 4 to 6 times in a food processor fitted with the metal chopping blade.

3. Quickly whisk together the buttermilk, corn oil, and eggs in a 1-quart measure, pour evenly over the combined dry ingredients, then pulse 3 to 4 times to make a stiff batter. The mixture will be lumpy and there may be a few dry flecks here and there, but that is as it should be. The point is not to overbeat.

4. Scoop the batter into the prepared pan, spreading to the corners, then bake on the middle oven rack until the corn bread is nicely browned and begins to pull from the sides of the pan, 30 to 35 minutes.

5. Cut at once into large squares and serve with plenty of sweet butter.

Parmesan Corn Bread with Fresh Sage
Begin by coarsely chopping 12 fresh large sage leaves in the food processor—three 10-second churnings should do it if you scrape the work bowl and stir between churnings. Add ½ cup freshly grated Parmesan along with all the other dry ingredients called for in Step 2, and proceed as directed. Serve hot.

Parmesan Corn Bread with Olive Oil and Fresh Rosemary
Prepare the previous variation as directed but substitute 1 tablespoon fresh rosemary leaves for sage and olive oil for corn oil. Serve hot. This one reminds me of a bread I once ate in Italy.

Corn Bread with a Ribbon of Monterey Jack, Diced Tomatoes, and Green Chiles

One of the things I've been trying to do as I work with the food processor is to simplify various processor techniques. With this recipe, for example, I wanted to see if I could chop the cheese with the metal chopping blade, eliminating the need for the shredding disk. It worked just fine. I first cut the cheese into half-inch cubes (with only two ounces of Monterey Jack, this goes zip-quick), I spread the cubes on a small square of aluminum foil, and set them on the "floor" of the freezer for half an hour. That brief stint "on ice" firmed the cheese up just enough that the chopping blade didn't buzz it into a spread. I ended up with chopped cheese about the texture of lentils. Exactly what I wanted.

SERVES 6 TO 8

2 ounces Monterey Jack cheese, cut into ½-inch cubes and partially frozen (see headnote)

1½ cups yellow cornmeal, preferably stone-ground

1 cup sifted all-purpose flour

2 tablespoons sugar

1 tablespoon baking powder

1 teaspoon baking soda

1 teaspoon dried leaf oregano

1 teaspoon salt

1 cup buttermilk

½ cup corn oil

2 large eggs

One 10-ounce can diced tomatoes with green chiles, drained and patted dry on paper toweling

1. Preheat the oven to 400°F. Lightly coat an 8 × 8 × 2-inch baking pan with nonstick cooking spray and set aside.

2. Place the partially frozen cheese cubes in a food processor fitted with the metal chopping blade and with two to three 10-second churnings, chop until the texture of lentils. Using a plastic spatula, scrape the work bowl between churnings and stir, pushing the larger pieces to the bottom. Tip the chopped cheese onto a piece of wax paper and reserve.

3. Add the cornmeal, flour, sugar, baking powder, soda, oregano, and salt to the work bowl and pulse 4 to 6 times.

4. Quickly whisk together the buttermilk, corn oil, and eggs in a 1-quart measure, pour evenly over the dry ingredients, then pulse 3 to 4 times to make a stiff batter. The mixture will be lumpy and that's okay—overbeating at this point will toughen the corn bread.

5. Scoop half the batter into the prepared pan, spreading to the corners, sprinkle half the cheese on top, then scatter the diced tomatoes and green chiles evenly over all. Sprinkle with the remaining cheese, then add the remaining batter, smoothing the surface and spreading to the corners.

6. Bake on the middle oven rack until the corn bread is nicely browned and begins to pull from the sides of the pan, 30 to 35 minutes.

7. Cut at once into large squares and serve with plenty of sweet butter.

Jalapeño Corn Bread with Sweet Corn Kernels

Prepare as directed but omit the diced tomatoes with green chiles. In Step 5 after you've spread half the batter in the pan and sprinkled it with half the cheese, scatter 1½ cups thawed and drained frozen whole-kernel corn and one well drained 4½-ounce can diced jalapeño peppers on top (I also pat both dry on paper toweling before adding). Cover with the remaining cheese and batter, then complete the recipe as directed. Serve hot. This corn bread should be eaten up right away because it doesn't keep.

Brethren Cheddar Bread

When I lived in New York, I used to rent a car on weekends and go exploring—Upstate New York, Connecticut, Massachusetts. I loved stumbling upon places and my most serendipitous discovery was Hancock Shaker Village near Stockbridge, Massachusetts (Norman Rockwell's town). The old Shaker commune is now a museum village with red brick buildings of rare architectural purity and a perfect round stone barn. There are cooking demonstrations and Shaker foods for sale. On a visit years ago I tasted this rich cheese bread and I was eager to work up a processor version. Given the Shakers' own ingenious laborsaving devices, I feel certain that they would have embraced the food processor.

Note: Use well-aged Cheddar here—lesser cheeses will ooze oil during baking. Wait until the bread is completely cold before you slice it; if you rush, you'll compact the delicate texture.

MAKES ONE 8½ × 4½ × 3-INCH LOAF

4 ounces refrigerator-cold sharp Cheddar cheese, cut in columns to fit the processor's small inner feed tube (see note)
2 cups sifted all-purpose flour
1 tablespoon sugar
2 teaspoons baking powder
1 teaspoon salt
½ teaspoon dill weed
6 tablespoons (¾ stick) refrigerator-cold butter, diced
1 large egg
1 cup cold milk

1. Preheat the oven to 400°F. Coat an 8½ × 4½ × 3-inch loaf pan well with nonstick cooking spray and set aside.

2. Equip the food processor with the medium shredding disk, then pulse the columns of cheese one by one down the small inner feed tube and through the shredding disk. Remove the shredding disk and insert the metal chopping blade, swiveling it back and forth to whisk the cheese aside, and anchor it firmly.

3. Add the flour, sugar, baking powder, salt, and dill weed and incorporate using 3 staccato pulses. Scatter the bits of butter evenly on top, then pulse 5 times. Scrape the work bowl and stir, pushing larger bits to the bottom. Pulse 5 times more or until the texture of coarse meal.

4. Add the egg and milk and pulse briskly 4 to 5 times. Scrape the work bowl and stir, then pulse 3 to 4 times more just until a soft dough forms. It should be lumpy.

5. Remove the chopping blade and scrape the dough clinging to it back into the work bowl. Stir once round the bowl—no more lest you toughen the bread.

6. Scoop the dough into the prepared pan, spreading to the corners, then bake on the middle oven rack until lightly browned and firm to the touch, 35 to 40 minutes.

7. Cool the bread in the upright pan on a wire rack 15 minutes, carefully loosen around the edge with a thin-blade spatula, and turn out.

8. Cool the bread right-side-up to room temperature, slice about ½ inch thick, and serve.

Irish Soda Bread

I've managed to make this dense loaf altogether in the food processor. I even begin mixing the liquid and dry ingredients right in the work bowl with a stiff long-handled plastic spatula—this avoids overchurning and toughening the dough. But do heed this warning: stir the processor mixture ever so slowly, keeping your fingers far away from the chopping blade. Because Irish soda bread is unusually heavy, it must bake for nearly an hour, otherwise it may be doughy inside. It must also cool completely before you slice it. Use a sharp serrated knife and instead of cutting the loaf into wedges, divide it in half, then slice each half crosswise, spacing the cuts about a half inch apart.

Note: This bread makes wonderful toast. Butter lightly, arrange buttered sides up on a small baking sheet, then set in a preheated 350°F oven just until nicely browned, about 10 minutes.

MAKES ONE 7-INCH ROUND LOAF

2 cups sifted all-purpose flour

2 cups unsifted whole-wheat flour

2 tablespoons sugar

2 teaspoons baking soda

1 teaspoon salt

6 tablespoons (¾ stick) refrigerator-cold unsalted butter, cut into pats (use the wrapper markings)

1 cup dried currants

1¾ cups buttermilk

1. Preheat the oven to 400°F. Coat a 2-quart casserole (one about 7 inches across and 3½ to 4 inches deep) with nonstick spray and set aside.

2. Combine the all-purpose flour, whole-wheat flour, sugar, baking soda, and salt by pulsing 3 to 4 times in a food processor fitted with the metal chopping blade.

3. Scatter the butter pats evenly on top and with 8 to 10 fairly long pulses, cut in until the mixture resembles coarse meal. Add the currants and pulse quickly 4 to 5 times.

4. Pour the buttermilk evenly over all, then with a plastic spatula and keeping your hands out of the processor work bowl, carefully stir the buttermilk into the dry ingredients—2 or 3 times round the bowl should do it.

5. Set the work bowl lid back in place and pulse the dough quickly 4 to 5 times, just until it begins to hold together.

6. Carefully lift out the chopping blade, turn the dough onto a lightly floured surface, and with lightly floured hands, shape into a ball.

7. Place in the prepared casserole and using a floured sharp knife, make a deep cut across the middle of the loaf, then a second deep cut at a right angle to it.

8. Bake 50 to 60 minutes, until the loaf is richly browned and hollow sounding when thumped. A cake tester inserted deep in the center should come out clean.

9. Cool the bread in the upright casserole on a wire rack 15 minutes, loosen around the edge, and turn out on the rack. Turn right-side-up, then cool for at least 2 hours before cutting.

Banana-Walnut Bread with Lemon

Like most fruit-nut breads, this one browns richly, rises impressively, then breaks in the center. Exactly as it should be. The trick here is not to overmix the batter—the liquid and dry ingredients should be folded together ever so gently—and yes, the batter will be lumpy.

MAKES ONE 9 × 5 × 3-INCH LOAF

1½ cups shelled walnuts

2½ cups unsifted all-purpose flour

Zest of 1 medium lemon, removed in strips with a vegetable peeler

¾ cup firmly packed light brown sugar

1½ teaspoons baking powder

1 teaspoon freshly grated nutmeg

½ teaspoon salt

2 large ripe bananas (about 1 pound), peeled and cut into 1-inch chunks

⅔ cup vegetable oil

2 large eggs

1 tablespoon vanilla

1. Preheat the oven to 350°F. Grease and flour a 9 × 5 × 3-inch loaf pan well or coat with non-stick oil-and-flour baking spray and set aside.

2. Pulse the nuts with 2 tablespoons of the flour 6 to 8 times in a food processor fitted with the metal chopping blade until coarsely chopped, then empty into a large mixing bowl.

3. Add the lemon zest and sugar to the processor and churn 30 seconds. Scrape down the work bowl sides and churn 30 seconds longer until the zest is finely grated.

4. Add the remaining flour, the baking powder, nutmeg, and salt and pulse briskly 8 to 10 times to combine. Add to the bowl of nuts, toss well, and make a well in the center.

5. Purée the bananas in the processor by churning 15 seconds. Scrape the work bowl, and with the motor running, add the oil, eggs, and vanilla down the feed tube. Churn 15 to 20 seconds until smooth and fluffy.

6. Pour the banana mixture into the well in the dry ingredients and using a large rubber spatula, gently fold the liquid ingredients into the dry—the batter will be lumpy. No matter if a few specks of white show.

7. Pour the batter into the prepared pan, spreading to the corners. Bake on the middle oven rack until the loaf is springy to the touch and a cake tester, inserted in the center, comes out clean, about 1 hour and 10 minutes.

8. Cool the bread in the upright pan on a wire rack 15 minutes, loosen around the edges with a thin-blade spatula, then turn out on the rack, making sure the loaf is right-side-up. Cool to room temperature, then cut into thin slices and serve.

Note: This bread can be made well ahead of time and frozen. Double-wrap in plastic food wrap, overwrap in aluminum foil, then label, date, and store in a 0°F freezer. Serve within two months.

Butternut Squash–Hazelnut Bread

For this loaf you'll need a 10 × 5 × 4- inch loaf pan—most good kitchen shops carry these. If you don't want to buy this pan (a good size, by the way, for full loaves of bread or cake, even meat-loaves), use a 9 × 5 × 3-inch loaf pan, but fill it only two-thirds with batter. Spoon the remaining batter into crinkly paper cup–lined muffin-pan cups, filling each two-thirds full, fill any empty cups halfway with water. The muffins should be done in 20 to 25 minutes.

Tip: The fastest way to thaw frozen squash is to empty the package into a 2-quart ovenproof glass measuring cup, set uncovered in the microwave oven, and microwave on DEFROST for 8 to 10 minutes, stirring at halftime. The recipe's remaining four ingredients (melted butter, milk, eggs, and vanilla) can be added to the measuring cup, then poured all at once into the food processor. No muss, no fuss.

MAKES ONE 10 × 5 × 4-INCH LOAF

2 cups shelled hazelnuts (about 12 ounces)

2½ cups unsifted all-purpose flour

1½ cups firmly packed light brown sugar

2 teaspoons baking powder

1 teaspoon baking soda

½ teaspoon freshly grated nutmeg

½ teaspoon salt

¼ teaspoon freshly ground black pepper

One 12-ounce package frozen cooked winter squash, thawed but not drained (see tip)

¾ cup (1½ sticks) unsalted butter, melted (no substitute)

½ cup milk or evaporated milk (use fat-free evaporated milk, if you like)

3 extra-large eggs

2 teaspoons vanilla extract

1. Preheat the oven to 350°F. Grease and flour a 10 × 5 × 4-inch loaf pan well or coat with nonstick oil-and-flour baking spray.

2. Spread the hazelnuts on an ungreased jelly roll pan or baking sheet, set uncovered in the oven, and toast for 15 minutes or until golden brown. Cool until easy to handle, then bundle the nuts, about half of the total amount at a time, in a clean dry dish towel and rub briskly to remove the skins. Don't worry about any stubborn bits of skin clinging to the nuts—they will add color and texture to the bread.

3. Pulse the hazelnuts with 2 tablespoons of the flour in a food processor fitted with the metal chopping blade 12 to 15 times until finely chopped and transfer to a large mixing bowl.

4. Add the remaining flour, the brown sugar, baking powder, soda, nutmeg, salt, and pepper to the processor and pulse quickly to combine. Add to the bowl of nuts and toss until well mixed. Make a well in the center of the dry ingredients.

5. Add the squash, melted butter, milk, eggs, and vanilla to the processor and pulse 5 to 6 times, just enough to combine.

6. Pour the squash mixture into the well in the dry ingredients and using a large rubber spatula, fold in gently until all dry ingredients are incorporated—do not beat or stir or you will toughen the bread. The batter will be stiff.

7. Scoop the batter into the prepared pan, spreading to the corners, and bake in the lower third of the oven until the loaf is springy to the touch and a cake tester, inserted in the center, comes out clean, about 1 hour and 15 minutes. The bread will hump a bit in the middle and break, but that is as it should be.

8. Cool the bread in the upright pan on a wire rack 15 minutes, loosen around the edges with a thin-blade spatula, then turn out on the rack, making sure the bread is right-side-up. Cool to room temperature, then cut into half-inch slices and serve.

Note: This bread freezes well. Wrap in a double thickness of plastic food wrap, pressing out all air, then overwrap in aluminum foil. Label and date and store in a 0°F freezer. Serve within three months.

Cinnamon-Oatmeal Loaf
with Dried Cranberries

Dried cranberries, now available nearly everywhere, make better bread than the fresh or frozen because they're chewy, slightly sweet, slightly tart, and never lose their rich ruby color. This loaf is unusually tender, so cool it completely before you slice it. And use a serrated knife.

MAKES ONE 9 × 5 × 3-INCH LOAF

1 cup dried cranberries

2¾ cups sifted all-purpose flour

1 cup firmly packed light brown sugar

2 teaspoons baking powder

1 teaspoon baking soda

1 teaspoon ground cinnamon

¼ teaspoon salt

1 cup old-fashioned rolled oats

1 cup buttermilk

¾ cup vegetable oil

2 large eggs

1 teaspoon vanilla extract

1. Preheat the oven to 350°F. Lightly coat a 9 × 5 × 3-inch loaf pan with nonstick spray and set aside. Place the dried cranberries in a large mixing bowl and set aside also.

2. Churn the flour, brown sugar, baking powder, soda, cinnamon, and salt about 10 seconds in a food processor fitted with the metal chopping blade. Add the rolled oats and pulse 3 to 4 times to combine. Empty all into the bowl with the cranberries and toss well. Make a well in the middle of the dry ingredients.

3. Add the buttermilk, oil, eggs, and vanilla to the processor and pulse 3 to 4 times to combine.

4. Pour into the well in the dry ingredients and, using a rubber spatula, gently fold the liquid ingredients into the dry—the batter will be lumpy. No matter if a few specks of white show. Resist the temptation to continue beating for if you do, your bread will be tough.

5. Scoop the batter into the prepared pan, spreading to the corners. Bake on the middle oven rack until the loaf is springy to the touch and a cake tester, inserted in the center, comes out clean, 55 to 60 minutes.

6. Cool the bread in the upright pan on a wire rack 15 minutes, loosen around the edges with a thin-blade spatula, then turn out on the rack, making sure the loaf is right-side-up. Cool to room temperature, then slice and serve.

Note: This bread freezes well. Double-wrap in plastic food wrap, overwrap in aluminum foil, then label, date, and store in a 0°F freezer. Serve within two months.

Pão (Portuguese Farm Bread)

What I wanted to do here was turn the food processor into a bread machine, that is, to see if I could proof the yeast, mix and knead the dough, even let it rise in the processor. I'm pleased to say that it worked perfectly. I don't recommend this technique for bigger batches of yeast dough, for more complex recipes, and certainly not for wimpy food processors with small work bowls (you need at least an 11-cup capacity). For this simple five-ingredient loaf, however, a big, powerful machine does it all. This "daily bread" of Portugal is both crusty and chewy thanks to the steam ovens in which it's baked (I bake my bread at very high temperature over a shallow pan of water). Because Portuguese flours are milled of hard wheat, I've fortified our softer-wheat all-purpose flour with semolina and find the texture exactly right. This dough is unusually stiff and for that reason I use the metal chopping blade throughout—the stubby dough blade merely spins the dough against the sides of the work bowl. I also use high-speed churning throughout (the ON button) instead of a "dough mode" because it does a better job of developing the gluten (wheat protein) that forms the framework of this bread.

MAKES ONE 8-INCH ROUND LOAF

1 tablespoon active dry yeast

¾ cup unsifted semolina (durum) flour

1 cup very warm water (110° to 115°F)

3 cups sifted unbleached all-purpose flour

1 teaspoon salt

1. Combine the yeast, semolina flour, and water by churning 10 seconds in a large heavy-duty food processor fitted with the metal chopping blade. Scrape down the sides of the work bowl, re-cover, and let stand until foamy, about 15 minutes.

2. With the machine running, add half the all-purpose flour down the feed tube. It's easier if you pour the flour from a spouted measuring cup into a wide-mouth canning funnel inserted in the feed tube or failing that, a stiff piece of paper rolled into a cone (the opening at the bottom should be at least 1 inch across).

3. Using a plastic spatula, scrape the work bowl, and if necessary, redistribute the dough so that it evenly surrounds the blade—take care! Add the salt and remaining flour, distributing evenly over the dough, and churn for 10 seconds. Again scrape the work bowl and redistribute the dough.

4. Churn the dough for 20 seconds nonstop, shut the machine off, and let the dough rest in the sealed work bowl for 5 minutes. Now churn for another 20 seconds.

5. Leaving the blade in place, carefully redistribute the dough until it's of uniform thickness. Re-cover the work bowl, keeping the pusher in. Note the level of the dough, estimate what it should be when doubled in bulk, and mark that level on the side of the work bowl.

6. Let the dough rise in the sealed work bowl until doubled in bulk, about 1 hour. Meanwhile, lightly coat an 8-inch springform pan or 8-inch pie pan lightly with nonstick cooking spray and set aside.

7. When the dough has fully doubled, pulse quickly 4 to 5 times to punch down, then churn for 20 seconds nonstop. Let the dough rest in the sealed work bowl for 5 minutes, then churn for another 20 seconds. The dough will roll into a ball and leave the sides of the work bowl reasonably clean.

8. Turn the dough onto a lightly floured surface, shape into a ball, then roll in the flour to dust lightly. Place the loaf in the prepared pan, cover with a clean, dry dish towel, and set in a warm, dry spot until nearly doubled in bulk— this will take about 30 minutes.

9. When the dough has risen for 10 minutes, position one rack in the middle of the oven and slide a second rack in the slot just below. Place a large shallow baking pan on the lower rack—I use a 15½ × 10½ × 1-inch jelly roll pan—and half-fill with water. Preheat the oven to 500°F.

10. Center the risen loaf on the middle rack and bake for 15 minutes. Reduce the oven temperature to 400°F and continue baking until richly browned and hollow sounding when thumped, 20 to 25 minutes longer.

11. Remove the bread from the pan as soon as it comes from the oven, set right-side-up on a wire rack, and cool to room temperature before cutting.

Cornell Bread

As white breads go, this one's the best: best in flavor, best in texture, and far and away the best in nutritive value. It's a high-protein loaf developed in the late 1940s by Dr. Clive McCay of Cornell University (hence the recipe's name) at the request of New York Governor Thomas E. Dewey. The reason? Patients in the state's mental institutions were malnourished because they were eating mostly high-carbohydrate white bread. McCay's solution was to boost the protein, vitamins, and minerals in white bread by adding soy powder, nonfat dry milk solids, and wheat germ. Choose a sunny day for making this bread. In damp weather, some of the ingredients may absorb atmospheric moisture and you'll have to add more flour, which puts a strain on the food processor. It's a good idea, as a matter of fact, to stop the machine after it's kneaded this heavy dough for twenty seconds. Open the work bowl and feel the dough. If it seems overly warm, let the machine rest for five minutes, then knead for another twenty seconds.

MAKES ONE 10 × 5 × 4-INCH LOAF

1½ cups water

½ cup milk

1 tablespoon active dry yeast

3 tablespoons sugar

6 tablespoons soy flour or soy powder

6 tablespoons nonfat dry milk powder

2 tablespoons wheat germ

5 to 6 cups sifted all-purpose flour
(see headnote)

2 teaspoons salt

4 tablespoons (½ stick) refrigerator-cold unsalted butter, cut into small dice

1. Heat the water and milk in a small heavy saucepan over moderately low heat until an instant-read thermometer registers 120°F.

2. Meanwhile, combine the yeast, sugar, soy flour, dry milk powder, wheat germ, 2 cups of the flour, and the salt by churning 10 seconds in a heavy-duty food processor fitted with the metal chopping blade.

3. Add the butter, distributing evenly, then with a plastic spatula, push the butter down into the dry ingredients. Churn 10 seconds, then scrape down the work bowl with the spatula making sure to loosen any solid bits at the bottom of the bowl—mind the blade. Churn 10 seconds longer or until the texture of coarse meal.

4. Add another 3 cups flour and churn 10 seconds to combine. Remove the chopping blade, scrape the work bowl, and insert the dough blade, pushing it down as far as it will go.

5. With the machine running, pour half the warm water mixture down the feed tube—but no faster than the dry ingredients can absorb it. Scrape the work bowl, again loosening any solid clumps at the bottom. Add the remaining warm water mixture the same way and churn until the dough rolls into a ball. Once again, scrape down the work bowl. If the dough is too sticky to form a ball, add another ½ cup flour and churn 5 seconds. If that doesn't bring the dough together, add the final ½ cup flour and churn until a ball forms and rides up on the central spindle.

6. Set the machine in the "dough mode" and knead the dough by churning for 20 seconds. Open the work bowl, feel the dough, and if it seems hot, give it and the machine a 5-minute rest. Knead for another 20 to 25 seconds in the dough mode—no longer because you risk overheating the dough and killing the yeast.

Note: If your machine has no dough mode, churn just until the dough rolls into a ball and leaves the sides of the work bowl relatively clean.

7. Scoop the dough into a large mixing bowl that has been lightly coated with nonstick cooking spray. Shape the dough into a ball, then turn in the bowl so that the coated side is up. Cover with plastic wrap, set in a warm dry spot, and let rise until doubled in bulk. This will take about 1 hour, or perhaps 15 to 20 minutes longer.

8. Punch the dough down and knead 2 to 3 minutes on a lightly floured surface until smooth and elastic. Shape into a loaf and place in a 10 × 5 × 4-inch loaf pan that has been lightly coated with nonstick cooking spray.

9. Cover with plastic wrap and set in a warm dry spot until not quite doubled in bulk. This will take 40 to 45 minutes. Toward the end of rising, preheat the oven to 400°F.

10. Remove the plastic wrap and bake the loaf on the middle oven rack until dark brown and hollow sounding when thumped, about 45 minutes.

11. Remove the loaf from the pan at once, place right-side-up on a wire rack, and cool to room temperature before slicing.

Whole-Wheat Bread

It took me several tries to get this recipe right. The first time around I used too much whole-wheat flour, which has too little gluten to make a good loaf. I next tried melting the butter in the warm milk–molasses mixture and found it difficult to combine the liquid and dry ingredients. But the third time was the charm. This recipe produces a high-rising loaf of unusually good flavor and texture. Properly baked, the crust will be as brown as coffee.

MAKES ONE 10 × 5 × 4-INCH LOAF

1½ cups milk

¼ cup unsulfured molasses

3 cups sifted unbleached all-purpose flour

2 tablespoons raw sugar or light brown sugar

1 tablespoon active dry yeast

2 teaspoons salt

¾ teaspoon ground ginger

½ teaspoon freshly ground black pepper

3 cups unsifted whole-wheat flour

6 tablespoons (¾ stick) refrigerator-cold unsalted butter, cut into pats (use the wrapper markings)

1. Heat the milk and molasses in a small heavy saucepan over moderately low heat until an instant-read thermometer registers 120°F.

2. Meanwhile, churn the all-purpose flour, sugar, yeast, salt, ginger, and pepper in a heavy-duty food processor fitted with the metal chopping blade 10 seconds to combine. Add the whole-wheat flour and churn 10 seconds longer. Scrape down the work bowl.

3. Scatter the butter pats on top, and with a plastic spatula, push the butter down into the dry ingredients. Churn 10 seconds, scrape down the work bowl with the spatula making sure to loosen any solid bits at the bottom of the bowl. Churn 10 seconds longer or until the texture of coarse meal. Remove the chopping blade, scrape down the work bowl, and insert the dough blade.

4. With the machine running, pour half the warm milk mixture down the feed tube—but no faster than the dry ingredients can absorb it. Scrape down the work bowl sides, again loosening any solid clumps at the bottom of the bowl. Add the remaining milk mixture the same way, churning until a soft dough is formed. Once again, scrape down the work bowl.

5. Set the machine in the "dough mode" and knead the dough by churning 40 seconds—any longer and you risk overheating the dough and killing the yeast.
   Note: If your machine has no dough mode, churn just until the dough rolls into a ball and leaves the sides of the work bowl relatively clean.

6. Scoop the dough into a large mixing bowl that has been lightly coated with nonstick cooking spray. Shape the dough into a ball, then turn in the bowl so that the coated side is up. Cover with plastic wrap, set in a warm dry

spot, and let rise until doubled in bulk. This will take about 1 hour and 20 minutes.

7. Punch the dough down and knead 2 to 3 minutes on a lightly floured surface until smooth and elastic. Shape into a loaf and place in a 10 × 5 × 4-inch loaf pan that has been lightly coated with nonstick cooking spray.

8. Cover with plastic wrap and set in a warm dry spot until not quite doubled in bulk. This will take 40 to 45 minutes. Toward the end of rising, preheat the oven to 400°F.

9. Remove the plastic wrap and bake the loaf on the middle oven rack until dark brown and hollow sounding when thumped, about 40 minutes.

10. Remove the loaf from the pan at once, place right-side-up on a wire rack, and cool to room temperature before slicing.

Rosemary and Ricotta Bread

I never thought I'd choose a dried herb over fresh, but I've tried this recipe both ways and I honestly think dried leaf rosemary (not ground) is preferable. Fresh rosemary is so resinous it gives the bread a soapy taste—to my palate, at least. If you want to try fresh rosemary, use one tablespoon of leaves (the smaller the better) and churn them with the sugar, salt, and pepper for about 60 seconds, pausing every 20 seconds and pulsing them briskly three to four times. The rosemary should be fairly finely chopped. This dough is so sticky you can't work it by hand—no problem because the machine does the mixing, kneading, and punching down. I used a new generation food processor, a heavy-duty one ("wimps" won't do) with a "dough mode" to do the kneading. But instead of kneading with the dough blade, I left the chopping blade in place and it worked just fine. For a stiffer dough I would switch blades.

MAKES AN 8- OR 9-INCH ROUND LOAF

One ¼-ounce envelope active dry yeast

⅓ cup warm water (110° to 115°F)

3 tablespoons sugar

1½ teaspoons dried leaf rosemary (see headnote)

1 teaspoon salt

½ teaspoon freshly ground black pepper

1 small yellow onion (about 2 ounces), peeled and quartered

1 cup firmly packed part-skim ricotta cheese, at room temperature

1 large egg, at room temperature

1 tablespoon olive oil

2½ to 2¾ cups sifted all-purpose flour

1. Sprinkle the yeast over the water in the measuring cup, whisk briskly with a fork, then let stand at room temperature for 5 minutes.

2. Meanwhile, pulse the sugar, rosemary, salt, and pepper in a food processor fitted with the metal chopping blade 4 to 5 times until the rosemary is fairly finely chopped. Add the onion and pulse quickly 8 to 10 times until moderately finely chopped. Scrape down the sides of the work bowl.

3. Add the ricotta, egg, and olive oil and pulse 4 to 5 times to combine; scrape down the work bowl sides. Add the yeast mixture and pulse once or twice.

4. Add 2½ cups of the flour and pulse about 5 times. Scrape down the work bowl and if the dough seems too soft (almost runny), add the remaining ¼ cup flour and pulse quickly to incorporate. Now with the machine at the "dough" setting, churn (knead) for 1 minute. Scrape down the work bowl sides.

Note: If your machine has no "dough" setting, churn 30 seconds, scrape down the work bowl, and churn 20 to 30 seconds longer until the dough is very elastic.

5. Leave the dough in the sealed processor until doubled in bulk, 45 minutes to 1 hour.

Meanwhile, coat a straight-sided 2-quart casserole well with nonstick cooking spray and set aside.

6. When the dough has doubled in bulk, punch it down by pulsing the machine quickly 2 to 3 times. Scoop the dough into the prepared casserole, cover with plastic wrap, and set in a warm, dry spot for 30 minutes. Toward the end of rising, preheat the oven to 350°F.

7. Remove the plastic wrap and bake the bread in the lower third of the oven until richly browned and hollow sounding when thumped, about 40 minutes.

8. Cool the bread in the upright casserole on a wire rack for 25 minutes, loosen around the edge with a thin-blade spatula, turn out on the rack, then cool right-side-up to room temperature.

9. Cut into wedges and serve as is or lightly brushed with a richly fruity olive oil.

Ricotta Bread with Fresh Dill

Prepare as directed but substitute 2 tablespoons fresh dill or 1 teaspoon dill weed for the rosemary, pulsing with the sugar, salt, and pepper until coarsely chopped.

Parsley-Parmesan Bread

Prepare as directed but substitute ¼ cup fresh Italian parsley leaves for rosemary, pulsing with the sugar, salt, and pepper until moderately finely chopped. Also add ⅓ cup freshly grated Parmesan cheese along with the ricotta.

Focaccia

I absolutely adore this Italian bread and was delighted to learn how easily it can be made by food processor. But there's a danger: the machine kneads the dough so effortlessly it's easy to overheat and kill the yeast. For most yeast doughs, 45 seconds nonstop is the maximum safe kneading time, so keep an eye on the second hand of your watch or timer. This recipe contains semolina flour or as it's sometimes labeled "pasta flour." Pale yellow in color, it is milled from durum wheat, an exceptionally hard grain used in many Mediterranean breads.

MAKES ONE 15½ × 10½ × 1-INCH LOAF

¾ cup water

6 tablespoons olive oil

2 cups sifted unbleached all-purpose flour

1 cup unsifted semolina (durum) flour

2 tablespoons sugar

1 teaspoon salt

One ¼-ounce envelope active dry yeast

1. Heat the water with 4 tablespoons of the olive oil in a small heavy saucepan over moderately low heat until it registers 120°F on an instant-read thermometer.

2. Meanwhile, pulse the all-purpose flour, semolina, sugar, salt, and yeast in a heavy-duty food processor fitted with the metal chopping blade 4 to 5 times to combine.

3. Remove the chopping blade, scrape the work bowl, and insert the dough blade. With the machine running, pour the warm water mixture down the feed tube—but no faster than the dry ingredients can absorb it. Scrape down the work bowl, then knead the dough by churning 45 seconds in the "dough mode"—no longer.

Note: If your machine has no dough mode, churn just until the dough rolls into a ball and leaves the sides of the work bowl relatively clean.

4. Scoop the dough into a large mixing bowl lightly coated with nonstick cooking spray, shape into a ball, then turn in the bowl so the coated side is up. Cover with plastic wrap and let rise in a warm, dry spot for about 1 hour or until doubled in bulk.

5. Punch the dough down and knead 2 to 3 minutes on a lightly floured surface until smooth and elastic. Shape into a ball, cover with plastic wrap, and let rest 15 minutes. This relaxes the dough so it's easier to roll. Meanwhile, lightly coat a 15½ × 10½ × 1-inch jelly roll pan with nonstick cooking spray.

6. Roll the dough on the lightly floured surface into a rectangle about the size of the pan, then ease into the pan, patting and stretching it into the corners. Cover with plastic wrap, and let rise in a warm, dry spot until not quite doubled in bulk. This will take about 45 minutes. Toward the end of rising, preheat the oven to 425°F.

7. With your fingers, dimple the dough all over, pressing right through to the pan, then brush or drizzle evenly with the remaining 2 tablespoons olive oil.

8. Bake the focaccia on the middle oven rack until golden brown, about 20 minutes.

9. Cut into large squares and serve warm.

Note: The way most New York City restaurants serve focaccia is with extra virgin olive oil, an intensely fruity one, puddled on bread plates for dipping.

Rosemary Focaccia

Prepare as directed, but in Step 2, pulse 1 teaspoon crumbled dried leaf rosemary along with the all-purpose flour, semolina, sugar, salt, and yeast. In Step 7, just before dimpling the dough with your fingers, scatter 1½ tablespoons coarsely chopped fresh rosemary leaves evenly over the focaccia. Then dimple, pressing the rosemary firmly into the dough. Drizzle with the 2 tablespoons olive oil and bake as directed.

Desserts

Puddings, Ice Creams, Pies, Cakes, Cookies, and Frostings

WHEN IT COMES to desserts, the newest generation of food processors can replace the ice cream machine, the blender, electric mixers both hand-held and standing, even—depending upon the brand—the citrus juicer. I am constantly amazed by their versatility, their power and prowess.

Food processors can chop nuts, mince them, or grind them to paste. They can grate citrus zest as coarse or fine as you like. They can churn soft ice creams in seconds. They can buzz up the creamiest frostings you ever saw and purée puddings, cream fillings, and sauces to silk.

They can combine flours, leavenings, and spices (no longer any need to sift them together), they can cut in butter or shortening until the mixture resembles coarse meal, they can whiz liquids until smooth, and if you develop a fast trigger-finger on the pulse button, food processors can combine liquid and dry ingredients without toughening a batter or dough.

When I began developing recipes for this chapter, I wasn't at all sure that I could make decent cakes or cookies in the food processor. I needn't have worried because I soon discovered that if I abandoned traditional techniques and developed new ones, if I upended the order of mixing, working always from dry ingredients to wet, I could make almost any baked goods in the food processor. (Well, not angel food, sponge, or chiffon cakes, but truly, nearly everything else.)

And as you'll see in the pages that follow, that includes pies and tarts, cheesecakes, cobblers, shortbread, and butter cakes not to mention a variety of cookies.

Note: Before beginning any of these recipes, read Processor Bread-Making Tips (page 194) because much of that information also applies here.

Swedish Cream

I first began making this dessert pre-processor (in the early sixties) and what I found particularly tiresome was having to stir the sugar-gelatin-cream mixture nonstop over low heat until no sugar or gelatin granules remained. A matter of 25 to 30 minutes. The food processor, I've learned, can trim cooking time by as much as 20 to 25 minutes because it combines the sugar, gelatin, and cream so completely they're very nearly dissolved before you cook them. Thanks to this new method, Swedish Cream couldn't be easier to make. Top it with whole or sliced fresh berries, or berries plus Ruby Raspberry Sauce (page 271), layering everything in balloon goblets. And do try the rum variation that follows. It's best with sliced fresh peaches, nectarines, or blood oranges.

SERVES 4

⅔ cup sugar

1 envelope plain gelatin

Pinch salt

1¼ cups half-and-half cream

1 cup heavy cream

1 pint sour cream

2 teaspoons vanilla extract

1. Combine the sugar, gelatin, and salt by pulsing 2 to 3 times in a food processor fitted with the metal chopping blade. Pour the half-and-half and heavy cream down the feed tube and pulse 4 to 5 times. Scrape down the work bowl sides and pulse 4 to 5 times more.

2. Transfer the gelatin mixture to a medium-size heavy saucepan and let stand, uncovered, at room temperature for 20 minutes.

3. Meanwhile, add the sour cream and vanilla to the food processor (no need to wash) and churn 5 seconds. Scrape down the work bowl sides, pulse once or twice, and let stand while you proceed with the recipe.

4. Set the gelatin mixture over moderate heat and cook, stirring often, until the sugar and gelatin dissolve completely, about 5 minutes.

5. Remove the food processor lid, pour in the gelatin mixture, lock the lid in place, and pulse 3 to 5 times until creamy-smooth.

6. Pour into a medium-size mixing bowl and rap sharply on the counter several times to expel large air bubbles. Let stand for 10 minutes, then again rap the bowl on the counter.

7. Cover the Swedish Cream with plastic wrap and refrigerate several hours until softly set; better yet, refrigerate overnight.

8. To serve, spoon into goblets and top with fresh berries, sweetened to taste.

Rum Cream

Prepare as directed but substitute ½ cup firmly packed light brown sugar for the ⅔ cup granulated sugar. Omit the vanilla and flavor instead with 1 tablespoon dark rum and 1 to 2 teaspoons rum extract. Chill until softly set. Spoon into dessert goblets and top with sliced fresh peaches, nectarines, or blood oranges that have been sweetened to taste.

Soft Peach-Amaretto "Ice Cream"

I put quotes around "ice cream" because this is really a supremely smooth milk sherbet with the mouth-feel of premium ice cream. Omit the Amaretto, if you like, and flavor instead with almond extract, but the results won't be the same. It's best to serve this frozen dessert as soon as it's made. Leftovers can be refrozen, but don't expect them to be as smooth as freshly made ice cream.

Note: It's important for the evaporated milk to be refrigerator-cold if this ice cream is to whip up properly in the food processor. The reason for using superfine sugar is that it dissolves more quickly and completely than granulated sugar in icy mixtures.

SERVES 6

One 16-ounce package solidly frozen unsweetened sliced peaches

⅓ cup superfine sugar

2 tablespoons solidly frozen orange juice concentrate

2 tablespoons Amaretto or 1 teaspoon almond extract

Pinch freshly grated nutmeg

Pinch salt

One refrigerator-cold 12-ounce can fat-free evaporated milk

1. Place all ingredients except the milk in a heavy-duty food processor fitted with the metal chopping blade and churn 1½ minutes nonstop. Scrape down the work bowl sides.

2. With the motor running, drizzle the evaporated milk down the feed tube and continue churning until the mixture is soft and fluffy, 1½ to 2 minutes more.

3. Spoon at once into dessert goblets and serve.

Frozen Lemongrass-Mango Mousse

Once rarely seen beyond big metropolitan areas, lemongrass is now sold across the country at farmer's markets and specialty food shops. You can even buy it potted (set in a sunny window and water often). When buying cut lemongrass, choose stalks that are moist and fresh.

Tip: The fastest way to dice a mango is to halve the fruit lengthwise, cutting on each side of the big fuzzy pit. Next, lay the mango halves skin-side down on a cutting board and score each half criss-cross fashion, spacing the cuts ½-inch apart and slicing to—but not through—the skin. To free the dice, slide the knife flat along the skin.

SERVES 6 TO 8

10 scallion-size stalks lemongrass (about 1 pound)

½ cup fresh lemon juice

1 envelope plain gelatin

¼ cup light corn syrup

3 large firm-ripe mangoes (about 2¾ pounds), peeled, pitted, and diced (see tip)

⅓ cup superfine sugar

2 ounces light cream cheese (Neufchâtel)

1 cup packed Yogurt Cheese (see page 270)

1. Trim the green tops from the lemongrass, strip the coarse outer sheathing from each stalk, then cut the tender inner stalks into 1-inch chunks. Drop the chunks into a heavy-duty food processor fitted with the metal chopping blade and churn 30 to 40 seconds until finely chopped; set aside.

2. Place the lemon juice in a small nonreactive saucepan, sprinkle the gelatin on top, and let stand 5 minutes. Add the corn syrup and lemongrass and bring to a boil over high heat. Set off the heat and steep for 1 hour. Wipe the food processor bowl and blade clean.

3. Place the diced mangoes in the food processor, sprinkle with the sugar, and let stand while the lemongrass steeps.

4. Strain the lemongrass infusion through a fine sieve directly into the food processor, pressing out as much liquid as possible; discard the solids. Add the cream cheese and yogurt cheese to the processor and purée 60 seconds. Scrape down the work bowl sides and purée 60 seconds longer or until smooth.

5. Pour the mango mixture into an ungreased 9 × 5 × 3-inch loaf pan, set in a 0°F freezer, and freeze until firm, about 5 hours.

6. Break into chunks, scoop into the food processor, and churn 20 to 30 seconds until light and fluffy.

7. Serve at once or pack into a ½-gallon freezer container; label, date, and store in the freezer. Use within 3 to 4 weeks, and soften slightly before serving.

Frozen Lemongrass-Papaya Mousse
Prepare as directed, substituting papayas for mangoes (weight for weight) and ⅓ cup fresh lime juice for the lemon juice.

Soft Raspberry-Lime "Ice Cream"

Here's another of my jiffy processor "ice creams," made this time with frozen unsweetened raspberries (and please note the two variations). You can substitute orange extract for Grand Marnier, just be sure you use pure orange extract, not imitation, which has a fake, flowery flavor.

Note: If the ice cream is to be soft and fluffy, the raspberries must be frozen hard and the evaporated milk refrigerator-cold.

SERVES 4

One 12-ounce package solidly frozen unsweetened raspberries

⅓ cup superfine sugar

¼ cup solidly frozen limeade concentrate

2 tablespoons Grand Marnier or 2 teaspoons orange extract

¾ cup refrigerator-cold fat-free evaporated milk

1. Place all ingredients except the milk in a heavy-duty food processor fitted with the metal chopping blade and churn 1½ minutes nonstop. Scrape down the work bowl sides.

2. With the motor running, drizzle the evaporated milk down the feed tube and continue churning until the mixture is soft and fluffy, 1 to 1½ minutes more.

3. Spoon at once into dessert goblets and serve.

Rasberry-Orange Ice Cream
Prepare as directed, increasing the sugar to ½ cup and substituting 2 tablespoons frozen orange juice concentrate for the limeade concentrate.

Raspberry-Orange Sorbet
Prepare Raspberry-Orange Ice Cream as directed but substitute cranberry juice cocktail or ice water for the evaporated milk.

Mocha Semifreddo

If you serve this straight from the food processor, it will have the texture of softly whipped cream—*semifreddo* (half-frozen), the Italians call it. For firmer texture, freeze for several hours, beating often with a wooden spoon to break up any ice crystals.

SERVES 6

¼ cup coffee liqueur

1 envelope plain gelatin

1½ cups nonfat dry milk powder

½ cup unsweetened Dutch process cocoa powder

⅓ cup superfine sugar

2 tablespoons instant espresso crystals

1 quart ice cubes

2 tablespoons dark corn syrup

2 teaspoons vanilla extract

1. Pour the coffee liqueur into a heatproof 1-cup measure, sprinkle in the gelatin, and let stand 5 minutes. Set in a small pan containing about 2 inches of simmering water and warm 5 minutes over moderately low heat until the gelatin dissolves completely; remove from the pan and cool 5 minutes.

2. Combine the dry milk powder, cocoa, sugar, and espresso crystals by pulsing 5 to 6 times in a heavy-duty food processor fitted with the metal chopping blade.

3. With the motor running, drop half the ice cubes down the feed tube, one by one at about 5-second intervals, covering the feed tube after each addition to keep the cocoa mixture from flying out. When the ice cubes are incorporated, pulse in the corn syrup, vanilla, and cooled gelatin mixture.

4. With the motor running, add the remaining ice cubes the same way, then churn for 4 to 5 minutes until the consistency of softly whipped cream. During the long churning, pulse the mixture occasionally to shatter the ice chunks.

5. Spoon into stemmed balloon goblets and serve at once. Or scoop into an ungreased 9 × 5 × 3-inch loaf pan and set in a 0°F freezer for 3 to 4 hours until softly frozen, beating every hour with a wooden spoon to keep the mixture from becoming crystalline.

6. Serve at once or pack into a 6-cup freezer container; label, date, and store in the freezer. Use within 3 to 4 weeks, and soften slightly before serving.

Lemon Chess Pie

I had barely gotten my first food processor when I began whipping up this old Southern classic for fund-raisers in my Gramercy Park neighborhood in New York City. Thanks to the processor, I could turn the pies out twice as fast and raise twice as much for community good works. Where did the name "chess" originate? It may be a corruption of the English lemon "cheese," or maybe of the word "chest" because these were "chest" pies so rich they required no refrigeration.

SERVES 6 TO 8

1 recipe Processor Pastry for Tarts and Pies (page 72), prepared as directed

1 large egg white, whisked until frothy

1½ cups sugar

2 tablespoons flour

Zest of 2 lemons, removed in strips with a vegetable peeler

¼ teaspoon salt

Juice of 2 lemons

5 large eggs

6 tablespoons unsalted butter, melted

1. Preheat the oven to 325°F.

2. Roll the pastry on a well-floured pastry cloth with a stockinette-covered rolling pin into a circle 12 inches across. Ease into a 9-inch pie pan, pressing over the bottom and up the sides. Trim the pastry so it overhangs the pan 1 inch all around, then roll under onto the rim, and crimp. Slide the pan onto a baking sheet, brush the pastry with the egg white, and set aside.

3. Churn the sugar, flour, lemon zest, and salt in a food processor fitted with the metal chopping blade for 15 seconds. Using a plastic spatula, scrape the bowl and stir, keeping your fingers well away from the blade. Continue churning in 15-second increments, scraping and stirring after each, until the zest is finely grated.

4. Pulse in the lemon juice and eggs, then with the motor running, drizzle the melted butter down the feed tube.

5. Lift the work bowl off the processor base, remove the lid, then holding your fingers on the top of the hub, rap the bowl lightly against the counter several times to expel large air bubbles. Pour the filling into the pie shell.

6. Bake the pie on the baking sheet on the middle oven rack until the filling puffs and is softly set, 50 to 60 minutes.

7. Transfer at once to a wire rack and cool the pie to room temperature.

8. When serving, cut into slim wedges—this pie is as rich.

Orange Chess Pie
Prepare as directed but substitute the zest of 1 navel orange for the lemon zest.

Lime Chess Pie
Prepare as directed but substitute the zest and juice of 3 large limes for the lemon zest and juice.

Oh-My-God Cheesecake

Why "Oh-My-God?" Because that's what people always say when they first taste this cheesecake. I've had the recipe for years but have reworked it completely for the food processor. The beauty of it is that the crust, filling, and topping can all be whizzed up by machine and there's no need to wash any processor parts in between. Do try the variations—I developed them specifically for this book.

Tip: Unwrap the cream cheese while it's cold, then let it come to room temperature. Soft cream cheese sticks to the wrapper and you waste a lot of time scraping it off.

SERVES 10 TO 12

CRUST
Ten 4¾ × 2½-inch graham crackers

¼ cup sugar

¼ teaspoon salt

⅛ teaspoon freshly grated nutmeg

5 tablespoons (½ stick + 1 tablespoon) unsalted butter, melted

FILLING
Two 8-ounce packages cream cheese, at room temperature (use light cream cheese or Neufchâtel, if you like) (see tip)

½ cup sugar

2 teaspoons vanilla extract

2 large eggs

TOPPING
1 cup sour cream

¼ cup sugar

1 teaspoon vanilla extract

1. Preheat the oven to 375°F.

2. For the crust: Crumble the graham crackers into a food processor fitted with the metal chopping blade, add the sugar, salt, and nutmeg and with four to five 5-second churnings, reduce to fine crumbs. With the motor running, drizzle the melted butter down the feed tube. Stop the machine and with a plastic spatula, scrape the work bowl and stir. Pulse 4 to 5 times briskly until the mixture is uniformly crumbly.

3. Scoop the crumb mixture into an ungreased 9-inch springform pan, then pat firmly over the bottom and about halfway up the sides. Scrape the work bowl and blade well, letting any remaining crumbs fall into the crumb crust. Pat firmly into place.

4. For the filling: Reassemble the food processor—no need to wash or rinse anything. Add the cream cheese, sugar, and vanilla and with three 5-seconds churnings, process until smooth, scraping the work bowl and stirring in between. Add the eggs and pulse quickly to combine. Pour the filling into the crust, scraping the work bowl and blade as clean as possible. Smooth the filling and spread to the edges, taking care not to dislodge any crumbs.

5. Set the springform pan on a baking sheet, slide onto the middle oven rack, and bake the cheesecake for 20 to 25 minutes, just until the filling quivers slightly when you nudge the pan. Remove from the oven and cool on a wire rack for 15 minutes.

6. Meanwhile, prepare the topping: First raise the oven temperature to 475°F. Place all topping ingredients in the food processor (still no need to wash the bowl or blade) and churn for 5 seconds. Scrape the work bowl and stir, then pulse quickly 3 to 4 times. Let the topping remain in the work bowl while the cheesecake cools.

7. Quickly pulse the topping and pour over the cheesecake, carefully smoothing and spreading, again taking care not to dislodge any crumbs—an offset spatula is the best tool for this.

8. Return the cheesecake, still on the baking sheet, to the oven and bake uncovered for 10 minutes exactly.

9. Remove the cheesecake from the oven and from the baking sheet, and cool to room temperature in the upright pan on a wire rack. Cover with foil and refrigerate overnight.

10. To serve, remove the springform pan sides, then cut the cheesecake into slim wedges.

Caramel Cheesecake

Prepare as directed but in the filling, substitute ½ cup firmly packed dark brown sugar for granulated sugar.

Chocolate Cheesecake

Prepare as directed but in the filling, substitute ½ cup firmly packed light or dark brown sugar for granulated sugar, add ¼ cup unsweetened cocoa powder (I favor Dutch process cocoa) and, if you like, add 1 teaspoon instant espresso crystals. The espresso isn't necessary but it does deepen the flavor of the chocolate.

Note: If you want to go whole-hog-chocolate, substitute the Chocolate Crumb Crust (page 74) for the crust here.

Toasted Hazelnut Tart

If you're planning an elegant dinner, this is the dessert to impress guests. The idea for it came to me while I was eating pecan pie. As fond as I am of pecans, I'm even fonder of hazelnuts, so I began thinking, why not . . . ? Creating this hazelnut tart wasn't quite as simple as substituting hazelnuts for pecans. But almost.

SERVES 10 TO 12

1 recipe Processor Pastry for Tarts and Pies (page 72), prepared as directed

1 large egg white, whisked until frothy

1½ cups shelled hazelnuts (about 8 ounces)

½ cup (1 stick) unsalted butter

¾ cup firmly packed light brown sugar

¾ cup light corn syrup

¼ cup heavy cream, half-and-half, or milk

1 tablespoon vanilla extract

¼ teaspoon salt

3 extra-large eggs

1. Preheat the oven to 350°F.

2. Roll the pastry on a well-floured pastry cloth with a stockinette-covered rolling pin into a circle 13 inches across. Lop the pastry over the rolling pin and ease into a 10½-inch tart tin with a removable bottom. Press the pastry against the bottom of the tin and up the sides, then roll the rolling pin across the rim, cutting off the overhang. Place the tart tin on a heavy baking sheet and brush the bottom and sides of the pastry shell with the beaten egg white. Allow to air-dry while you prepare the filling.

3. Spread the hazelnuts in an ungreased 15½ × 10½ × 1-inch jelly roll pan, set uncovered in the oven, and toast until richly browned, 15 to 20 minutes.

4. Meanwhile, melt the butter in a small heavy saucepan over lowest heat, then allow to turn the color of topaz. This will take about 15 minutes but watch closely. Set off the heat.

5. When the nuts are done, cool until easy to handle, bundle in a clean dry dish towel, and rub briskly to remove the skins. Don't worry about any stubborn bits of skin—they will add color and texture.

6. Drop the nuts into a food processor fitted with the metal chopping blade and churn for 3 seconds. Tip the nuts into a pie pan, return any whole nuts and large chunks to the processor, and churn 3 seconds more. Repeat this sorting and churning until all hazelnuts are coarsely chopped. Some will be quite fine and that's okay. Scatter the nuts evenly over the bottom of the tart shell.

7. Place the sugar, corn syrup, cream, vanilla, and salt in the processor (no need to wash bowl or blade) and churn 5 seconds to combine. Pulse in the eggs, then with the motor running, drizzle the browned butter down the feed tube.

8. Lift the work bowl off the processor base, remove the lid, then holding your fingers on the top of the hub, rap the bowl lightly against the counter several times to expel large air bubbles. Pour the filling evenly over the nuts in the tart shell.

9. Set the tart, still on the baking sheet, on the middle oven rack and bake until the filling puffs and jiggles only slightly when the tin is nudged, 40 to 45 minutes.

10. Transfer at once to a wire rack and cool the tart to room temperature.

11. Cut into slim wedges—this tart is very rich—and serve as is. Or if you like, "cut the richness" with scoops of vanilla ice cream.

Pecan Tart

Prepare as directed but substitute 1 cup pecan halves for the 1½ cups hazelnuts and toast them for 10 minutes only. Do not chop the pecans; simply cool 10 minutes and scatter into the tart shell. In Step 7, reduce the amount of vanilla extract to 1 teaspoon and add 2 tablespoons bourbon along with the other ingredients. Finish the recipe as directed.

Frangipane Tart

Some frangipane tart recipes call for baking strawberries (or raspberries) on top of an almond filling. I prefer to bake the filling, then arrange fresh strawberries on top in a decorative pattern because baking causes the berries to weep and this thins and discolors the filling. My way the berries remain plump and fresh and, thanks to a melted jelly glaze, they glisten.

Note: Be picky about the strawberries you choose for this tart and reject those humongous specimens that look to have been fertilized with steroids. The majority are hollow or pithy inside and many, moreover, are misshapen and flavorless. I look for firm-ripe, farm-fresh berries of moderate size, the kind my father grew in our backyard. Don't make this recipe in wet or humid weather because the berries, crust, and filling will suffer.

SERVES 8

1 recipe Processor Pastry for Tarts and Pies (page 72), prepared as directed

2 cups blanched slivered almonds

¾ cup sugar

¼ teaspoon salt

½ cup (1 stick) unsalted butter, cut into pats (use the wrapper markings), at room temperature

1 teaspoon vanilla extract

½ teaspoon almond extract

¼ cup half-and-half cream

2 large eggs

¼ cup red currant jelly, melted

1 quart strawberries, washed, hulled, sliced ¼ inch thick, and patted dry on paper toweling

1. Preheat the oven to 425°F.

2. Roll the pastry on a well-floured pastry cloth with a stockinette-covered rolling pin into a circle 13 inches across. Lop the pastry over the rolling pin and ease into a 10½-inch tart tin with a removable bottom. Press the pastry against the bottom of the tin and up the sides, then roll the rolling pin across the rim, cutting off the overhang. Prick the crust all over with a fork, smooth a large sheet of heavy-duty aluminum foil over the bottom of the tart shell, then weight by filling with dried beans or rice. Slide the tart tin onto a heavy baking sheet.

3. Bake the tart shell on the middle oven rack until pale tan, about 15 minutes. Remove from the oven, carefully lift out the foil and beans, and cool the tart shell to room temperature. Reduce the oven temperature to 350°F.

4. Meanwhile, place the almonds, sugar, and salt in a food processor fitted with the metal chopping blade and with two 10-second churnings, grind the nuts very fine. Using a plastic spatula and being careful to avoid the blade, scrape the work bowl between churnings and stir, pushing any larger bits of almond to the bottom.

5. Add the butter, vanilla, and almond extract and churn until smooth, about 5 seconds. Add

the half-and-half and eggs and pulse until smooth.

6. Pour the almond mixture into the cooled tart shell (still on the baking sheet), spreading to the edge and smoothing the top. Bake on the middle oven rack just until puffed and lightly browned, about 20 minutes. Remove the tart from the oven and from the baking sheet, set on a wire rack, and cool to room temperature.

7. Brush the filling with some of the melted jelly, then beginning in the center of the tart and working all the way to the rim, arrange the sliced strawberries in concentric rings as artistically as possible. Glaze the berries by brushing with a little more of the melted jelly, but don't overdo it. You only want the berries to glisten.

8. Let the finished tart stand at room temperature for about an hour before cutting.

Note: This tart does not keep well at room temperature. Cover loosely with wax paper (plastic wrap seals in the moisture and makes the tart soggy) and store in the refrigerator.

Apple-Oatmeal-Walnut Crumble

The processor can't peel and core the apples, but it does do everything else. I don't worry about this being a big recipe because it's the kind of homespun dessert people never tire of. Moreover, it keeps for days and doesn't have to be refrigerated.

Tip: I've tried processor-slicing apples several different ways and the most efficient method, it seems to me, is to quarter the apples lengthwise, then core and peel (for me the paring knife works best). I stand the apple quarters on end in the feed tube with the concave sides all facing the same way. My processor feed tube can accommodate four apple quarters in a single row plus a fifth piece just behind. This makes for a snug fit and that's important if the apples are to slice cleanly. What also helps is pulsing the apples down the feed tube instead of running the machine full tilt.

SERVES 8

TOPPING

1 cup shelled walnuts or pecans

⅓ cup unsifted all-purpose flour

½ cup firmly packed light brown sugar

⅛ teaspoon salt

6 tablespoons (¾ stick) unsalted butter, cut into pats and at room temperature

1 cup quick-cooking rolled oats

FILLING

¼ cup firmly packed light brown sugar

¼ cup unsifted all-purpose flour

1 teaspoon ground cinnamon

½ teaspoon ground ginger

½ teaspoon freshly grated nutmeg

Pinch salt

6 large Golden Delicious apples (about 3½ pounds), peeled, cored, and quartered lengthwise

2 tablespoons fresh lemon juice

⅓ cup cold water

1. Preheat the oven to 400°F. Lightly coat a 13 × 9 × 2-inch baking pan with nonstick cooking spray and set aside.

2. For the topping: Place the walnuts and flour in a food processor fitted with the metal chopping blade. Break the brown sugar into small clumps, letting them drop into the work bowl, add the salt, and churn for 5 seconds. Scrape down the work bowl and pulse 5 seconds longer.

3. Scatter the butter pats evenly over all and pulse 8 to 10 times until the texture of coarse meal. Add the oats and pulse 5 to 6 times to incorporate. Tip all onto a piece of wax paper and reserve.

4. For the filling: Combine the sugar, flour, cinnamon, ginger, nutmeg, and salt by pulsing 5 to 6 times in the food processor (no need to wash the blade or bowl). Scrape the spice mixture into a large mixing bowl and set aside.

5. Remove the chopping blade from the processor work bowl and fit the medium slicing disk into place. Stand as many apple quarters in

the feed tube as will fit (see tip), and exerting gentle pressure on the pusher, pulse the apples down the feed tube. Repeat until all apples have been sliced.

6. Add the sliced apples, lemon juice, and water to the mixing bowl and toss well with the spice mixture.

7. Spread the apple mixture over the bottom of the prepared pan, then scatter the topping evenly over all.

8. Bake on the middle oven rack until bubbling and nicely browned, 40 to 45 minutes. Remove from the oven and cool at least 20 minutes before serving.

9. Spoon into dessert bowls and serve as is or add a trickle of cream or a scoop of vanilla, dulce de leche, or butter pecan ice cream. This apple crumble is as good at room temperature as it is warm. In fact, I even like it better that way.

Clafouti with Dark Cherries, Almonds, and Dried Cranberries

According to *Larousse Gastronomique*, clafouti is a "fruit pastry or thick fruit pancake from the Limousin, usually made with black cherries." It's a humble French country dessert that could not be easier to make. I use fresh dark sweet cherries, but their season is so short (late spring to early summer) I sometimes substitute canned dark sweet cherries, draining them as dry as possible. Almonds and cherries are one of those culinary marriages made in heaven, so I've added ground almonds to the batter, and then just before the Clafouti goes into the oven, scattered it with thinly sliced almonds (available in every good supermarket). If you opt for the whipped cream topping, let the food processor do the whipping. But bear these points in mind: Choose regular whipped cream, not ultrapasteurized, chill the cream well, and use the metal chopping blade to do the job. Churn the cream for about 10 seconds, scrape the work bowl, then churn in 5-second increments—watching closely—until the cream thickens and billows. Don't expect stiff peaks.

Note: If you don't have a cherry pitter, the easiest way to pit cherries is to lay several thicknesses of paper toweling on the counter, then gently whack the cherries, a few at a time, with a cutlet bat or rolling pin. The idea is not to mash the cherries, only to expose the pits so they can be lifted out. The paper toweling helps "tame" the spurting juices.

SERVES 6

2 teaspoons unsalted butter, at room temperature (to grease the pan)

CHERRIES
½ pound dark sweet cherries, stemmed and pitted (see note)

2 tablespoons dried cranberries

1 tablespoon Grand Marnier or other orange liqueur

½ teaspoon almond extract

BATTER
½ cup granulated sugar

½ cup blanched slivered almonds

2 tablespoons all-purpose flour

¼ teaspoon salt

⅔ cup heavy cream

2 large eggs

2 large egg yolks

⅓ cup thinly sliced unblanched almonds

TOPPING
2 tablespoons confectioners' (10X) sugar

1 cup heavy cream, softly whipped, optional (see headnote)

1. Preheat the oven to 350°F. Grease a 9-inch pie pan well with the 2 teaspoons butter and set aside.

2. For the cherries: Place the cherries, cranberries, Grand Marnier, and almond extract in a small nonreactive bowl, toss well, and allow to macerate while you prepare the batter.

3. For the batter: Place the granulated sugar, slivered almonds, flour, and salt in a food processor fitted with the metal chopping blade and with three 5-second churnings, grind until uniformly fine. Between churnings, scrape the work bowl with a plastic spatula and, keeping your distance from the blade, stir the mixture, pushing any larger chunks of almond to the bottom.

4. Add the cream, eggs, and egg yolks and churn for 3 seconds. Scrape the bowl, stir, then churn for another 3 seconds or until creamy.

5. Remove the work bowl from the processor base, then holding the blade in place by pressing your thumb on the top of the hub, lightly rap the work bowl on the counter once or twice to expel large air bubbles.

6. Pour half the batter into the prepared pan, toss the cherry mixture well, then scatter evenly over the batter, drizzling the juices over the fruit. Pour in the remaining batter and scatter the sliced almonds evenly on top.

7. Bake on the middle oven shelf until puffed, lightly browned, and set, about 30 minutes. Transfer to a wire rack and cool for 30 minutes.

8. For the topping: Dust the clafouti lightly with the 10X sugar.

9. To serve, cut into wedges and top each portion, if you like, with softly whipped cream.

Peach (or Apricot or Plum) Clafouti

Prepare as directed but substitute 1½ cups diced, peeled, and pitted firm-ripe peaches, apricots, or plums for the cherries. Depending on size, you'll need 2 to 3 peaches and 4 to 5 apricots or plums. It's important that these fruits be firm because if they are soft and juicy, they will water down the batter.

Blueberry Cobbler with Whole-Wheat Topping

My family tells me this is the best cobbler they've ever eaten and can't believe that I made the whole thing in a food processor. I even puréed some of the berries in the processor to help bind the whole berries. Blueberries, by the way, are now believed to be about as nutritionally perfect as a berry can be because in addition to vitamins and minerals, they contain valuable phytochemicals, which some researchers say may help prevent cancer.

Note: Whole-wheat flour contains less gluten than all-purpose flour—this is the wheat protein that can toughen biscuits, cakes, muffins, and other baked goods if overbeaten. For that reason, this cobbler topping remains moist and tender even though the food processor does the mixing.

Tip: A quick way to stem and dry blueberries in a single operation is to line a shallow baking pan with several thicknesses of paper toweling, then to add the washed berries and tilt the pan quickly from side to side so that the berries roll about, drying and stemming themselves.

SERVES 6 TO 8

BERRIES
2 quarts fresh blueberries, washed, stemmed, and patted dry on paper toweling (see tip)

1 cup sugar

One 1-inch cube fresh ginger, peeled and halved

Zest of 1 medium lemon, removed in strips with a vegetable peeler

⅓ cup unsifted cornstarch

½ teaspoon ground cinnamon

TOPPING
1 cup sifted all-purpose flour

½ cup unsifted whole-wheat flour

2 teaspoons baking powder

½ teaspoon salt

½ cup (1 stick) refrigerator-cold unsalted butter, cut into pats (use the wrapper markings)

½ cup milk

1. For the berries: Coat a 3-quart casserole with nonstick cooking spray, then add all but 1 cup of the berries.

2. Place the sugar, ginger, and lemon zest in a food processor fitted with the metal chopping blade and with three 10-seconds churnings, chop the ginger and zest very fine. Stop the machine between churnings, then minding the blade and using a plastic spatula, scrape the work bowl and stir. Add the cornstarch and cinnamon and pulse quickly 5 to 6 times to combine. Add to the casserole of berries.

3. Place the reserved 1 cup blueberries in the processor and churn 10 seconds to purée. Add to the berries, mix well, and let stand at room temperature for ½ hour. Meanwhile, rinse and dry the food processor parts and reassemble.

4. For the topping: Preheat the oven to 400°F. Place the two flours, the baking powder, and salt in the work bowl and combine by pulsing 5

to 6 times. Scatter the butter pats evenly on top and cut in until the texture of coarse meal—this will take three 5-second churnings. Scrape the work bowl and stir the mixture with the spatula between churnings, pushing larger flecks of butter to the bottom. If flecks are still visible after three churnings, pulse quickly 3 to 5 times.

5. Drizzle the milk evenly over the butter-flour mixture and with two 3-second churnings, mix in forming a soft dough. Remove the chopping blade and set aside.

6. Stir the berry mixture well, then using a tablespoon or large rubber spatula, scoop the dough from the work bowl, and drop in clumps on top of the berries.

7. Bake on the middle oven rack until the berries bubble and the topping is tipped with brown, about 30 minutes.

8. Let the cobbler cool on a wire rack for at least half an hour before serving.

9. Serve as is (this is the way I like it), or, if you must, top with whipped cream or vanilla ice cream. Even a trickle of milk is good—and certainly lower in calories than whipped cream or ice cream.

Note: This cobbler keeps well at room temperature for several days.

Old-Fashioned Strawberry Shortcake

This is my mother's recipe, updated for the food processor. Her shortcake was a rich biscuit, not sponge cake. She'd pat the dough into a circle on a baking sheet, then quarter it as soon as it came from the oven. Each quarter was split and buttered, then sandwiched together with crushed strawberries. We grew our own berries—by the acre, it seemed to me because it was my job to separate the runners and do the picking. Backbreaking work, I can tell you.

SERVES 4

BERRIES
3 pints ripe strawberries, washed, hulled, halved, and patted dry on paper toweling

½ cup sugar (preferably superfine)

1 tablespoon fresh lemon or lime juice

SHORTCAKE
1¾ cups sifted all-purpose flour

¼ cup sugar

2 teaspoons baking powder

½ teaspoon salt

6 tablespoons (¾ stick) refrigerator-cold unsalted butter, cut into pats (use the wrapper markings)

½ cup milk whisked with 1 large egg yolk

2 tablespoons unsalted butter, softened

OPTIONAL GARNISHES
1 cup heavy cream, whipped to soft peaks

4 perfect strawberries with the stems still on

4 small sprigs lemon geranium, lemon verbena, or mint

1. Preheat the oven to 450°F.

2. For the berries: Pulse the strawberries, sugar, and lemon juice 5 times in a food processor fitted with the metal chopping blade. Scrape the work bowl and pulse 3 times more until coarsely chopped. Transfer the berries to a nonreactive bowl and set aside. Rinse, dry, and reassemble the food processor.

3. For the shortcake: Churn the flour, sugar, baking powder, and salt in the food processor 5 seconds to combine, then pulse quickly 3 times. Scatter the butter pats evenly on top and churn 5 seconds. Scrape the work bowl, then pulse 4 to 5 times. Again scrape the work bowl and pulse 4 to 5 times until the texture of coarse meal.

4. Pour the milk-egg mixture evenly over all and pulse 4 to 5 times just until the dough comes together. This is a soft, sticky dough. Turn onto an ungreased baking sheet and with well-floured hands, shape the dough into a circle about 7 inches across and ⅝ inch thick.

5. Bake on the middle oven rack until nicely browned, 12 to 15 minutes. Cut the hot shortcake into 4 wedges, quickly split each wedge, and spread the bottom halves with the softened butter, dividing the total amount evenly.

6. Place the buttered wedges on dessert plates, spoon half the berries on top, then set the top halves in place, and cover with the remaining berries. Garnish, if you like, with whipped cream, whole strawberries, and sprigs of lemon geranium.

Chopped Apple–Sour Cream Cake

I frankly think Golden Delicious apples are better cooked than raw because heat somehow develops their flavor. They're a good choice for this recipe because they do not cook down to mush and thus give the cake a bit of texture. This cake is unusually tender and must be cooled to room temperature before it's cut. I don't think it needs frosting, but skim-coat, if you like, with Lemon Glaze (page 276).

MAKES A 13 × 9 × 2-INCH LOAF CAKE

1½ cups shelled walnuts or pecans

3 cups sifted all-purpose flour

1½ teaspoons baking powder

1 teaspoon baking soda

1½ teaspoons ground cinnamon

1 teaspoon freshly grated nutmeg

¼ teaspoon salt

1¼ cups sugar

2 large Golden Delicious apples (about 1½ pounds), peeled, cored, and cut into eighths

1 cup vegetable oil

½ cup sour cream

¼ cup fresh lemon juice

2 large eggs

2 teaspoons vanilla extract

1. Preheat the oven to 350°F. Lightly coat a 13 × 9 × 2-inch baking pan with nonstick oil-and-flour baking spray and set aside.

2. Place the walnuts in a food processor fitted with the metal chopping blade and pulse 8 to 10 times until coarsely chopped. Add ¼ cup of the flour and pulse quickly to combine. Tip into a large mixing bowl.

3. Add the remaining flour to the processor work bowl along with the baking powder, soda, cinnamon, nutmeg, and salt and pulse quickly 4 to 5 times to combine. Add the sugar and churn 3 to 4 seconds. Add to the mixing bowl, toss well with the dredged walnuts, then make a well in the center of the dry ingredients.

4. Add the apples to the food processor, churn 3 seconds, then scrape down the work bowl. Repeat twice until the apples are moderately finely chopped. Add the oil, sour cream, lemon juice, eggs, and vanilla and pulse quickly to combine.

5. Scoop into the well in the dry ingredients and mix gently but thoroughly with a wooden spoon, reaching again and again to the bottom of the bowl until no dry specks show. Do not beat the batter because you will toughen the cake.

6. Scrape the batter into the prepared pan, spreading to the corners, and bake on the middle oven rack until springy to the touch and a cake tester inserted in the middle of the loaf comes out clean, about 35 minutes.

7. Remove the cake from the oven, set right-side-up on a wire rack, and cool to room temperature.

8. Cut into bars and serve.

Big-As-Texas Chocolate Cake
with Pecan-Fudge Frosting

What I've done here is turn the classic Texas Sheet Cake upside down so that it can be made in a food processor. And I have to say that despite the machine's ferocious churning, this cake is amazingly tender. Frost it the instant it comes from the oven (the frosting is buzzed up by processor, too).

Note: I always measure all ingredients before I begin this cake so that there's no stop/start. All dry ingredients go into a spouted 2-quart measure (the easier to add them to the processor work bowl) and all liquids into a 1-quart liquid measure.

MAKES A 15½ × 10½ × 1-INCH SHEET CAKE

CAKE

2 cups sifted all-purpose flour

1¾ cups granulated sugar

⅓ cup unsweetened cocoa powder

1 teaspoon baking soda

¼ teaspoon salt

½ pound (2 sticks) refrigerator-cold unsalted butter, cut into pats (use the wrapper markings)

¾ cup buttermilk

¾ cup water

2 large eggs

2 teaspoons vanilla extract

FROSTING

1 cup pecan halves

¼ pound (1 stick) unsalted butter, cut into pats and brought to room temperature

¼ cup unsweetened cocoa powder

⅓ cup heavy cream, half-and-half, or milk

1 pound confectioners' (10X) sugar

2 teaspoons vanilla extract

1. For the cake: Preheat the oven to 400°F. Coat a 15½ × 10½ × 1-inch jelly roll pan well with nonstick spray and set aside.

2. Place the flour, sugar, cocoa, baking soda, and salt in a food processor fitted with the metal chopping blade and pulse 5 to 6 times to combine.

3. Scatter the butter pats evenly on top and pulse quickly 10 times. Scrape down the work bowl, then repeat the pulsing and scraping three more times until the mixture is as fine as cornmeal. Transfer all to a large mixing bowl and make a well in the middle.

4. Add the buttermilk, water, eggs, and vanilla to the processor and pulse 4 to 5 times to combine.

5. Pour into the well in the dry ingredients and mix gently but thoroughly with a wooden spoon, reaching again and again to the bottom of the bowl until no dry specks show. Do not beat the batter—you will toughen the cake.

6. Pour the batter into the prepared pan, spreading to the corners, and bake until springy to the touch and a cake tester inserted in the middle of the cake comes out clean, about 20 minutes. Meanwhile, wash and dry the processor bowl and blade.

7. About 10 minutes before the cake is done, begin the frosting: Pulse the pecans in a food processor fitted with the metal chopping blade 8 to 10 times until coarsely chopped. Tip onto a piece of wax paper and set aside.

8. Place the butter, cocoa, and cream in a small heavy saucepan and bring quickly to a boil. Meanwhile, place the confectioners' sugar and vanilla in the food processor (no need to wash the bowl or blade).

9. Pour the boiling cocoa mixture evenly over the sugar in the food processor and pulse quickly once or twice to combine. Scrape down the work bowl sides, then churn the frosting until creamy, about 5 seconds. Add the reserved pecans and pulse 2 to 3 times to incorporate.

10. Remove the cake from the oven, set right-side-up on a wire rack, and frost at once.

11. Cool to room temperature, cut into 24 bars of equal size, and serve.

Mexican Chocolate Cake

Prepare as directed, adding 1 teaspoon ground cinnamon to the cake's dry ingredients. Omit the pecans from the frosting and add ½ teaspoon ground cinnamon.

Mocha Cake with Chocolate-Hazelnut Frosting

Prepare as directed, adding 1 tablespoon instant espresso crystals to the cake's dry ingredients. In the frosting, omit the pecans and substitute 1 cup coarsely ground toasted hazelnuts (see page 210 for directions on how to toast hazelnuts). Also add 2 teaspoons instant espresso crystals along with the confectioners' sugar and vanilla.

Pecan-Zucchini Cake

For rich cakes, I prefer light-colored aluminum pans because there's less chance of overbrowning. This recipe makes a full loaf, a bit too full for a 9 × 5 × 3-inch loaf pan, so I use a 10 × 5 × 4-inch pan, a handy size to have on hand and one that's available in every good kitchen shop. If you don't have this pan and don't want to buy one, use the 9 × 5 × 3, adding only enough batter to fill two-thirds of the pan. Spoon the remaining batter into crinkly paper cup-lined muffin-pan cups, filling each two-thirds full; half-fill any empty cups with water. The cupcakes should be done in 20 to 25 minutes. This cake is so moist, so rich, it needs no frosting.

MAKES ONE 10 × 5 × 4-INCH LOAF

3 cups shelled pecans (10 to 12 ounces)

1 cup granulated sugar

½ cup packed light brown sugar

Zest of 1 large lemon, removed in strips with a vegetable peeler

2½ cups unsifted all-purpose flour

2 teaspoons baking powder

1 teaspoon baking soda

1½ teaspoons ground cinnamon

1 teaspoon ground ginger

1 teaspoon freshly grated nutmeg

½ teaspoon salt

¼ teaspoon freshly ground black pepper

3 medium tender young zucchini (about 1½ pounds), trimmed but not peeled, halved lengthwise, and each half cut into 1-inch chunks

⅔ cup vegetable oil

3 extra-large eggs

1 tablespoon vanilla extract

1 tablespoon orange extract

1. Preheat the oven to 350°F. Grease and flour a 10 × 5 × 4-inch loaf pan well or coat with nonstick oil-and-flour spray; set aside.

2. Pulse the pecans in two batches in a food processor fitted with the metal chopping blade until coarsely chopped and transfer to a large mixing bowl.

3. Add the granulated and brown sugars and lemon zest to the processor and churn 1 minute. Scrape down the work bowl sides and churn 1½ to 2 minutes longer until the zest is finely grated. Scrape the bowl once again.

4. Add the flour, baking powder, soda, cinnamon, ginger, nutmeg, salt, and pepper and pulse quickly to combine. Add to the bowl of nuts and toss until well mixed. Make a well in the center of the dry ingredients.

5. Add the zucchini chunks to the processor, distributing evenly, and pulse 6 to 8 times. Scrape down the work bowl sides and pulse 6 to 8 times more until moderately finely chopped. Add the oil, eggs, vanilla and orange extracts and pulse 5 to 6 times, just enough to combine.

6. Pour the zucchini mixture into the well in the dry ingredients and using a large rubber spatula, fold in gently until all dry ingredients are incorporated—do not beat or stir or you will toughen the cake. The batter will be very stiff.

7. Scoop the batter into the prepared pan, spreading to the corners, and bake on the middle oven rack until the loaf is springy to the touch and a cake tester, inserted in the center, comes out clean, about 1 hour and 15 minutes. The cake will hump a bit in the middle and break, but that is as it should be.

8. Cool the cake in the upright pan on a wire rack 15 minutes, loosen around the edges with a thin-blade spatula, then turn out on the rack, making sure the cake is right-side-up. Cool to room temperature, then cut into ½-inch slices and serve.

Fresh Ginger Gingerbread

I call this "grown-up" gingerbread because it's intensely gingery and not very sweet. Do not over-mix the batter when you combine liquid ingredients with the dry—the gingerbread will be tough.

Tip: I find that the easiest way to deal with the convolutions of fresh ginger is to divide it into chunks by breaking off the "fingers," then to peel both "fingers" and "trunk" with a vegetable peeler. Once peeled, the ginger can quickly be cut into 1-inch chunks. To keep molasses from clinging to a measuring cup, coat the cup with nonstick cooking spray.

MAKES ONE 9 × 5 × 3-INCH LOAF

2¾ cups unsifted all-purpose flour

1 cup sugar

1 teaspoon baking powder

½ teaspoon baking soda

1 teaspoon ground ginger

1 teaspoon ground cinnamon

½ teaspoon freshly grated nutmeg

½ teaspoon salt

¼ teaspoon freshly ground black pepper

6 ounces fresh ginger, peeled and cut into 1-inch chunks (see tip)

Zest of 1 medium orange, removed in strips with a vegetable peeler

⅔ cup vegetable oil

½ cup fresh orange juice

¼ cup molasses

3 large eggs

1. Preheat the oven to 350°F. Grease and flour a 9 × 5 × 3-inch loaf pan well or coat with non-stick oil-and-flour baking spray.

2. Pulse the flour, ½ cup of the sugar, the baking powder, soda, ground ginger, cinnamon, nutmeg, salt, and pepper in a food processor fitted with the metal chopping blade 3 to 4 times, then transfer to a large mixing bowl. Make a well in the center of the dry ingredients.

3. Add the remaining sugar, fresh ginger, and orange zest to the processor and churn 30 seconds. Scrape the work bowl and churn 30 seconds longer until reduced to mush.

4. Add the oil, orange juice, molasses, and eggs and combine with 3 to 4 long pulses. Scrape the work bowl and pulse once or twice more.

5. Pour the molasses mixture into the well in the dry ingredients and using a large wooden spoon, stir gently until all dry ingredients are incorporated—the batter will be lumpy.

6. Pour the batter into the prepared pan, rap once on the counter to expel air bubbles, and bake on the middle oven rack until the loaf is springy and a cake tester, inserted in the center, comes out clean, about 1 hour. The gingerbread will hump slightly in the middle and crack, but that's okay.

7. Cool the gingerbread in the upright pan on a wire rack 15 minutes, loosen around the edges with a thin-blade spatula, then turn out on the rack, making sure the gingerbread is right-side-up. Cool to room temperature, then cut into thin slices and serve.

Blonde Gingerbread with Fresh Blueberries

Unlike the gingerbread that precedes, this one is unusually delicate. Serve it straight up or, if you like, top with whipped cream or vanilla ice cream. I like it straight up.

Note: Small to medium blueberries are best for this recipe. The easiest way to make the topping is to swirl the sugar and cinnamon in a small deep bowl.

SERVES 16

1 cup firm-ripe blueberries, washed, stemmed, and patted very dry on paper toweling (see note)

1¾ cups unsifted all-purpose flour

1 cup sugar

1 teaspoon ground cinnamon

1 teaspoon ground ginger

½ teaspoon freshly grated nutmeg

½ teaspoon salt

¼ cup (½ stick) unsalted butter, melted

¼ cup vegetable oil

3 tablespoons molasses

1 extra-large egg

2 teaspoons orange extract

1 teaspoon baking soda

1 cup buttermilk

2 tablespoons sugar blended with ½ teaspoon ground cinnamon (cinnamon sugar), for topping

1. Preheat the oven to 350°F. Grease and flour a 9 × 9 × 2-inch baking pan well or coat with nonstick oil-and-flour baking spray. Place the blueberries in a large mixing bowl and set aside.

2. Pulse the flour, sugar, cinnamon, ginger, nutmeg, and salt in a food processor 3 to 4 times to combine, then transfer to the bowl of berries. Toss the berries in the dry ingredients until evenly dredged, then make a well in the center of the dry ingredients.

3. Add the melted butter, oil, molasses, egg, and orange extract to the food processor. Quickly stir the baking soda into the buttermilk, pour down the processor feed tube, and pulse 4 to 5 times until all ingredients are well blended.

4. Pour the molasses mixture into the well in the dry ingredients and using a large rubber spatula, gently fold the wet ingredients into the dry—no matter if a few floury specks show. They will disappear as the gingerbread bakes.

5. Pour the batter into the prepared pan, spreading to the corners, then sprinkle the cinnamon-sugar topping evenly over the batter.

6. Bake on the middle oven rack until the gingerbread is springy to the touch and a cake tester, inserted in the center, comes out clean, 35 to 40 minutes.

7. Cool the gingerbread to room temperature in the upright pan on a wire rack. Cut into large squares (4 cuts from left to right and 4 from top to bottom), then serve.

Carrot Cake

Except for the final mixing of wet and dry ingredients, this cake is made entirely by processor. It's an unusually light carrot cake and for that reason must be completely cool before it's frosted. As with all processor recipes, sequence is everything here. Start with the dry ingredients and work your way to the wet. That way, there's no need to stop and wash the work bowl or blade.

MAKES A 13 × 9 × 2-INCH LOAF CAKE

2 cups shelled walnuts or pecans

2¼ cups sifted all-purpose flour

¾ cup granulated sugar

Zest of 1 medium orange, removed in strips with a vegetable peeler

¾ cup firmly packed light brown sugar

2 teaspoons baking powder

1 teaspoon baking soda

1½ teaspoons ground cinnamon

1 teaspoon ground ginger

½ teaspoon ground allspice

¼ teaspoon salt

1 cup seedless golden raisins (Sultanas)

3 medium carrots (about ½ pound), peeled and cut into chunks 2½ inches long

1 cup vegetable oil

½ cup fresh orange juice

4 large eggs

2 teaspoons vanilla extract

1 recipe Orange Sour Cream Frosting (page 275)

1. Preheat the oven to 350°F. Coat a 13 × 9 × 2-inch baking pan well with nonstick oil-and-flour baking spray and set aside.

2. Place the walnuts in a food processor fitted with the metal chopping blade and pulse 8 to 10 times until coarsely chopped. Add ¼ cup of the flour and pulse quickly to combine. Tip into a large mixing bowl.

3. Add the granulated sugar and orange zest to the processor and churn 30 seconds. Scrape down the work bowl sides and churn 15 seconds more until the zest is finely grated.

4. Add the brown sugar and pulse quickly 5 to 6 times. Add the remaining 2 cups flour, the baking powder, soda, cinnamon, ginger, allspice, and salt and pulse 4 to 6 times to combine. Add the raisins and pulse quickly once or twice. Transfer all to the bowl with the nuts and toss well with your hands. Make a well in the middle of the dry ingredients.

5. Lift out the chopping blade and set aside. Equip the processor with the fine shredding disk and snap the lid into place. Arrange the carrots in the feed tube so they don't wobble. Insert the pusher and gently pulse the carrots through the shredding disk.

6. Remove the shredding disk but not the shredded carrots, then set the chopping blade back in place. Add the oil, orange juice, eggs, and vanilla and pulse 4 to 5 times to combine.

7. Pour into the well in the dry ingredients and mix gently but thoroughly with a wooden spoon, reaching again and again to the bottom of the bowl until no dry specks show. Do not beat the batter because you will toughen the cake.

8. Scoop the batter into the prepared pan, spreading to the corners, and bake on the middle oven rack until springy to the touch and a cake tester inserted in the middle of the loaf comes out clean, 40 to 45 minutes.

9. Remove the cake from the oven, set right-side-up on a wire rack, and cool for 2 hours. Toward the end of the cooling period, prepare the Orange Sour Cream Frosting as the recipe directs.

10. With the cake still in the pan, spread the frosting on top and as soon as it hardens, score in a criss-cross pattern forming 24 bars of equal size.

11. Cut into bars and serve.

Irish Country Christmas Cake

This quick loaf is for those who loathe fruitcake. It's buttery, it bakes in 40 to 45 minutes, but best of all, it can be made almost entirely by food processor. Compare that with long-winded fruitcakes that take days to prep, hours to bake, then months to age in whiskey-soaked cloths.

Note: I'm afraid you'll have to chop the candied cherries by hand (a three- to five-minute operation) because the food processor, despite my best efforts, reduces them to sludge. I'd hoped that freezing the cherries would harden them enough to chop in the processor. Alas, candied cherries do not freeze—they're too sweet. The same holds true for dates but these, at least, can be bought already diced. So can candied citron and orange rind although for this recipe I needed smaller pieces. Fortunately, I was able to freeze, then processor-chop both. Finally, by using short, fierce pulses, I also managed to give the golden raisins a decent chop.

MAKES A 13 × 9 × 2-INCH LOAF CAKE

¼ cup diced candied citron (see note)

¼ cup diced candied orange rind (see note)

⅔ cup slivered almonds

3¼ cups sifted all-purpose flour

¾ cup seedless golden raisins (Sultanas)

¾ cup dried currants

½ cup coarsely chopped candied red cherries (see note)

½ cup diced pitted dates (see note)

1 cup sugar

1 teaspoon baking powder

1 teaspoon ground cinnamon

½ teaspoon ground nutmeg (or better yet, freshly grated)

½ teaspoon ground allspice

½ teaspoon salt

½ pound (2 sticks) refrigerator-cold unsalted butter, cut into pats (use the wrapper markings)

1 cup milk

1 large egg

2 teaspoons vanilla extract

ICING AND DECORATION
1 recipe Almond Icing (page 274)

6 candied red cherries, halved

6 candied green cherries, halved

1. The night before you make the cake, line a small baking sheet with aluminum foil, shiny-side up. Arrange the pieces of candied citron and orange rind on the foil, not touching, set uncovered in the freezer, and leave overnight.

2. When ready to proceed, preheat the oven to 350°F. Coat a 13 × 9 × 2-inch baking pan well with nonstick oil-and-flour baking spray and set aside.

3. Place the almonds in a food processor fitted with the metal chopping blade and churn 10 to 15 seconds until uniformly fine. Add ¼ cup of the flour and pulse quickly to combine. Tip into a large mixing bowl.

4. Add the frozen candied citron and orange rind to the processor and with several quick, sharp pulses, reduce to a coarse chop. Add to the mixing bowl.

5. Add the raisins to the processor and once again give quick sharp bursts of speed until coarsely chopped. Add to the mixing bowl along with the currants, cherries, and dates. Toss all until well dredged.

6. Add the remaining 3 cups flour to the processor along with the sugar, baking powder, cinnamon, nutmeg, allspice, and salt and pulse quickly several times to combine.

7. Scatter the butter pats evenly on top and pulse quickly 10 times. Scrape down the work bowl, then repeat the pulsing and scraping three more times until the mixture is as fine as cornmeal. This step is key because the butter must be reduced to tiny bits and these evenly incorporated. Add to the mixing bowl, and with your hands, mix lightly but thoroughly, reaching down to the bottom of the bowl again and again. Make a well in the center of the combined dry ingredients.

8. Add the milk, egg, and vanilla to the processor (no need to wash bowl or blade) and pulse 3 to 4 times to combine.

9. Pour into the well in the dry ingredients and mix gently but thoroughly with a wooden spoon, again reaching time and again to the bottom of the bowl until no dry specks show. Do not beat at any point because you will toughen the cake. The mixture will be very stiff—about like biscuit dough.

10. Scoop into the prepared pan, spreading to the corners, and bake on the middle oven rack until lightly browned and a cake tester inserted in the middle of the loaf comes out clean, 40 to 45 minutes.

11. Remove the cake from the oven, set right-side-up on a wire rack, and cool to room temperature. Meanwhile, prepare the Almond Icing as the recipe directs.

12. With the cake still in the pan, smooth the icing on top and as soon as it hardens, score in a criss-cross pattern forming 24 bars of equal size. To decorate, stud the bars with the candied cherries, alternating the red and the green.

13. Cut into bars and serve.

Lemon-Poppy Seed Cupcakes

This recipe demonstrates as well as any how you can make almost any butter cake by food processor if you turn the order of mixing upside-down. The first two jobs here are to grate the lemon zest and grind the poppy seeds. Thanks to the abrasive power of sugar, the two can be done simultaneously. These cupcakes are deeply lemony and not too sweet. Serve them "nude" or add a lemon glaze.

Tip: The surest way to get cupcakes of equal size is to use an ice cream scoop—the No. 24 (meaning 24 scoops per quart) is just right.

MAKES 16 CUPCAKES

1 cup sugar

Zest of 1 large lemon, removed in strips with a vegetable peeler

2 tablespoons poppy seeds

2 cups sifted all-purpose flour

2 teaspoons baking powder

½ teaspoon baking soda

¼ teaspoon salt

½ cup (1 stick) refrigerator-cold unsalted butter, cut into pats (use the wrapper markings)

1 cup milk

2 large eggs

1 tablespoon fresh lemon juice

1 recipe Lemon Glaze (page 276), optional

1. Preheat the oven to 350°F. Line 16 standard muffin-pan cups with crinkly paper liners or lightly coat with nonstick cooking spray; set aside.

2. Churn the sugar, lemon zest, and poppy seeds in a food processor fitted with the metal chopping blade for 10 seconds. Using a plastic spatula and minding the blade, scrape the work bowl and stir, pushing larger pieces of zest to the bottom. Churn 10 seconds longer and if any largish pieces of lemon zest remain, pulse them out.

3. Add the flour, baking powder, soda, and salt and pulse 5 to 6 times to combine.

4. Scatter the butter pats evenly on top and with two 5-second churnings, cut in until the texture of coarse meal; scrape the work bowl and stir between churnings. If any large pieces of butter remain, pulse them out with staccato bursts.

5. Quickly whisk together the milk, eggs, and lemon juice, pour evenly over the dry ingredients, and with two to three 1-second churnings, process until a stiff batter forms. Remove the chopping blade and set aside.

6. Scoop the batter into the prepared muffin pans, two-thirds filling each cup, and bake on the middle oven rack until lightly browned and springy to the touch, 20 to 25 minutes.

7. Cool the cupcakes in the upright pans on a wire rack for 10 minutes, then remove from the pans, and cool to room temperature. Serve as is, or if you like, skim-coat the top of each cupcake with Lemon Glaze.

Double Chocolate Brownies with Ground Pecans

One of the challenges of working with the food processor is learning how much it can do to simplify recipes, even ones that aren't so difficult to begin with. Because I'm a chocoholic addicted to brownies, I wondered if I could re-sequence the order of mixing to make them wholly by food processor. As recipes go, dark, chewy brownies—my favorite kind—are not "critical" (apt to fail), so I turned an old recipe inside-out and discovered that I could make superior brownies using the food processor every step of the way. There are a few departures: I used unsweetened chocolate because that's all I had and to tell the truth, it produced brownies of awesome flavor. I also ground the pecans fine (I'll admit it, I added them too soon). But this, too, improved the brownies.

Tip: To break chocolate into small pieces, place the still-wrapped squares on a cutting board and whack with a cutlet bat or rolling pin. No piece should be more than ½ inch across.

MAKES SIXTEEN 2¼-INCH SQUARES

1½ cups granulated sugar

Two 1-ounce squares unsweetened chocolate, broken up (see tip)

1 cup shelled pecans

½ cup firmly packed light brown sugar

1 cup unsifted all-purpose flour (stir well before measuring)

¼ cup unsweetened cocoa powder

¼ teaspoon salt

½ pound (2 sticks) unsalted butter, cut into pats (use the wrapper markings)

4 large eggs

2 teaspoons vanilla extract

1. Preheat the oven to 350°F. Coat a 9 × 9 × 2-inch baking pan well with nonstick cooking spray. Also, if you like, spoon 2 tablespoons unsweetened cocoa powder into the pan and shake until the bottom and sides are lightly coated. Tip out the excess cocoa and set the pan aside.

2. Pulse the granulated sugar, chocolate, and pecans 2 to 3 times in a food processor fitted with the metal chopping blade, then churn for 5 seconds. Scrape the work bowl and push the larger pieces of chocolate to the bottom.

3. Crumble the brown sugar into the work bowl and pulse 3 to 4 times. Add the flour, cocoa, and salt and pulse 3 to 4 times more.

4. Scatter the butter pats evenly over all and churn 5 seconds. Scrape the work bowl and push the butter pieces to the bottom. Repeat twice more until the texture of coarse meal.

5. Add the eggs and vanilla and pulse 4 to 5 times. Scrape the work bowl, stir, and pulse 3 to 4 times to form a stiff batter.

6. Scoop into the prepared pan, and bake on the middle oven rack until there's only slight "give" when you press the top, 40 to 45 minutes.

7. Cool the brownies in the upright pan on a wire rack to room temperature, then cut into 16 bars of equal size, and serve.

Butterscotch Brownies

The brown sugar you use for this recipe must be soft. If it has hardened on the shelf, empty into a microwave-safe bowl, cover with plastic wrap, and microwave on HIGH (100 percent power) for 1 minute. If the sugar is still hard, re-cover, and microwave 30 seconds more. Check once again, and if necessary, re-cover and microwave for another 30 seconds.

Note: Once brown sugar has been softened by microwave, it must be used straight away. It hardens quickly and further microwaving will not bring it back.

MAKES SIXTEEN 2¼-INCH SQUARES

1 cup firmly packed light brown sugar (see headnote)

½ cup granulated sugar

1½ cups unsifted all-purpose flour (stir well before measuring)

1 teaspoon baking powder

¾ teaspoon salt

¾ cup (1½ sticks) refrigerator-cold unsalted butter, cut into pats (use the wrapper markings)

2 cups shelled pecans

2 large eggs

⅓ cup milk or half-and-half cream

1 tablespoon vanilla extract

1. Preheat the oven to 350°F. Coat a 9 × 9 × 2-inch baking pan well with nonstick oil-and-flour baking spray and set aside.

2. Churn the two sugars in a food processor fitted with the metal chopping blade for 5 seconds. Scrape the bowl and break up any lumps of sugar. Churn 5 seconds more and if lumps remain, repeat until uniformly fine.

3. Add the flour, baking powder, and salt and churn 5 seconds to combine. Scatter the butter pats evenly on top and churn 5 seconds. Scrape the work bowl, then minding the blade, stir and push any large chunks of butter to the bottom. Repeat until the texture of coarse meal.

4. Add the pecans, distributing evenly, then pulse five times. Scrape the bowl and stir the mixture well. Repeat until the nuts are fairly finely chopped.

5. Add the eggs, milk, and vanilla and pulse 5 times. Scrape the work bowl, stir, then pulse quickly 2 to 3 times until a batter forms.

6. Scoop into the prepared pan, spread to the corners, and bake on the middle oven rack until there's only slight "give" when you press the top, 45 to 50 minutes.

7. Cool the brownies in the upright pan on a wire rack to room temperature, then cut into 16 bars of equal size and serve.

Chocolate Chip Brownies

Prepare as directed through Step 5. Carefully lift out the processor chopping blade and set aside. Sprinkle 1 cup semisweet chocolate chips over the batter, stir in, then proceed as directed.

Double Butterscotch Brownies

Prepare as directed for Chocolate Chip Brownies, but substitute 1 cup butterscotch chips for chocolate chips.

Lemon Bars

Few recipes are more processor-perfect than these tart, two-ply bars. The bottom shortbread layer can be buzzed up in seconds, and while it bakes, the lemon zest grated and lemon curd mixed—all by machine. You don't even have to wash the work bowl or blade.

MAKES 32 BARS, EACH MEASURING APPROXIMATELY 2¼ × 1¾ INCHES

SHORTBREAD
⅔ cup confectioners' (10X) sugar

½ teaspoon vanilla extract

¼ teaspoon salt

10 ounces (2½ sticks) refrigerator-cold unsalted butter, cut into pats (use the wrapper markings)

2½ cups sifted all-purpose flour

LEMON CURD
Zest of 1 large lemon, removed in strips with a vegetable peeler

2 cups granulated sugar

¼ teaspoon salt

½ cup sifted all-purpose flour

1 teaspoon baking powder

6 tablespoons fresh lemon juice

4 large eggs

3 tablespoons confectioners' (10X) sugar, for dusting

1. Preheat the oven to 350°F. Lightly coat a 13 × 9 × 2-inch baking pan with nonstick cooking spray and set aside.

2. For the shortbread: Place the confectioners' sugar, vanilla, salt, and butter in a food processor fitted with the metal chopping blade, distributing the butter pats evenly. Churn for 30 seconds. Scrape down the work bowl sides, then churn 30 seconds longer until creamy. With 5 brisk pulses, incorporate the flour; scrape down the work bowl. Pulse 5 more times, turn the dough into the prepared pan, and pat evenly over the bottom.

3. Bake the shortbread on the middle oven rack until lightly browned and fairly firm to the touch, about 25 minutes.

4. Meanwhile, prepare the lemon curd: In the same food processor (no need to wash the bowl or blade), churn the lemon zest, granulated sugar, and salt for 1 minute. Scrape down the work bowl and pulse 3 to 4 times until the lemon zest is finely grated. Add the flour and baking powder and pulse several times.

5. Add the lemon juice and eggs and combine using 4 to 5 long pulses. Let stand undisturbed in the work bowl.

6. As soon as the shortbread tests done, pulse the lemon curd several times, then pour evenly over the hot shortbread.

7. Return to the oven and bake until the lemon curd is lightly browned and set, about 25 minutes.

8. Remove the pan from the oven, set right-side-up on a wire rack, and cool the lemon bars to room temperature.

9. Sift the dusting sugar evenly on top, cut into bars, and serve.

Highland Shortbread

I used to watch a Scottish friend make shortbread and it seemed to take forever. First she creamed the butter and sugar until no sugar grains were discernible, then at a snail's pace, she worked in the flour with her fingers. That was years ago and much as I adored her shortbread, I think this processor version is just as good. I call for low-gluten cake flour because if there's one thing a food processor's vigorous churning does, it's develop gluten (wheat protein). And that's the surest way to toughen shortbread. For the same reason, I've substituted gluten-free cornstarch for some of the flour because I wanted a processor shortbread that was truly short and tender. I'm only sorry my Scottish friend is no longer around to taste it.

MAKES FORTY 1 × 2-INCH BARS

3 cups sifted cake flour

½ cup sifted cornstarch

⅔ cup sugar

½ pound (2 sticks) unsalted butter, cut into pats (use the wrapper markings) and brought to room temperature (the butter should be about the consistency of vegetable shortening)

1 teaspoon vanilla extract

¼ teaspoon salt

1. Preheat the oven to 350°F. Sift the flour and cornstarch together onto a piece of wax paper and set aside.

2. Cream the sugar, butter, vanilla, and salt in a food processor fitted with the metal chopping blade by churning 5 seconds. Scrape the work bowl, pushing the butter toward the center of the work bowl, and churn 5 seconds more. Again scrape the bowl and churn 5 seconds until light and creamy. Scrape the work bowl once again.

3. Add the sifted dry ingredients, churn 5 seconds, and scrape the work bowl well. Pulse briskly 3 to 5 times just until the mixture is crumbly and begins to come together.

4. Scrape onto an ungreased 15½ × 10½ × 1-inch jelly roll pan, gather up all bits and crumbs of dough and press firmly into a ball. Now pat the dough into a rectangle 10 inches long, 8 inches wide, and ½ inch thick, straightening the sides and squaring the corners. It's important that the shortbread be the same thickness throughout, otherwise the thinner portions will overbrown.

5. Bake on the middle oven shelf until the shortbread is evenly pale tan—slightly darker than a manila file folder. This will take 20 to 25 minutes.

6. Set the pan upright on a wire rack and while the shortbread is still hot score the top, creating 40 bars of equal size.

Tip: If you use an 18-inch ruler, letting it rest on the rim of the pan, this is easy.

7. Cool the shortbread to room temperature before cutting into bars and serving.

Orange-Almond Macaroons

Before baking parchment became widely available, we would bake these macaroons on sheets of heavy brown paper. The cookies always stuck fast and to loosen them we'd slide a damp towel underneath the paper. That made the macaroons soggy so the next step was to air-dry them on racks. Baking parchment eliminates all of these steps. And it goes without saying that the food processor simplifies the mixing.

Tip: The easiest way to dice almond paste is to halve the roll lengthwise, give it a quarter turn, and halve lengthwise again. Next, slice the roll crosswise at half-inch intervals.

If you "butter" the underside of each corner of the parchment with a bit of macaroon dough and press against the baking sheet, the paper will lie flat throughout baking.

MAKES ABOUT 4 DOZEN COOKIES

1 cup granulated sugar

½ cup unsifted confectioners' (10X) sugar

Four 3-inch strips orange zest, removed with a vegetable peeler

⅛ teaspoon salt

One 7-ounce roll almond paste, diced (see tip)

3 large egg whites

1. Place the oven rack in the lowest position and preheat the oven to 300°F. Line two baking sheets with baking parchment; set aside.

2. Place the granulated sugar, confectioners' sugar, orange zest, and salt in a food processor fitted with the metal chopping blade and with three 20-second churnings, grind the zest very fine. Using a plastic spatula and skirting the chopping blade, scrape the work bowl between churnings and stir the sugar mixture.

3. Scatter the diced almond paste evenly over all and with two to three 10-second churnings, cut in until the texture of coarse meal. Scrape the work bowl and stir between churnings.

4. Add the egg whites and mix in with two 5-second churnings, scraping the work bowl and stirring at halftime. Remove the chopping blade and set aside.

5. Working directly from the work bowl, scoop up the dough by rounded ½ teaspoons and drop onto the parchment-lined baking sheets, spacing the cookies 2 inches apart. They will spread considerably as they bake.

6. Bake the cookies, one sheet at a time, until lightly browned and crackly on top, 20 to 25 minutes.

7. Remove from the oven, transfer to a wire rack, and cool the cookies completely on the baking parchment.

8. To remove, loosen the cookies carefully around the edges with a small pancake turner or offset spatula using short quick strokes. Fortunately, these cookies are not very brittle. After you've loosened a few cookies, you'll get the hang of it and things will go faster.

9. Layer the macaroons between sheets of wax paper in airtight containers and store in a cool dry spot.

Rugelach

I'd lived in New York City for many years before I tasted these wonderful little Jewish pastries. Or are they cookies? Whatever they are, they soon became an addiction, so I was eager to learn if I could make them in a food processor. I quickly found my answer. The processor does them to perfection.

Note: If the pastry is to be flaky, you must use regular cream cheese. The fat-reduced is too wet, and the fat-free—well, I don't think it's good for much of anything.

MAKES ABOUT 4 DOZEN (INCLUDING REROLLS)

PASTRY

2¼ cups sifted all-purpose flour

½ cup sugar

¼ teaspoon salt

½ pound (2 sticks) refrigerator-cold unsalted butter, cut into pats (use the wrapper markings)

One 8-ounce package refrigerator-cold cream cheese, diced (see note)

FILLING

1½ cups shelled walnuts

⅓ cup sugar

2 teaspoons ground cinnamon

¼ teaspoon salt

¼ cup confectioners' (10X) sugar, for dusting

1. For the pastry: Combine the flour, sugar, and salt by pulsing 4 to 6 times in a food processor fitted with the metal chopping blade.

2. Scatter the butter pats on top and with two 5-second churnings, cut in until the texture of oatmeal. Between churnings, scrape the work bowl with a plastic spatula and minding the blade, stir and push the larger pieces of butter to the bottom.

3. Scatter the bits of cream cheese on top, churn 5 seconds, scrape and stir, then churn 5 seconds more until the mixture rolls into a ball. Remove the blade and set aside.

4. Transfer the dough to a piece of plastic food wrap, divide into 5 equal parts, then roll each into a ball the size of a tennis ball. Wrap each ball individually in plastic wrap and refrigerate for several hours, or better yet, overnight.

5. Meanwhile, prepare the filling: Place all ingredients except the 10X sugar in a food processor fitted with the metal chopping blade and churn until reduced to fine crumbs, about 10 seconds. I make the filling as soon as the pastry is made and don't find it necessary to wash, or even rinse, the processor work bowl or blade. Transfer the filling to a plastic zipper bag, seal, and refrigerate until ready to proceed.

6. Preheat the oven to 350°F. Using an 8½-inch-round plate or pan lid as a guide, trace a circle on cardboard and cut it out. This will serve as a template.

7. Working with one ball of dough at a time, roll on a lightly floured pastry cloth into a circle as thin as pie crust. Place the cardboard template on top and with a floured sharp knife, cut the dough into a circle; reserve the trimmings for rerolls.

8. Divide the circle into 8 wedges of equal size but do not separate these until you've scattered 3 tablespoons of the filling on top. Carefully separate the wedges and beginning at the base, roll each one up toward the point. Arrange the rugelach points-down on an ungreased baking sheet, spacing 1 inch apart. Repeat until all dough and filling are gone.

9. Bake the rugelach in the upper third of the oven until pale tan, 15 to 18 minutes. Transfer at once to wire racks and cool to room temperature.

10. Just before serving, dust with the confectioners' sugar.

Note: Layered into an airtight container between pieces of wax paper and stored in a cool, dry spot, rugelach remain amazingly fresh-tasting for several weeks.

Toasted Hazelnut Biscotti

I had no idea whether I could make good biscotti in a food processor and feared that its awesome power might produce cookies too tough to chew. Not so, because I've added butter to a fairly classic Tuscan recipe. That single addition guarantees that there are no jaw-breakers here. If you want biscotti that are good and crisp, however, do not make this recipe when it's humid or rainy.

Note: Instead of greasing the baking sheets, I line them with foil. After the first baking (*biscotti*, by the way, is Italian for *twice-baked*), the foil can be peeled right off. Properly stored, biscotti will remain crisp and fresh for several weeks.

MAKES ABOUT 2 DOZEN COOKIES

1½ cups shelled hazelnuts (about 8 ounces)

1 cup sugar

2½ cups sifted all-purpose flour

2 teaspoons baking powder

½ teaspoon ground cinnamon

¼ teaspoon salt

¾ cup (1½ sticks) refrigerator-cold unsalted butter, cut into pats (use the wrapper markings)

3 large eggs

2 teaspoons vanilla extract

1. Preheat the oven to 350°F. Line two baking sheets with aluminum foil, dull-side-up; do not grease the foil. Set the pans aside.

2. Spread the hazelnuts in an ungreased 15½ × 10½ × 1-inch jelly-roll pan, set uncovered in the oven, and toast until lightly browned, 12 to 15 minutes. Cool the nuts until easy to handle, bundle in a clean dry dish towel, and rub briskly to remove the skins. It doesn't matter if you can't remove all bits of skin.

3. Drop ½ cup of the nuts into a food processor fitted with the metal chopping blade and with 4 to 5 rapid-fire pulses, chop until about the texture of lentils. Tap onto a piece of wax paper and reserve. Some of the nuts will be quite finely ground and that is okay, but if any large pieces remain, break these apart with your fingers.

4. Add the remaining 1 cup nuts and the sugar to the work bowl and churn until the nuts are finely ground, about 10 seconds. Scrape the work bowl, add the flour, baking powder, cinnamon, and salt and pulse 4 to 6 times to combine.

5. Scatter the butter pats evenly on top and with three 5-second churnings, process until the texture of oatmeal. Between churnings, scrape the work bowl with a plastic spatula and minding the blade, stir, pushing larger bits of butter to the bottom.

6. Add the eggs and vanilla and with two 3-second churnings, process into a soft dough, again scraping the work bowl and stirring between churnings.

7. Turn the dough onto a well-floured surface and knead in the reserved chopped hazelnuts.

Working at one end of a prepared baking sheet, shape half the dough into a rectangle 8 inches long, 4 inches wide, and ¾ inch thick that lies crosswise in the pan. Shape the remaining dough into an identical rectangle at the opposite end of the pan, leaving 4½ to 5 inches between the two and wide margins at each end—this dough expands quite a bit as it bakes.

8. Bake on the middle oven rack until firm to the touch and irresistible smelling, about 35 minutes.

9. Cool the biscotti on the pan on a wire rack for 20 minutes. Peel the foil from one block of biscotti, place the biscotti on a cutting board, and using a very sharp knife, slice crosswise and slightly on the bias at ½ inch intervals. You should have 12 slices.

10. Lay the slices on their sides on the second foil-lined baking sheet, spacing about an inch apart. Return to the 350°F oven and bake just until lightly browned and crisp, 12 to 15 minutes.

11. Meanwhile, reline the first baking sheet with foil, and slice the remaining biscotti the same way. Arrange on the baking sheet just as you did the first batch and when that one comes from the oven, bake the second batch 12 to 15 minutes.

12. Cool the biscotti to room temperature on the baking sheets on wire racks—this furthers the drying process.

13. When the biscotti are completely cold, layer into a large airtight cannister between sheets of wax paper, and store in a cool dry spot.

Mocha-Hazelnut Biscotti

Prepare as directed, but in Step 4, add ⅓ cup unsweetened cocoa powder and 1 tablespoon instant espresso crystals along with the flour and other dry ingredients.

Almond Biscotti

Next to Toasted Hazelnut Biscotti, which precedes, this is my favorite.

MAKES ABOUT 2 DOZEN COOKIES

1 cup unblanched whole almonds (about 3½ ounces)

1 cup sugar

2½ cups sifted all-purpose flour

2 teaspoons baking powder

½ teaspoon freshly grated nutmeg

¼ teaspoon salt

¾ cup (1½ sticks) refrigerator-cold unsalted butter, cut into pats (use the wrapper markings)

3 large eggs

1 teaspoon vanilla extract

1 teaspoon almond extract

½ cup sliced unblanched almonds

1. Preheat the oven to 350°F. Line two baking sheets with aluminum foil, dull-side-up; do not grease the foil. Set the pans aside.

2. Process the 1 cup almonds and the sugar in a food processor fitted with the metal chopping blade until the nuts are finely ground, about 10 seconds. Scrape the work bowl, add the flour, baking powder, nutmeg, and salt and pulse 4 to 6 times to combine.

3. Scatter the butter pats evenly on top and with three 5-second churnings, process until the texture of oatmeal. Between churnings, scrape the work bowl with a plastic spatula and minding the blade, stir, pushing larger bits of butter to the bottom.

4. Add the eggs, vanilla, and almond extract and with two 3-second churnings, process into a soft dough, again scraping the work bowl and stirring between churnings.

5. Turn the dough onto a well-floured surface and knead in the ½ cup sliced almonds. Working at one end of a prepared baking sheet, shape half the dough into a rectangle 8 inches long, 4 inches wide, and ¾ inch thick that lies crosswise in the pan. Shape the remaining dough into an identical rectangle at the opposite end of the pan, leaving 4½ to 5 inches between the two and wide margins at each end—this dough expands quite a bit as it bakes.

6. Bake on the middle oven rack until firm to the touch and irresistible smelling, about 35 minutes.

7. Cool the biscotti on the pan on a wire rack for 20 minutes. Peel the foil from one block of biscotti, place the biscotti on a cutting board, and using a very sharp knife, slice crosswise and slightly on the bias at ½ inch intervals. You should have 12 slices.

8. Lay the slices on their sides on the second foil-lined baking sheet, spacing about an inch apart. Return to the 350°F oven and bake just until lightly browned and crisp, 12 to 15 minutes.

9. Meanwhile, reline the first baking sheet with foil, and slice the remaining biscotti the same way. Arrange on the baking sheet just as you did the first batch. When the first batch comes from the oven, bake the second batch 12 to 15 minutes.

10. Cool the biscotti to room temperature on the baking sheets on wire racks—this furthers the drying process.

11. When the biscotti are completely cold, layer into a large airtight cannister between sheets of wax paper, and store in a cool dry spot.

Chocolate-Almond Biscotti

Prepare as directed, but increase the sugar to 1¼ cups and in Step 2 add ⅓ cup unsweetened Dutch process cocoa powder along with the flour and other dry ingredients.

Chocolate Chip Cookies

I so wish that people would go back to making cookies from scratch instead of using mixes and rolls of refrigerated cookie dough (on my latest supermarket prowl I saw refrigerated dough already divided into cookies). Maybe this quick, one-bowl processor version of America's favorite cookie will encourage cooks to make their own once again. I hope so. I must say that these chocolate chip cookies are amazingly crisp and tender.

Note: Baking sheets lightly coated with nonstick cooking spray do not need to be resprayed between batches. But you should rub lightly with a crumple of paper toweling to remove any browned bits. You should also cool the baking sheets before dropping on another batch of cookies.

Tip: If you freeze the pecans, you'll find that the food processor will chop them more crisply and uniformly—especially important when you want a coarse chop.

MAKES ABOUT 4 DOZEN COOKIES

1 cup frozen shelled pecans (see tip)

1¼ cups sifted all-purpose flour

½ cup firmly packed light brown sugar

⅓ cup granulated sugar

½ teaspoon baking soda

¼ teaspoon salt

6 tablespoons (¾ stick) refrigerator-cold unsalted butter, cut into pats (use the wrapper markings)

4 tablespoons refrigerator-cold vegetable shortening, diced (use stick shortening, cut into tablespoons using the wrapper markings, then quarter each tablespoon)

1 large egg

2 teaspoons vanilla extract

1 cup semisweet chocolate chips

1. Preheat the oven to 375°F. Lightly coat two baking sheets with nonstick cooking spray and set aside.

2. Coarsely chop the pecans in a food processor fitted with the metal chopping blade—two 5-second churnings should do it. Using a plastic spatula and minding the blade, scrape the work bowl between churnings and stir, pushing larger pieces of nut to the bottom. Tip the chopped pecans onto a piece of wax paper and reserve.

3. Add the flour, brown sugar, granulated sugar, baking soda, and salt to the work bowl and churn 10 seconds to combine, then pulse quickly 2 to 3 times.

4. Scatter the butter pats and bits of shortening evenly on top and cut in until the texture of coarse meal with three 3-second churnings. Scrape the work bowl and stir between churnings, pushing larger pieces to the bottom.

5. Add the egg, vanilla, chocolate chips, and chopped pecans and with three to four 1-

second bursts of speed, churn to a soft dough. Scrape and stir between churnings. Remove the chopping blade and set aside.

6. Working directly from the work bowl, scoop up the dough by rounded ½ teaspoons and drop onto the prepared baking sheets, spacing the cookies 2 inches apart.

7. Bake on the middle oven rack until lightly ringed with brown, about 10 minutes.

8. Allow the baked cookies to firm up on the baking sheets 10 to 15 seconds, then transfer to wire racks, and cool to room temperature. Store in airtight containers.

Kourabiedes (Greek Christmas Cookies)

Christmastime in Greece means joyous feasting with plenty of holiday sweets. Among them are bound to be these buttery almond cookies shaped like little logs or crescents, then rolled while warm in confectioners' sugar.

Note: To toast almonds, spread in a pie pan and set uncovered in a preheated 350°F oven for 6 to 8 minutes until uniformly golden; cool before using.

MAKES ABOUT 4½ DOZEN COOKIES

⅔ cup blanched slivered almonds, lightly toasted (see note)

2 tablespoons granulated sugar

¼ teaspoon salt

⅔ cup sifted confectioners' (10X) sugar

3½ cups sifted all-purpose flour

1¼ cups (2½ sticks) refrigerator-cold unsalted butter, cut into pats (use the wrapper markings)

1 tablespoon vanilla extract

1 tablespoon brandy

1 teaspoon almond extract

1 extra-large egg yolk

1½ cups unsifted confectioners' (10X) sugar, for dredging

1. Place the almonds, granulated sugar, and salt in a food processor fitted with the metal chopping blade and with two 10-second churnings, grind the nuts very fine. Using a plastic spatula and being careful to avoid the blade, scrape the work bowl between churnings and stir, pushing any larger bits of almond to the bottom.

2. Add the ⅔ cup confectioners' sugar and the flour and incorporate using two 5-second churnings. Scatter the butter pats evenly on top and cut in with three to four 5-second churn-ings. Scrape the work bowl between churnings and stir, pushing bits of butter to the bottom. Now pulse 3 to 4 times until the texture of coarse meal.

3. Add the vanilla, brandy, almond extract, and egg yolk and with three to four 1-second bursts of speed, churn to a stiff but soft dough. Scrape and stir between churnings. Remove the chopping blade and set aside.

4. Turn the dough onto a lightly floured sur-face and shape into two disks about 1 inch thick. Wrap in plastic food wrap and refrigerate for at least 1 hour. When ready to proceed, pre-heat the oven to 350°F.

5. Pinch off pieces of dough about the size of walnuts and shape into small logs or crescents. Space 1½ inches apart on ungreased baking sheets.

6. Bake, one sheet at a time, on the middle oven rack until the cookies are uniformly tan and irresistible smelling, 12 to 15 minutes. Meanwhile, place the 1½ cups dredging sugar in a pie pan.

7. When the cookies are done, cool for 1 minute on the baking sheets, then roll in the confectioners' sugar until snowy.

8. Arrange the cookies on large racks set over a wax paper–covered counter and cool to room temperature. Sift any remaining dredging sugar on top. The cookies should be thickly coated.

9. Layer the cookies in airtight canisters between sheets of wax paper and store in a cool dry spot.

"Moldy Mice"

Prepare as directed but substitute 1½ cups untoasted pecans for the ⅔ cup slivered almonds, and omit the brandy and almond extract. Instead of shaping the dough into logs or crescents, roll into 1-inch balls and flatten slightly with your palm, smoothing out any ragged edges. Bake 10 to 12 minutes until pale tan and soft-firm to the touch, then dredge, and cool as directed. This old Southern favorite, like Kourabiedes, is a Christmas favorite. Makes 4½ to 5 dozen.

Mexican Wedding Cakes

Prepare Moldy Mice as directed, substituting 1½ cups toasted hazelnuts (see page 262) for pecans. Makes about 5 dozen.

Yogurt Cheese

You do not need a food processor to make yogurt cheese, but you will find this thick, smooth curd useful in all manner of processor recipes—especially jiffy low-fat ice creams. It's also good in cheesecakes and as a dessert topping.

MAKES 2 CUPS

One 32-ounce container plain yogurt (use low-fat, if you like)

1. Line a large fine sieve with coffee filters or several thicknesses of cheesecloth and set over a 2-quart glass measure.

2. Dump in the yogurt and with a sharp knife, score criss-cross fashion, cutting deep into the curd. Cover and refrigerate for 24 hours. At halftime, score the curd once again. If you've used coffee filters, replace them after 12 hours.

3. Discard the whey (liquid), transfer the curd to a 1-pint jar, screw the lid down tight, and store in the refrigerator. Use within 7 to 10 days.

Ruby Raspberry Sauce

Few dessert sauces are more versatile, prettier, or easier to make than this one. I thaw the berries, dissolve the sugar, and melt the jelly in a single operation in the microwave because doing so in a saucepan over moderate heat not only takes longer but also tends to give the berries a cooked taste. If you have no microwave, place the frozen berries, sugar, and jelly in a large nonreactive saucepan, and cook and stir over moderate heat just until the berries thaw—10 to 12 minutes. Stored in a tightly capped jar in the refrigerator, this sauce keeps about a week.

MAKES 3½ CUPS

Two 12-ounce packages solidly frozen unsweetened raspberries, chunks broken up

⅔ cup sugar

¼ cup red currant jelly

¼ cup fresh lime juice

¼ cup Grand Marnier or other orange liqueur

3 tablespoons frozen orange juice concentrate

1. Place the berries, sugar, and jelly in a large, shallow microwave-safe mixing bowl and stir gently to mix. Set uncovered in a microwave oven and microwave on MEDIUM (50 percent power) for 4 minutes. Stir well and microwave, uncovered, 4 minutes more.

2. Transfer the berry mixture to a food processor fitted with the metal chopping blade, add all remaining ingredients, and purée until smooth, about 1 minute nonstop.

3. Scoop the purée into a large fine sieve set over a large mixing bowl (use the one in which you microwaved the berries), then with a large rubber spatula or the bowl of a large ladle, force the purée through the sieve. Discard the raspberry seeds.

4. Pour the sauce into a 1-quart preserving jar, cap, and refrigerate until ready to use.

5. Ladle over sponge cake, angel food, or poundcake, or over vanilla ice cream, fruit ice cream, sorbet, or ice. Ruby Raspberry Sauce is also delicious over fresh raspberries, strawberries, blueberries, or blackberries (or any combination or them) not to mention over sliced full-of-flavor peaches. But I like it best over Swedish Cream (page 224).

Cream Cheese Frosting

Here's the classic frosting for carrot cake, but it's equally delicious swirled over any firm fruit-and-nut-studded cake. Make sure the cream cheese is at room temperature before you begin.

MAKES ABOUT 2 CUPS, ENOUGH TO FROST ONE 13 × 9 × 2-INCH LOAF, 24 CUPCAKES,
OR FILL AND FROST AN 8- OR 9-INCH, 2-LAYER CAKE

Two 3-ounce packages cream cheese (use light, if you like), at room temperature

One 1-pound box confectioners' (10X) sugar

1 tablespoon vanilla extract

1 to 3 tablespoons milk or half-and-half cream, as needed for good spreading consistency

1. Churn the cream cheese, confectioners' sugar, and vanilla in a food processor fitted with the metal chopping blade until light and fluffy, 8 to 10 seconds. Scrape the work bowl well.

2. With the motor running, add the milk down the feed tube, tablespoon by tablespoon, until the frosting is a good spreading consistency.

Chocolate Cream Cheese Frosting

Prepare as directed, adding 2 ounces melted unsweetened chocolate at the outset in Step 1. Also increase the milk as needed for good spreading consistency. Use to fill and frost chocolate, caramel, or yellow cake.

Mocha Cream Cheese Frosting

Prepare Chocolate Cream Cheese Frosting as directed, adding 1 tablespoon instant espresso crystals along with the chocolate. Use to fill and frost chocolate or yellow cake.

Coffee Cream Cheese Frosting

Prepare the basic cream cheese frosting as directed, adding 2 tablespoons instant espresso crystals along with the other ingredients in Step 1. For less intense coffee flavor, add only 1 tablespoon instant espresso crystals. Use to fill and frost chocolate or yellow cake.

Lemon or Orange Cream Cheese Frosting

Using a vegetable peeler, strip the zest from 1 large lemon or 1 medium orange. Place in a food processor fitted with the metal chopping blade, add 1 cup of the confectioners' sugar, and churn 15 seconds. Scrape the work bowl, then continue churning until finely grated, 15 to 20 seconds longer. Add the cream cheese and remaining confectioners' sugar but omit the vanilla. Churn as directed until fluffy, then add 1 to 3 tablespoons fresh lemon or orange juice instead of milk, spooning down the feed tube with the motor running. Continue churning until a good spreading consistency. Use to fill and frost lemon, orange, or yellow cake.

Basic Buttercream Frosting

My mother used this frosting, or one of its variations, to ice every cake she ever baked. With her Mixmaster it was easy, although the machine did send the powdered sugar flying. Not a problem in the sealed work bowl of a food processor. Mother never lived to see the food processor, but she would have loved this speed demon.

MAKES ABOUT 2 CUPS, ENOUGH TO FROST ONE 13 × 9 × 2-INCH LOAF, 24 CUPCAKES, OR FILL AND FROST AN 8- OR 9-INCH, 2-LAYER CAKE

One 1-pound box confectioners' (10X) sugar

6 tablespoons (¾ stick) unsalted butter, at room temperature

1 tablespoon vanilla extract

¼ teaspoon salt

3 to 5 tablespoons milk, half-and-half, or heavy cream

1. Place the confectioners' sugar in a food processor fitted with the metal chopping blade and scatter the butter on top. Add the vanilla and salt and churn until light, 8 to 10 seconds. Scrape the work bowl well.

2. With the motor running, add the milk down the feed tube, tablespoon by tablespoon, until the frosting is a good spreading consistency.

Coffee Buttercream Frosting

Prepare as directed, adding 1 tablespoon instant espresso crystals along with the vanilla and salt. Use to frost chocolate, white, or yellow cake.

Chocolate Buttercream Frosting

Prepare as directed, adding ½ cup unsweetened Dutch process cocoa powder along with the vanilla and salt. Also increase the milk as needed for good spreading consistency. Use to fill and frost chocolate, caramel, or yellow cake.

Mocha Buttercream Frosting

Prepare Chocolate Buttercream Frosting as directed, adding 1 tablespoon instant expresso crystals along with the cocoa. Use to fill and frost chocolate or yellow cake.

Buttercream-Pecan Frosting

Spread ½ cup pecans in a pie tin and set uncovered on the middle rack of a 350°F oven for 10 minutes; cool, then place in a food processor fitted with the metal chopping blade along with 1 cup of the confectioners' sugar. Churn until the nuts are finely chopped, 10 to 15 seconds. If any large pieces remain, quickly pulse them out; scrape the work bowl well. Add 4 tablespoons (½ stick) unsalted butter, the vanilla, and the remaining confectioners' sugar, and churn until light. Add the milk as directed and continue churning until a good spreading consistency. Use to fill and frost chocolate, caramel, or yellow cake.

Citrus Buttercream Frosting

Using a vegetable peeler, strip the zest from 1 large lemon, 2 large limes, 1 medium orange, or

¼ medium grapefruit. Place in a food processor fitted with the metal chopping blade, add 1 cup of the confectioners' sugar, and churn 15 seconds. Scrape the work bowl, then churn until finely grated, 15 to 20 seconds longer. Add the butter and remaining confectioners' sugar but omit the vanilla. Churn as directed until light, 8 to 10 seconds, then add 3 to 5 tablespoons fresh lemon, lime, orange, or grapefruit juice, respectively, instead of milk, spooning down the feed tube with the motor running. Continue churning until the frosting is a good spreading consistency. Use to fill and frost lemon, orange, white, or yellow cake.

Almond Icing

Why resort to ready-made frostings when you can buzz this one up in a food processor in less than two minutes? It's delicious on Irish Country Christmas Cake (page 252), and for that matter, on any white, yellow, or chocolate cake.

MAKES ABOUT 1¼ CUPS, ENOUGH TO FROST ONE 13 × 9 × 2-INCH LOAF
OR THE TOP AND SIDES OF AN 8-INCH, 2-LAYER CAKE (BUT NOT ENOUGH TO FILL IT)

3 cups unsifted confectioners' (10X) sugar

2 teaspoons vanilla extract

1 teaspoon almond extract

4 to 6 tablespoons heavy cream

1. Place the confectioners' sugar, vanilla, and almond extract, and 4 tablespoons of the heavy cream in a food processor fitted with the metal chopping blade. Churn 5 seconds until creamy.

2. Scrape down the work bowl sides and if the icing is too stiff to spread easily, add an additional 1 to 2 tablespoons cream. Pulse until creamy, then use to frost cake.

Vanilla Icing
Prepare as directed but increase the vanilla extract to 1 tablespoon and omit the almond extract. For a slightly richer frosting, add 2 tablespoons softened unsalted butter in Step 1 along with the other ingredients.

Orange Sour Cream Frosting

Whenever I make Carrot Cake (page 250), I frost it with this sweet-sour icing instead of the more traditional Cream Cheese Frosting (page 272), which is richer.

MAKES ABOUT 1½ CUPS, ENOUGH TO FROST A 13 × 9 × 2-INCH LOAF OR
THE TOP AND SIDES OF AN 8- OR 9-INCH, 2-LAYER CAKE (BUT NOT ENOUGH TO FILL IT)

1 pound confectioners' (10X) sugar

Zest of ½ medium orange, removed in strips with a vegetable peeler

¼ teaspoon salt

⅓ cup sour cream (about)

1 teaspoon vanilla extract

1. Place 1 cup of the confectioners' sugar, the orange zest, and salt in a food processor fitted with the metal chopping blade and churn 60 seconds. Scrape down the work bowl sides and pulse quickly until the orange zest is finely grated. Add the remaining sugar and pulse just enough to combine.

2. Add the sour cream and vanilla and pulse 4 to 5 times until creamy. If the icing seems too stiff to spread easily, add another 1 tablespoon sour cream or, if you prefer, 1 tablespoon heavy cream or milk. Again pulse until creamy and use to frost cake.

Lemon Sour Cream Frosting
Prepare as directed but substitute the zest of 1 large lemon for orange zest and lemon extract for the vanilla.

Grapefruit Sour Cream Frosting
Prepare as directed but substitute the zest of ½ small grapefruit for orange zest and orange extract for the vanilla.

Lemon Glaze

Just the thing to buzz up in a mini food processor—5 seconds is all it takes. You can use these proportions for a variety of glazes. Only the liquid ingredient changes. You might, for example, substitute fresh lime, grapefruit, or even orange juice for lemon. You might use cream (half-and-half, light, or heavy) and flavor with a teaspoon of vanilla, orange, or rum extract. Or you might use a liqueur as the liquid—Grand Marnier, Cointreau, Frangelica, Cherry Heering, Tía Maria, Kahlúa, crème de menthe, whatever you fancy.

Tip: The easiest way to glaze (or frost) cupcakes is to pour the glaze into a small bowl, then dip the cupcakes into it upside-down (only the tops should be coated). For cookies, especially fancy cutouts, I paint the glaze on with a pastry brush applying, if necessary, a second thin coat after the first has dried.

MAKES ABOUT ½ CUP, ENOUGH TO SKIM-COAT ONE 9 × 5 × 3-INCH LOAF,
1½ DOZEN CUPCAKES, OR 4 DOZEN MEDIUM-SIZE COOKIES

1½ cups unsifted confectioners' (10X) sugar

3 tablespoons fresh lemon juice (see headnote)

1. Churn the sugar and lemon juice in a mini food processor fitted with the metal chopping blade 3 to 5 seconds until smooth.

2. Use to frost cupcakes or cookies (see tip).

Index

caramel cheesecake, 230–31

carrot cake, 250–51

chocolate-almond biscotti, 264–65

chocolate cheesecake, 230–31

chocolate chip brownies, 256

chocolate chip cookies, 266–67

chopped apple–sour cream cake, 243

clafouti with dark cherries, almonds, and
dried cranberries, 238–39

double butterscotch brownies, 256

double chocolate brownies with ground
pecans, 255

frangipane tart, 234–35

fresh ginger gingerbread, 248

frozen lemongrass–mango mousse, 226

frozen lemongrass–papaya mousse, 226

Highland shortbread, 258

Irish country Christmas cake, 252–53

kourabiedes, 268–69

lemon bars, 257

lemon chess pie, 229

lemon-poppy seed cupcakes, 254

lime chess pie, 229

Mexican chocolate cake, 244–45

Mexican wedding cakes, 268–69

mocha cake with chocolate-hazelnut frosting,
244–45

mocha-hazelnut biscotti, 262–63

mocha semifreddo, 228

"moldy mice," 268–69

oh-my-God cheesecake, 230–31

old-fashioned strawberry shortcake, 242

orange-almond macaroons, 259

orange chess pie, 229

pecan tart, 230–32

pecan-zucchini cake, 246–47

raspberry-orange ice cream, 227

raspberry-orange sorbet, 227

rugelach, 260–61

rum cream, 224

soft peach–Amaretto "ice cream," 225

soft raspberry–lime "ice cream," 227

Swedish cream, 224

toasted hazelnut biscotti, 262–63

toasted hazelnut tart, 232–33

dill:

egg salad with, 101–2

fresh, in ricotta bread, 219–20

fresh, in salmon loaf with sweet red pepper,
149–50

mushrooms paprika with parsley and,
173–74

Swedish cucumbers with sour cream and,
188

dips, 89, 90, 94, 96

baba ghanouj, 96

black olive mayonnaise, 88

coyote caviar, 89

guacamole, 87–88

hummus, 94

tapenade, 92

see also spreads

double butterscotch brownies, 256

double chocolate brownies with ground pecans,
255

dough, bread, processing of, 194–95

egg(s):

hard-cooked, preparation of, 18

Provençal spinach and basil omelet, 157

raw, preparation of, 18

eggplant:

dip, *see* baba ghanouj

preparation of, 17–18

egg salad, 101–2

dilled, 102

even easier, 101

with tarragon, 102

equivalents, table of, 36–41

falafel, 158–59

sandwich, 158–59

skordalia (Greek garlic spread), 95
slaw:
    Down South marinated, 189
    red, with sauerkraut and caraway, 190
sorbet, raspberry-orange, 227
sorrel soup, 130
soups, 103–31
    chestnut, 111
    cold cress, pear, and potato, 126–27
    cool summer, of roasted beets and cucumbers, 107–8
    cream of cauliflower, 110
    curried cauliflower, 110
    fennel, with pancetta and Parmigiano-Reggiano, 113–14
    golden bell pepper, with rosemary and marjoram, 123
    good, quick gazpacho, 119–20
    green pea–scallion with buttermilk and mint, 125
    instant icy avocado, 104
    leek and potato, 128
    Madeira onion, 112
    minestrone, 115–16
    mixed mushroom, 117–18
    New England fish chowder, 131
    potage Crécy, 109
    roasted garlic and red pepper, with tomatoes, 121–22
    sopa de palmito (Brazilian hearts-of-palm soup), 124
    sorrel, 130
    sweet potato, with coconut milk, lemongrass, and cilantro, 129
    Tuscan white bean, 105–6
    Vichyssoise, 128
sour cream:
    -chopped apple cake, 243
    cucumber sauce, 51
    -grapefruit frosting, 275
    Green Goddess dressing, 60

    -lemon frosting, 275
    mustard-caper sauce, 50
    mustard-dill sauce, 50
    -orange frosting, 275
    Swedish cucumbers with dill and, 188
    sweet-sour mustard sauce, 50
    Viennese beets and horseradish with, 165
spinach and basil omelet, Provençal, 157
spreads, 90, 92–102
    dilled egg salad, 101–2
    egg salad, 101
    egg salad with tarragon, 101–2
    even easier egg salad, 101
    ham salad, 99
    jalapeño cheese, 98
    Liptauer cheese, 97
    mushroom caviar, 90
    olivada, 93
    skordalia, 95
    spicy pimiento cheese, 98
    spicy potted shrimp, 100
    tapenade, 92
    see also dips
squash:
    butternut, and hazelnut bread, 210–11
    crookneck casserole, 185
    summer, preparation of, 34
    winter, *see* purées
stir-fry:
    of beef, red onion, and bell peppers, 145–46
    of chicken, red onion, and bell peppers, 145–46
stocks, 43–46
    beef, 44
    chicken, 43
    fish, 45
    vegetable, 46
strawberry(ies):
    preparations of, 34
    shortcake, old-fashioned, 242
stuffing, for artichokes, 163